Cheese

and the 12.39 to Wigan

Cheese Butties

and the 12.39 to Wigan

Andrew Mellor

RAILWAY HERITAGE
from
The **NOSTALGIA** *Collection*

**For my wife Valerie,
my son and daughter,
my late mother and father,
and my late mother-in-law
and father-in-law**

First published in 2011

British Library Cataloguing in Publication Data

A catalogue record for this book is available from the British Library.

ISBN 978 1 85794 354 2

Silver Link Publishing Ltd
The Trundle
Ringstead Road
Great Addington
Kettering
Northants NN14 4BW

Tel/Fax: 01536 330588
email: sales@nostalgiacollection.com
Website: www.nostalgiacollection.com

Printed and bound in the Czech Republic

Contents

Preface

Collecting railway engine numbers was a respectable hobby for a good many schoolboys in the 1950s. Railway enthusiasts, however, had been around since the late Victorian era, although not as number-collectors. They compiled notes on locomotive performances and made general observations of the railway of their day. It was in 1944 that one enterprising young gentleman, by the name of Ian Allan, commenced publication of his now famous *ABC* series of booklets listing locomotive running numbers (or fleet numbers); they also gave basic technical details, such as cylinder and driving wheel sizes. Thus youngsters could underline the numbers of locomotives they saw, and the hobby of number-collecting was born. (Actually, the activity was commonly referred to as 'train-spotting'. This was something of a misnomer, as it was not the trains we were spotting, but the locomotives that pulled them!).

My interest in trains and railways was inherited from my late father, whom I refer to as Dad throughout my story. Dad grew up in the West Derby district of Liverpool, which had a station on the Cheshire Lines Committee's branch line described in the first chapter. Prior to the Grouping of the many and varied railway companies into what became known as the 'Big Four' in 1923, he often used to spend time at West Derby station just to watch the trains, but was never a number-spotter in that pre-Ian Allan age. Not long before the Second World War my parents married and chose a house in Childwall, the rear of which happened to overlook the very same railway line. I was born towards the end of the war, and having a railway at the bottom of our garden naturally sparked off my interest at a very early age.

This, then, is the story of my adventures. From the early beginnings of days out and visits to relatives by train, they continued, through the years of 'shed-bashing' and early interests in photography, to the post-spotting era, culminating in the recording of railway sounds. The saga concludes in 1969, the year in which *Flying Scotsman*, by then privately preserved, was the only steam locomotive allowed to haul trains on British Rail's main-line network.

1
Beginning at the start

'There's a train coming!'

This exclamation was heard quite frequently at home during my formative years. Home was in the Childwall district of Liverpool, and backed onto a branch line of the Cheshire Lines Committee heading from Halewood at the south-east corner of the city to the north. Northbound trains worked hard against a gradient of 1 in 264/170, and could be heard a while before they passed, particularly if the wind was from the east. Then the sound of the engine was all but cut off, as it passed under the nearby bridge. Childwall was still 'out in the country' when the line was built, and the bridge was one of two in the vicinity built for the purpose of farming access. Never carrying roads, they were constructed with two arches, as the CLC was optimistic that increasing traffic volume would eventually warrant quadrupling of the line. However, the line remained double, and the second arches were used to allow telephone wires to pass through, linking the various signal boxes. During time of war concrete pyramids, about 5 feet high, were placed on the bridges in an effort to hinder enemy tanks etc, should invasion have taken place. More of these pyramids lined an open field adjacent to the railway embankment. Here, football was enjoyed with the local lads until the land was developed into a school playing-field. The line had become mainly freight by the early 1950s, but what a variety of motive power there was, as we shall see shortly. This, then, was my world of railways for the time being; the main lines carrying the long expresses headed by big engines were, for the present, in another world.

During the austere period after the Second World War (which practically lasted as long as the war itself), trips away from home were considered as rare treats. One of those treats took the form of a family outing to Southport, and provides some of my earliest recollections of railway travel. Judging from photographs from the family album, I guess this trip took place in about 1948. Gateacre, on the CLC branch, was our local station (Childwall had closed in 1931), where we boarded our train. This was hauled by what I later knew as a Class 4F 0-6-0 of

LMS origin, and comprised a rake of suburban non-corridor coaches. I caught an unfamiliar view of home as the train headed northward, handkerchiefs waving at our neighbours, who in turn waved theirs at us! The bridge having put an abrupt end to this frivolity, our train continued to Southport via Aintree, Altcar, and through the sand dunes to reach Lord Street station. Ahh! The sheer novelty of it all: the swaying carriage, the telegraph wires seemingly dancing to the rhythm of the wheels clicking over the rail joints, and the sounds coming from the engine, accompanied by the occasional smell of smoke.

Noticing my growing interest in the trains that passed by our garden, Dad suggested I took up number-spotting as a hobby. He set me up with my first two spotter's books: the London Midland Region and the Eastern & North Eastern Region editions of Ian Allan's famous *ABC* series, in which I could underline the numbers of engines I saw. The Eastern edition was necessary, for although Liverpool was geographically in the LMR, there was a strong presence on the CLC system of engines of 'eastern' origin. A brief synopsis of the CLC's history will explain why.

As its name suggests, the system had its roots in Cheshire. A consortium comprising the Manchester, Sheffield & Lincolnshire Railway (later renamed the Great Central Railway) and the Great Northern Railway, joined later by the Midland Railway, jointly took under its wings a number of small railways in that county. The CLC was set up to operate the system, and the owning companies used this as a tool to gain access to other railways' territory. Thus, CLC tracks soon expanded into Lancashire, and by 1864 had reached Brunswick on the banks of the River Mersey in south Liverpool, an area dominated by the London & North Western Railway up to that time. The branch from Halewood was constructed to reach the deeper waters of the north Mersey, where the larger ships could berth. At Fazakerley Junction the branch divided; one line veered west through Walton to reach the CLC's Huskisson Dock, which was the main intention, while the other was constructed northward to reach Aintree. At Aintree a connection was made with the LYR's Liverpool to Preston line, while the CLC gained access to Southport over the metals of the Cheshire Lines Extension Railway, another separate entity. These veered north-westward away from Aintree to reach the resort via the route taken by our train referred to above.

From 1923, following the Railways Act of 1921, the GCR and GNR were vested in the London & North Eastern Railway (LNER), while the MR became part of the London Midland & Scottish Railway (LMS). The fact that the former two companies were so firmly entrenched business-wise in what was virtually LMS territory resulted in the CLC retaining its separate identity until nationalisation in 1948. The Eastern Region then administered the Liverpool CLC engine sheds of Brunswick and Walton-on-the-Hill for the following 12 months. After this period, these sheds were transferred to the London Midland Region, but they retained much of their LNER motive power. At the Manchester end, Trafford Park and Gorton sheds supplied motive power for the CLC. The former shed had been jointly owned by the LMS and LNER and possessed engines belonging to both companies, but Gorton shed, east of Manchester, was purely LNER (being GCR in origin). Thus it follows that LNER types predominated on most CLC lines, particularly during the first few years under BR ownership. From further field, LNER types visited from Yorkshire, Nottinghamshire and Lincolnshire, while those of the former LMS travelled from an area stretching from Carlisle to the Midlands. So, as my interest blossomed, this is how the stage was set. Actors came and went, LMS and BR Standard locomotives replacing LNER types as time elapsed through into the 1960s.

Nos 63631 and 63633 were the first two numbers I recorded as a spotter. Dad explained how these particular engines had a 2-8-0 wheel arrangement, which meant one pair of supporting wheels leading on a pony truck, followed by four pairs of driving wheels, the zero indicating that there were no trailing supporting wheels. Their numbers were listed in the Eastern & North Eastern *ABC* book, all ex-LNER locos having numbers between 60000 and 69999 after nationalisation (LMS types gained numbers between 40000 and 59999). The *ABC* book also informed me that both these engines were of GCR origin and became LNER Class 'O4'[1] at the Grouping of 1923. These 2-8-0s, together with the WD and LMS 8F versions, were a common sight on the CLC system. Many of the 'O4s' seen at home were based at Gorton, as was No 63631, but No 63633 was from Ardsley, near Wakefield[2]. BR bought the WD locos from the Ministry of Supply following cessation of the Second World War. (There were also some 'WD' 2-10-0s, and one of these, No 90763, made occasional appearances while based at Carlisle King moor.) Aintree had a plentiful supply of 'WD' 2-8-0s, as

---

[1] There were variations of the class, all differing in detail, which the LNER sub-classified between 'O4/1' and 'O4/8'. Engines of Class 'O4/2' were built for the ROD (Railway Operating Division) for operation at home and overseas during the First World War. The Class 'WD' 2-8-0s became their equivalent during the Second World War.

[2] I wasn't aware of such trivia at the time, nor did I care. There was a *Locoshed Book* available in the Ian Allan *ABC* series, which listed shed allocations of all BR locomotives. It wasn't until 1956 that I bought my first shed book.

well as a few Fowler 7F 0-8-0s, which it sent down the line regularly. These handsome but ill-fated 0-8-0s suffered the indignity of becoming extinct ahead of the type they were supposed to replace, namely the LNWR 'G2' 0-8-0s ('Super Ds'), which were also classed as 7F. Inadequate wheel bearing surfaces and other details demanded frequent attention, thus inflating maintenance costs, and it was this factor that led to the withdrawal of about 80% of the class by the early 1950s. After that, the withdrawal rate slowed down, with the last survivor, No 49508, being withdrawn in 1962, two years ahead of the last of the LNWR 'Super Ds'. The 0-6-0 type was well represented by LNER 'J39s', and the occasional 'J11', and LMS 3Fs and 4Fs. Although by now in the LMR, Brunswick and Walton sheds clung on to a handful of LNER 'J10' 0-6-0s together with some 'N5' 0-6-2Ts, both veteran types of MSL origin, and these regularly exercised themselves along the branch in their advancing years.

The LMS 2-6-0 ('Mogul') type was represented by the Hughes 'Crabs', Stanier's version of these, and H. G. Ivatt's Class 4s, while 'K3s' and, less commonly, 'K2s' made up the LNER contingents. The 'Crabs' had large cylinders perched at a high angle in order to clear the leading pony wheels, giving a massive front-end appearance, which somehow inspired their nickname. These engines, together with Gresley's 'K3s' and Ivatt's LMS Class 4s were the most visually impressive to this young spotter before he ventured to pastures new. The 'K3s' looked huge, as they possessed a 5ft 6in-diameter boiler, giving them a rather top-heavy appearance on their relatively short wheelbase. They also had three cylinders, Dad informed me, which emitted six exhaust beats through the chimney for each wheel revolution. (The more commonly appreciated four-beat came from two- and four-cylindered locomotives.) The exhaust rhythm of the 'K3s' was very distinctive. Instead of employing three sets of valve gear for the valves of each cylinder, Gresley specified his 'derived motion' to drive the valves for the middle cylinder. This comprised a system of levers linked to the outside valve rods, which were of course driven by the two sets of outside gear. Through general 'wear and tear' within the lever system, the middle valve setting generally became somewhat desynchronised, hence there was an uneven exhaust beat. The predecessors of the 'K3s', the two-cylindered 'K2s', were also Gresley engines and to me appeared more aesthetically pleasing.

By contrast, the Ivatt Class 4 2-6-0s, which were introduced on the LMS just prior to nationalisation, were quite a common, if rather ugly, sight at home during my early observations. BR adopted them as a precursor standard type, and they were making their presence known on other regions as well as the LMR. The first 50 of the class were originally built with double blastpipes and chimneys in an attempt to maximise draughting of the fire. The draughting worked too well, and in practice the arrangement had a rather detrimental effect. It seems that when these locos were worked hard, much unburned fuel was sucked through the boiler tubes to be thrown straight out of the chimney by the blast. By the mid-1950s all of the double-chimneyed engines had been provided with the single variety. Interestingly, No 43029 was fitted with a single 'stovepipe' design, and made appearances in Childwall in this form before later receiving a standard single chimney. Some 2-6-0s of Ivatt's Class 2 version, which emerged new around the same time, appeared at home in later years.

The only examples of 4-6-0s to pass regularly in those early years were LNER 'B1s'. A couple from York worked daily into Liverpool on freights from Normanton and Mottram. Although these trains ran to Aintree, the 'B1s' usually resided at Walton shed until their time came to return eastward. Occasionally Walton used them on fill-in turns, which took them back and forth along the branch. What handsomely proportioned locos the 'B1s' were, like their freight counterparts, the Class 'O1' 2-8-0s (rebuilds of 'O4s' that also made spasmodic appearances at home). Oddly, 'Black 5' 4-6-0s, the LMS equivalent of the 'B1s', were a rarity during the early 1950s. Some of the 'B1' 4-6-0s carried names; indeed, the first 40 commemorated African wildlife. 'Copping' a namer was considered very prestigious, and there was some quiet satisfaction when underlining one in the *ABC* book in preference to just a number.

Other namers such as the LNER 'Director' 4-4-0s of Classes 'D10' and 'D11/1', and LMS 'Patriot' and 'Jubilee' 4-6-0s, materialised hauling summer excursion traffic to Southport. This traffic produced a wide variety of motive power. Apart from the namers, locomotive types ranged from LMS Compound 4-4-0s, 'Black 5s' and Stanier and 'Crab' 2-6-0s, to the ubiquitous 4F 0-6-0s. The 'K3s' and 'B1s' completed the LNER's representation on these trains. Grand National Race Day, usually held at the end of March, produced a similar variety of locomotives, and included double-headers using various combinations of engines. Horse-box trains, usually with a single braked passenger coach at the rear, moved horses and trainers, etc, to and from Aintree in connection with the big race meeting. More about Race Day specials later.

Regular passenger services through to Southport Lord Street ceased in January 1952, and the direct Cheshire Lines Extension link from Aintree closed. Thereafter the summer excursions were routed from the CLC onto the Lancashire & Yorkshire Railway line from Aintree to Burscough Junction, from where they turned left to gain that company's line from Wigan Wallgate to Southport's Chapel Street station. The only passenger services to continue past home were three workers' trains, which ran between Aintree and Manchester, Warrington and Liverpool. They returned in the evening on weekdays, and at lunchtime on Saturdays. Class 4F 0-6-0s, together with Class 2P and Compound 4-4-0s were commonly used on these trains during my early years. Later, a trio of LMS Fairburn 2-6-4Ts were drafted to Walton shed to power these trains, namely Nos 42111, 42112 and 42113. Later still, these were supplemented by Stanier examples. The tanks also took a hand with local freight workings.

It wasn't long before I could tell what type of engine was approaching by listening to the sound it made. Apart from having four or six beats, exhaust sounds differed between the various types, and the ringing or clanging sounds emanating from their rods and valve gears also gave clues as to which type was approaching. Take the 2-8-0s as a case in point. While the rods of Stanier 2-8-0s clanked, 'WDs' clanged, but the O4s clanged even louder! I liked the sounds of 'B1' 4-6-0s, whose big 6ft 2in wheels rotated with a clank-clonk, in contrast to the 4-4-0s of Compound or 'Director' types, whose rods gave out a distinctive ringing sound. This peculiarity was common to most 4-4-0s, and to a lesser extent the 0-6-0s, no matter what their origin.

At school, I was pleased to discover that 'train-spotting' was a common interest among some of the other lads.

'You want to come to Broad Green with us,' said some, who lived not far from there. 'You'll get more namers than you do at home!'

And so I went, and I did, copping Nos 45538 *Giggleswick* and 45630 *Swaziland*, my first 'Patriot' and 'Jubilee' Class 4-6-0s. I was surprised to hear these two emitting a six-beat exhaust, until consultation with my *ABC* book revealed that it was not only the LNER that had given us three-cylindered engines!

Broad Green, on the pioneering Liverpool & Manchester Railway, was about three-quarters of a mile from home, from where in favourable conditions we could hear the Newcastle and Hull expresses speeding along the high embankment near Roby. At the time I didn't appreciate the historical significance of this line, being as it was the first inter-city railway in the world. Originally built as a double track in the late 1820s between Liverpool and Manchester, it was quadrupled at the Liverpool end in 1871 to accommodate a second pair of tracks as far as Huyton. There the two pairs diverged[3], the later tracks leading off to Wigan via

---

[3] Huyton is still a junction, although the line from Edge Hill is now only double-track. The M62 motorway has taken over domination of the area from the railway.

St Helens. Broad Green station was well equipped, with waiting rooms and toilets available on all four platforms. The signal box was situated on Platform 1 (inward-bound from Manchester), and a house was provided for the Station Master. Platforms 3 and 4 served the Wigan lines, and crossovers connected the two pairs of tracks, running from No 1 line to No 3 line westbound, and from No 4 line to No 2 line in the opposite direction.

We spotters soon sorted ourselves into cliques, and Scott, Roy and Will, all schoolmates, joined with me. Spike, also a school friend, was at present out of this world. A fan of Dan Dare, Pilot of the Future (these were pre-*Star Trek* days), he joined the spotting fraternity a few years later after coming back to earth! We sometimes used the station for spotting, but generally preferred to view the trains from some railings that lined the top of a wall close to the station.

How the mind conjures up warm sunny days from our childhood! Clinging to those railings, we watched a 'Super D' 0-8-0 shunt the morning pick-up goods in the coal yard on the opposite side of the line. Its job done, the crew parked their steed on the loop and brewed up as they waited for a path forward towards Liverpool. We gazed at the heat haze over the engine's boiler, then at the shimmering tracks to the east. The inward and outward Manchester lines were both 'pegged' (signals cleared) – time for the 11 o'clock expresses ('exies'). Normal power for these was a 'Royal Scot', 'Jubilee' or 'Patriot' 4-6-0 (which we called 'Scots', 'Jubs' and 'Pates'). Occasionally a pilot locomotive was provided, usually in the form of an LMS Class 5 4-6-0.

Then, with the 'exies' out of the way, the 'Super D' was signalled out of the yard, through the station, then across from No 1 track to No 3. It may have headed straight to the reception sidings at Edge Hill. Alternatively, it could have headed up the Bootle branch, which diverged from Nos 3 and 4 tracks at Olive Mount Junction, deep inside the well-known cutting of that name. Along this branch it would find more coal yards where it could shunt in peace without any hindrance from fast trains!

To experience the sight and sound of a 'Super D' was an education. These engines seemed to defy the laws of physics, wheezing and snorting as though suffering from some bronchial complaint. Yet they were very strong, as experienced drivers have testified. Shed staff, though, were not so enthusiastic. The 'Super Ds' were awkward to maintain, with difficult access to many critical parts. They were conceived and developed by the LNWR, and the LMS considered it worth its while to rebuild some of the early examples to conform to the ultimate LNWR version. We knew the 'Super Ds' as 'Bowen-Cookes', after the CME responsible for their introduction, and they were the only LNWR type familiar to us. All of that railway's mixed traffic and express passenger engines had been eliminated by 1952 and, of the few 0-6-0 and 0-6-2T goods engines left, none were allocated to areas within our spotting territory. At that time, there were approximately 260 Bowen-Cooke 0-8-0s on BR's books.

The next 'exie', from Hull, was about an hour and a quarter away, with maybe Nos 45705 *Seahorse* or 45708 *Resolution* at its head. 'Stinks' we called them if we had seen them before. So during the lull between all this activity, it was back to playing Hopalong Cassidy for a while, or maybe Flash Gordon, or…?

The 'set' we used for these enactments comprised some bushes and huts, situated close to the railings by Old Thomas Lane. This lane originally crossed the railway on the level by the station, and at this point stood a terrace of four former railway cottages, which had been built when the line was still double track. When quadrupling took place, one gable end was so close to track 4 that a 'limited clearance' warning sign (a square plate with two red and two white squares alternately) was affixed to the wall to warn engine drivers of its close proximity. During our spotting era three of the cottages were derelict, but one was occupied by an elderly gentleman with a dog. He seemed to be some sort of a recluse, but we didn't bother him, and he didn't bother us! By 1869 Old Thomas Lane had been diverted parallel to the railway to run east a little way to a junction with a new road, named just plain Thomas Lane, and this road then passed under the railway to join Broad Green Road. Also passing under the L&M line alongside Thomas Lane was the CLC Aintree branch line. Spotters sometimes took up position on Thomas Lane to observe both lines, but the view of the L&M was somewhat impaired from this point.

The main entrance to Broad Green station is still from the Broad Green Road, which bridges the tracks to the west. Underneath this bridge was a girder supporting three LNWR lower-quadrant semaphore signals (the centre one for the eastbound crossover). These signals continued in use after the remainder in the vicinity had been converted to upper-quadrant; presumably there was insufficient clearance under the arched bridge to accommodate the latter. All semaphores at Broad Green were replaced by colour-light apparatus in the 1960s. Incidentally, a little further on along Broad Green Road, at its intersection with the Queen's Drive ring road, is The Rocket public house. Its name is said to have been bestowed on an earlier establishment on this site at the behest of the navvies who built the railway. In time, 'The Rocket' became the unofficial title for the immediate surrounding area.

Reference to Broad Green Road prompts mention of another form of rail transport, the tramcars. Outward from the city, the No 6 tram route entered Broad Green Road. at The Rocket. From here they ran on reserved grassed-over tracks on the central reservation and continued thus down to the terminus at Bowring Park, near Roby. During school holidays, Liverpool Corporation allowed children a flat fare of 1 penny for each single tram journey. As a diversion from trains, Scott, Roy and myself took advantage of this facility, and devised grand circular bus and tram tours around Liverpool. About five tram routes remained at the time, and we enjoyed the lengthy rides to Kirkby and back to the Pier Head via the No 19 route. Liverpool's last tram ran in 1957.

Reminiscence of Broad Green also recalls the 'auto-trains' to Earlestown and Warrington, worked by Ivatt Class 2 2-6-2Ts, Edge Hill's only Compound 4-4-0 No 41121 on the Manchester 'stoppers', and brand-new BR Standard Class 5 4-6-0s, Nos 73090-99, which were allocated to Manchester's Patricroft shed. I hadn't seen any Standards at home, so this was an exciting time seeing some brand-new engines. Some Standard Class 4 4-6-0s soon appeared on the scene, sharing the Liverpool-Wigan services with LMS 2-6-4Ts. To my knowledge, Standard 2-6-4Ts never appeared on the L&M line.

The so-called Standards were a series of 12 types of locomotive, developed after nationalisation. Ranging from 4-6-2s down to diminutive 2-6-0s, they allegedly embodied the best features of locomotives built by the 'Big Four' companies, although basic LMS principles predominated. The intention was to use the Standards as a stopgap, the 'knock-on' effect releasing ageing pre-Grouping locos for scrapping while plans were afoot to electrify our main lines. Following nationalisation, electrification had been recommended in preference to wide-scale dieselisation but, as we shall see, events evolved rather differently. In the meantime, locomotives in the higher power bracket at Broad Green remained the Class 7Ps of the 'Royal Scot' and 'Patriot' classes, supplemented by the 6P 'Patriots' and 'Jubilees'.

It hadn't escaped my young notice that there was a similarity in appearance between the 'Royal Scots' and some of the 'Patriot' 4-6-0s. As detailed in my *ABC* book, the LMS had begun rebuilding the 'Scot' 4-6-0s in 1943, replacing their huge parallel boilers by examples that embodied a taper. BR continued the process, so that by 1955 all 70 of the class had been rebuilt. The unique No 46170 *British Legion* became the 71st member of the 'Royal Scot' Class following its rebuild in 1935 from the ill-fated experimental locomotive No 6399 *Fury*. Anticipating the appearance of the rebuilt 'Scots', *British Legion* differed with its non-standard boiler. The boilers used in the rebuilt 'Scots' were identical to those fitted to two 'Jubilee' 4-6-0s, rebuilt under Stanier's direction before the Second World War. The two 'Jubilees' were Nos 45735 *Comet* and 45736 *Phoenix*, and it seems logical to assume that they were rebuilt as 'guinea pig' prototypes for the planned modification of the 'Scots'. Obviously, the LMS considered that the remaining 'Jubilee' 4-6-0s were adequate for traffic requirements and no more were rebuilt. Instead, after the war 18 of the 'Patriot' 4-6-0s were rebuilt under H. G. Ivatt from 6P to 7P classification, using the same boiler. I liked the neat appearance of the rather old-fashioned-looking original 'Patriots', 33 of which thankfully remained with their smaller parallel boilers for the rest of their lives. As for *Comet*, *Phoenix* and, indeed, *British Legion*, they proved rather elusive for me for a few years.

The most outstanding of my recollections of Broad Green is the sight of preserved GNR 4-4-2 No 251 on 4 September 1954, which passed on a visit to Liverpool. The train was a Northern Rubber Co special of Alan Pegler's initiative (more about this gentleman later), and ran from Retford to Liverpool's Riverside station. The 'Atlantic', normally on static display at York's original railway museum at Queen Street, was specially steamed for the run, and double-headed the train with 'D11' 4-4-0 No 62663 *Prince Albert*. Approaching Broad Green station, they were slowed as they approached from Manchester, then the middle 'peg' was raised on the bracket signal for the train to cross to the Wigan tracks, necessary to access the line to Riverside station from Edge Hill. But the authorities weren't going to risk sending the celebrities through the long Waterloo Tunnel and across the dock gates. Instead, the honour fell to a pair of 'Super D' 0-8-0s. In the dark September evening, I returned to Broad Green with Dad, joining a small crowd to watch the pair pass through on their return run.

2
Distant horizons

Mum discovered that a friend of hers owned a cottage in the Welsh slate-mining town of Blaenau Ffestiniog and, as holidays had been scarce since the war, both Mum and Dad jumped at the chance of staying there. The year was 1953.

I don't know if Dad was aware at the time that a railway existed between Blaenau and Llandudno Junction, but he decided we'd travel by bus. Thus we found ourselves queuing at 8.00am one June Saturday morning at Crosville's depot in Edge Lane, Liverpool. Waiting for a bus, I thought, was far worse than waiting for a train. Well, for one thing, I wasn't into collecting bus fleet numbers. The buses were then not as powerful as today's. Acceleration was slow, and once into the Welsh hills there was a lot of first-gear work.

The cottage was one of a terrace, situated on the road from Betws-y-Coed as it entered Blaenau, and our bus set us down at the gate on the main road. Wow! The terrace lay at the foot of some high crags (the edge of Moel Penamnen). Of the two bedrooms, one was at ground-floor level, while the other was situated in the roof. It had a dormer window, from which there was a panorama of mountains of slate, built up from the quarries we had first encountered on the descent into Blaenau. But the aspect from here pleased me for another reason. About a quarter of a mile distant across a plateau was Blaenau Ffestiniog North, the terminus of the LNWR branch line from Llandudno Junction, and I could read the engine numbers by using Dad's binoculars.

But ... the engines were LMS-pattern, Ivatt Class 2 2-6-2Ts to be precise. Dad had told me it was the old GWR that had served Wales. So why were there LMS engines at Blaenau? Woefully infantile innocence! I hadn't even begun to understand our railway history, which would eventually tell me about the LNWR/LMS presence in Wales. The Ivatt 2-6-2Ts were the only type I recall seeing on this line, although history relates that Stanier's Class 3 version also appeared during this period. Anyway, a walk into the town happily revealed Central station, the terminus of the GWR branch from Bala. Not many trains there, though. I always seemed to be passing at the wrong time of day during periods of inactivity. Sometimes the inevitable 0-6-0PT snoozed away while awaiting its return duty to Bala, its crew probably away for a brew.

Blaenau itself was decked out with bunting. It was Coronation Year, and our new Queen was about to be crowned. The big day, 30 June, was miserably wet, but this didn't dampen the spirits of the locals, many of whom had donned fancy dress. There was a church, or church hall, in the town centre, to where children were invited to watch the Coronation service on one small TV set. This set was perched high on one of the roof joists, and we youngsters all craned our necks, trying to decipher the black and white images on the tiny screen. However, we were soon spared the discomfort, because at the moment the service commenced the TV picture was lost. Television development was then still in its infancy, having resumed after the break for war. But even today it can be difficult relaying terrestrial TV signals over mountainous regions. It was possible to get reasonable radio reception, however. The strains of Lita Roza singing 'How Much is that Doggie in the Window' and Frankie Lane belting out 'I Believe' came through on the cottage wireless, no problem.

The area around Blaenau Ffestiniog and Betws-y-Coed does have rather a wet reputation weather-wise. But if you are fortunate enough to catch the slate mountains in sunlight after a heavy downpour, you can behold a magnificent glistening sight. Although quarrying ceased after 1946, slate was still being moved in 1953, but by road transport and not by the narrow-gauge Ffestiniog Railway, which used to take it down to Porthmadog. However, at Blaenau the quarry railway, which was of the same narrow gauge, was in use. Shunting of the wagons at ground level was performed by diminutive 0-4-0 locomotives of either petrol or diesel propulsion. Rope haulage was used for the movement of wagons up and down the steep slopes of the slate mountains, from which the slate was being removed. With Alec, whose mother was caretaker of the cottage, I stole rides on the empty wagons as they were moved about the yard, but for obvious reasons we were banned from riding up and down the inclines.

The Ffestiniog Railway had closed in 1939, but there was talk among the locals of efforts to reopen the line. Amongst those involved was one Alan Pegler, whom we encountered earlier regarding the running of engine No 251. All this business completely confused the young mind! Why should anyone want to close a railway? Surely, railways were a necessary part of life…? Anyway, an FR engine, *Prince*, was stuck on a plinth outside North station as a symbolic goal to be reached by the railway's restorers. That goal was realised in May 1982, when the new Interchange station, built on the site of the old GWR Central terminus[4], linked the Ffestiniog system with BR's line from Llandudno Junction. North station was then closed.

I returned to stay with Alec and his family later in the year, but this sojourn was not railway-orientated. Our families were to become lasting friends.

In 1954 another family holiday saw us staying with an aunt and uncle who ran a farm some miles out of Stafford. The journey involved travelling by train from Liverpool Lime Street to Stafford, from where Auntie collected us with her car for the run to the farm. And what a run! 50mph along quiet narrow lanes – it's just as well they were quiet in those days! At the farm there was home-produced milk and eggs, and home-made cheese and butter, but I'm not certain where the bacon came from! Washing water had to be pumped by a small petrol engine up into a storage tank in the loft, and drinking water was obtainable from a hand pump in the yard. There were tractor rides through the fields, Smutty the black cat, and Auntie had a television – such a rarity. Football's World Cup Final was in progress. Germany beat Hungary 3-2. Served the Magyars right for bashing England 3-6 at Wembley!

Well, life had certainly been different out in the country, but this young townie was glad to return home. We caught a late train back, and much of the run was in darkness. Suddenly, Dad realised we had stopped at an unfamiliar station. Chester was not normally on the route taken to Liverpool! He quickly ascertained that our train was destined for Birkenhead, and that we'd got into the wrong portion at Stafford. That was OK, as there was a ferry to Liverpool's Pier Head, or the underground railway to Liverpool Central. As our train trundled out of Chester, pictures remain in the mind of rows of GWR engines as our train rounded the curve past Chester West shed (then coded 84K in the Western Region) and, at Birkenhead Woodside, of the Class '5100' 2-6-2T that had taken over our train at Crewe or Chester. My uncle died a few years later, but we continued to visit Auntie by train, and I managed the usual quota of about a dozen 'cops' each time. A few years later, Stafford engine shed, situated alongside the station, was used as a stabling point for locos withdrawn from service. LMS engines from far and wide congregated there while on their way to Crewe for scrapping. Unfortunately I didn't generate sufficient enthusiasm to visit this now historical mortuary.

Dad bought me a bike about now. He took me spotting at Halewood and Ditton Junction, Acton Bridge, and Moore, near Warrington. At Halewood the road to Ditton crossed the London line. From here,

---

[4] The GWR terminus closed when services from Bala Junction ceased in 1960. A freight link between the two lines had been installed earlier for BR to gain access to the Trawsfynydd Power Station from Llandudno Junction. It was used for the passage of nuclear flask trains.

about a mile distant, there was an unobstructed view of trains hurtling along the long straight embankment carrying the CLC main line to Manchester. There was no Ford Motor Co factory at Halewood then, nor was there a direct arterial road to Widnes; instead there were fields containing various crops. How idyllic it was without the droning noise of traffic, just bird song and the occasional cracking sound as the rails expanded on hot days. During autumn we saw the harvest being gathered during our wait for trains. One year one of the newfangled combined harvesters appeared instead of the traditional tractor-pulled apparatus. I considered it a rather unwelcome intrusion, as thoughts returned of the days spent at my aunt and uncle's farm near Stafford.

3
'Limehouse'

Spotting at Broad Green became rather tame after a year or so, and it wasn't long before Liverpool's Lime Street station beckoned. Answering the call, Scott, Roy and I duly caught a Wigan-Liverpool train one Saturday afternoon. The fare to Lime Street was sixpence for a child's day return. The train arrived, and we boarded a side-corridor compartment coach, shut the sliding door, and settled ourselves on the spring-interior seats (comfort no longer available on today's trains). The train moved off, and as it bounced gently over the crossovers and under the bridge, we thought, 'This is the life!' There was a pleasantly musty smell, characteristic in carriages of the steam railway, particularly the older examples.

We then passed through a shallow cutting, which progressively deepened to more than 100 feet by Olive Mount. Here the line slices through the sandstone ridge that stretches from Woolton in the south of the city. At Olive Mount Junction two tracks diverged right and burrowed through a huge embankment to form the branch northward to Bootle and the North Liverpool Docks. We looked in awe at the number of railway tracks that seemed to have appeared quite suddenly. Trains were spotted on top of the high embankment, a couple of lines crossed overhead before another link from the Bootle branch trailed in on our right.

The embankment was constructed by the LNWR in 1873, together with a system of sorting sidings, known as the 'gridiron', for the purpose of sorting goods wagons by making use of gravity. Trains arriving at Edge Hill were either pulled or pushed up the embankment to the reception sidings at Olive Mount. From there wagons were uncoupled as required and allowed to roll down into the sorting sidings, roughly halfway to Edge Hill. Wagons were then remarshalled into new trains before being taken to the departure sidings, which we could see from our train on the approach to Edge Hill station. The gridiron system eliminated various small goods yards, which had been constructed piecemeal since 1830. Congestion on the main-line tracks, previously caused by 'trip' workings between these yards, was thus alleviated.

Meanwhile, we had passed the local engine shed (coded 8A),

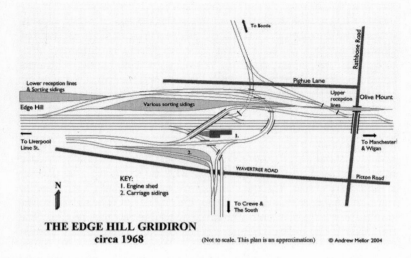

THE EDGE HILL GRIDIRON
circa 1968   (Not to scale. This plan is an approximation)   © Andrew Mellor 2004

situated on the other side of a wall to our left, just too high to spot any numbers. This was immediately followed by a junction with the line from Crewe, trailing in on the same side from under a ramp supporting a pair of tracks we'd passed under seconds earlier leading up to the Olive Mount embankment. Next came the long Wavertree Road viaduct, which carried our local No 79 bus route across the several tracks on its way into the city. There were finally more sidings seen on both sides, before our train drew to a halt in the sharply curved Edge Hill station. The sidings to our right served Edge Hill Goods Depot, from where three-wheeled 'mechanical horses' dragged trailers around delivering local consignments. Pause for thought for a moment. It's been said before what a considerable amount of activity there was around these and similar goods yards all those years ago. You could see work being done and people going about their business. Edge Hill Goods has long since gone. Also on the right, two tracks led away through the long Waterloo Tunnel to serve both the depot of the same name and Riverside station, owned by the Mersey Docks & Harbour Board. Trains to here connected with the transatlantic liners that berthed at the Prince's Landing Stage. (Riverside station closed in 1971 following the demise of the ocean-going liners.) Meanwhile, on our left was Spekeland Road coal yard, and tracks leading to Crown Street Goods, then through Wapping Tunnel to Park Lane Goods. Crown Street station was the original L&M terminus. The approach to it was virtually straight, so when in 1836 the company extended its line to Lime Street in the city, the sharp deviation curve on which Edge

Hill station is situated became necessary. By 1958 a new goods depot at Spekeland Road had been built on the site of the old coal yard, but the latter still functioned on a much reduced scale as the demand for coal changed.

Four tracks continued (as they do today) down through the tunnels for the last lap to the terminus. Local spotters always referred to the stretch between Edge Hill and Lime Street as 'the tunnels', but most were really bridges thrown across the top of the deep cutting. The cutting materialised when the original continuous single tunnel, accommodating a double track, was opened up and the line widened to accommodate the four tracks. However, four tunnels became requisite and, as our train left Edge Hill station, we passed under the first of these, which carried, would you believe, Tunnel Road across the tracks. Further down the line are the two twin-bore tunnels of Overbury Street and Mount Pleasant, and lastly the single-arched Russell Street Tunnel at the throat of the station. Beyond Mount Pleasant Tunnels, stop signals were positioned, permitting entry into the station. At the time, the lines here were designated 'up', 'up', 'down' and 'down', so that two trains could be held at the signals on adjacent tracks, waiting to drop down into their respective platforms. After electrification, the lines were redesignated 'up', 'down', 'up', 'down', and many of the open spaces between bridges were covered over as steam working became less frequent, and the need for smoke ventilation became unnecessary. A head shunt ran from the station between the two pairs of tracks as far as the Mount Pleasant Tunnels.

And so into 'Limehouse', so dubbed by the local spotters, with its cavernous twin-arched roof. We soon discovered that the best viewing platform was No 7, the longest and stretching almost into Russell Street Tunnel. The platform layout of Lime Street station today is much as it was during the 1950s, save for the abandonment of No 10 and the parcels platform beyond. The wide expanse of tarmac between Nos 7 and 8 platforms supports a roadway, which in former years accommodated limited car parking and a taxi rank. The top end of this roadway abutted a loading bay containing two short sidings. A ramp at the end of the roadway enabled early road vehicles, originally horse-drawn, to be loaded into vans through end doors. This little retreat often provided a resting place for the station pilots, usually 'Jinty' 0-6-0Ts, in between turns of duty.

I don't recall ever spending a whole day at Lime Street; it was a case of morning or afternoon shift. Up to 1955 Scott and Roy were my regular companions, but we seemed to see less of each other once Scott and I started at different secondary schools. By 1956 Spike had returned from space. One day he turned up on our doorstep and proudly announced that he had taken up 'train-spotting'. We teamed up to form a close friendship that lasted until I left school in 1960.

On the morning shift at Lime Street we always hoped to see the 'Merseyside Express' leaving for London. Timing of trains, including some principal expresses, could vary slightly from year to year, but the 'Merseyside' usually departed around 10.10am. It was normally hauled by an Edge Hill 'Princess Royal' 4-6-2 ('Prinny Royals' to the spotting fraternity), hence the attraction. There always seemed to be a train from Broad Green that would at least get to past Edge Hill in time to catch sight of the 'Merseyside', hopefully with a 'cop' on the front. There were then 12 'Princess Royals' in total[5], divided between Edge Hill and Crewe North sheds. The Crewe 'Royals' never showed in Liverpool during my time, but the allocations were occasionally swapped. It didn't take me long to see all but one; I eventually copped the elusive No 46211 *Queen Maud* at Lime Street in December 1958, when it returned to Edge Hill from a sojourn at Crewe.

Accompanied by Spike one morning, our train from Broad Green rolled into Lime Street with the 'Merseyside Express' still standing at Platform 7. At its head, not a Class 8P 4-6-2, but one of Edge Hill's Class 6P5F 'Patriot' 4-6-0s, No 45516 *The Bedfordshire and Hertfordshire Regiment*. Consternation! We quickly scurried around to Platform 7, nonchalantly walked between the open roadway gates unsighted by the ticket inspectors at the ticket barriers, then ran up to the platform end. Once there, we were greeted by the sight of another loco backing onto the front of *Beds and Herts*. It was another Class 6 'Patriot', the unnamed No 45544, also from Edge Hill, and obviously ex-works judging from the mirror-finish paintwork. It coupled up to No 45516, and before long the pair departed, both blowing off furiously at the safety valves and filling the tunnels with smoke and steam as they climbed away. The loco that had brought in the empty stock for such heavy trains usually gave banking assistance, sometimes dropping away at the platform end, sometimes going as far as the advanced starter signal in the tunnels. It's speculation, but maybe the 'Patriots' were replaced at Crewe by a 'Pacific'.

Shortly after the departure of the 'Merseyside', another train left for Birmingham, which could be hauled by a 'Jubilee' or 'Black 5'. Then a calm returned after this hectic 10 minutes or so, that is except when the Summer timetable was in operation. During the holiday season there was almost constant activity through to mid-afternoon. Summer extras

---

[5] No 46202 *Princess Anne* was scrapped in 1952 following the fateful accident at Harrow & Wealdstone. The engine had been converted from the experimental steam turbine loco, LMS No 6202, just six months previously.

were run to far-flung places such as the West Country, South Wales, the South Coast, and Kent. Some of these trains picked up through coaches at Crewe originating from, say, Glasgow or Manchester, then split up at some other station further south. Nearer home, extra trains ran to North Wales supplementing the normal services. Inevitably, 'Black 5s' powered many of these trains.

One autumn day in 1956 when I was at Lime Street on my own, there was a gleaming 'Standard 5' 4-6-0 at one of the shorter platforms. Its number was 73135, and as it drew out with its train its appearance seemed rather odd. Reference to the trusty *ABC* at home revealed that this loco was fitted with poppet valves operated by Caprotti rotary gear. These valves operated in a similar fashion to those of an internal combustion engine, and substituted the usual piston valves and Walschaerts gear found on most BR locos. There were 30 of these Standard Caprottis, Nos 73125 to 73154, marked with an asterisk in the *ABC* book. I felt 'dead chuffed' underlining my first Standard Caprotti in my *ABC* – underlining any number shown with an asterisk, dagger or whatever else was always considered a bit special. No 73135 was allocated new to Holyhead in October 1956, and may have been on its way there after a period of running-in from Derby, where it was built. There were in fact already 20 LMS Caprotti-fitted 'Black 5s' that employed inside drive to the valves from between the frames, hence the sight of No 73135 with its outside rotating gear completely flummoxing me! The precursors of the Standard Caprottis were in fact two 'Black 5s' that employed outside drive, Nos 44686 and 44687, engines I hadn't yet seen.

I once witnessed a mishap at Lime Street involving a 'Jinty' 0-6-0T that was manoeuvring a passenger coach. Somehow the coach became detached from the engine. Its severed vacuum brake pipe apparently had no effect, and the engine crew and a shunter could only stand and watch as the coach ran away down into the train shed. We heard an almighty thud as it hit the hydraulic buffers at the end of the track. Wandering back to the concourse, we saw that the coach had remained on the rails, but had rebounded about 50 yards back up the track!

Apart from the 'Merseyside Express', Edge Hill's 'Princess Royals' worked the up 'Shamrock' (a little too early for us at something past 8 o'clock in the morning), and occasionally the up 'Manxman', which left for London at 2.00pm. The latter, though, sometimes had a Class 7 'Royal Scot' 4-6-0, one of which also worked the unnamed up 4.05pm departure, which conveyed through coaches from Southport to the capital. Normally comprising two coaches, this working brought one of Southport's Stanier Class 3 2-6-2Ts to Lime Street. The route followed was the LYR electrified line as far as Bootle, there diverging onto the branch to Edge Hill and so to Lime Street. A little manoeuvring by the rostered London loco had the 'Southport throughs' tucked in at the front of the main train, and away they went. There was a turntable at Lime Street with a couple of sidings radiating from it, and the Southport engine stayed there until called upon to collect some homeward-bound coaches off a later arrival.

Of course, there were our beloved 'exies' we used to see at Broad Green. From 11.00am until teatime there were two departures for Hull and two for Newcastle, plus a Newcastle relief in summer. On the arrival side, one was from Leeds, one from Hull, and two from Newcastle. Farnley Junction 'Jubilees' and rebuilt 'Patriots' from Edge Hill were the regular performers on these trains, but very occasionally there might be a surprise from Leeds Holbeck shed in the form of a 'Royal Scot'. With the exception of No 45705 *Seahorse*, which had gone to Blackpool by 1957, the same old 'stinks' continued to show at Lime Street. Nos 45708 *Resolution*, 45646 *Napier* and 45581 *Bihar and Orissa* were the most common of Farnley Junction's offerings, while Edge Hill rostered Nos 45521 *Rhyl*, 45525 *Colwyn Bay* and 45531 *Sir Frederick Harrison* among others. 'Stinks' notwithstanding, these trains did provide some entertainment for the patient spotter. The stock of the 3.10pm arrival from Newcastle was used to form the 5.00pm return. The train remained at the platform, normally No 6, with the engine uncoupled and standing confined at the buffer stops. At departure time it gave starting assistance to the outgoing engine, the pair providing superpower for the initial climb into the tunnels. After a pause for the train to clear the next signal, the assisting engine reversed away, heading for the sheds.

Very shortly after all this came the star turn of the day, a 'Duchess' 'Pacific' taking out the 'Red Rose' for London at around 5.20pm. The 'Duchess' 4-6-2s were known as 'Semis' to us spotters. No one seems to know the origin of this name. Most of the 'Duchesses' had been streamlined as built, so it could have been related to the fact that, when the streamlined casing was removed from these examples, we had a semi-complete engine, if you like. Edge Hill didn't have any 'Duchesses' on its books during this period, and the daily visitor was always from Camden, to which 15 were allocated at the time. The only example of the class to visit Liverpool on a regular basis, it usually arrived in Liverpool at 11.30amSX (Saturdays excepted) or 12.45pm from the capital, after which it retired to Edge Hill shed for the afternoon. As with the Newcastle trains, the stock of the corresponding London arrival was used to form the up train. However, spotters were unfortunately spared the spectacle of 'Pacific' banking 'Pacific' out of the station! Instead, the empty stock was dragged into the tunnels by one of the two 'Jinty' station pilots, assisted by the incoming engine, normally a 'Princess Royal', sometimes a 'Royal Scot'. The train engine then headed off to the sheds, following which the second station pilot guided the coaches back into the station, usually Platform 7. During all this to-ing and fro-ing, the train's catering stewards could be seen resetting the tables in the restaurant cars for the next journey.

So, while the 'Jinty' simmered at the buffer stops and passengers climbed aboard, a reasonable crowd of spotters gathered at the platform end to await the arrival of the 'Duchess' from the sheds. Those who'd seen it at midday generally didn't hang around to see it again at teatime, but knowledge of its identity would have got to us on the afternoon shift via the usual grapevine. Anyway, whether we copped it or not, when the big tender showed itself in the tunnels, there was still a feeling of immense anticipation. We couldn't see the number until the engine had drawn almost level with us, then there were always cheers and jeers whichever 'Duchess' it was!

The guard's flag was out of sight around the S-curves on Platform 7. So when he called 'right away', the driver of the 'Jinty' pulled a series of blasts on his engine's whistle to call the attention of his counterpart on the 'Duchess'. There could be quite a din at the front end by now, as the 'Duchess' was likely to be blowing off at three of its four safety valves. Added to all this, the Stanier hooter answered the 'Jinty' and the big engine was set in motion. Perhaps slipping a little at first, the 'Pacific' got to grips and headed away into the tunnels. Then a column of smoke at the rear came into view as the 'Jinty', powering away at the back for all it was worth, snaked around the curves. On most occasions it continued up to the advanced starter in the tunnel before dropping back into the short bay between Platforms 7 and 8.

Well, the departure of the 'Red Rose' signalled the end of the afternoon shift for us, and we had a choice of both Wigan and Manchester trains, which would drop us off at Broad Green before 6.00pm. If I'd copped a 'Semi', I walked on air for the three-quarter-mile trek home from Broad Green; but if it had been a bad day – few or no cops – then it would be quite a trudge. The walk took me past CADWA[6] Hall, the local social club for the area, where in earlier years I'd attended concerts, fetes and film shows. During our Broad Green era a rainy day usually meant watching films instead of the trains. A Saturday matinee cost us sixpence to watch our heroes Laurel and Hardy, Charlie Chaplin … ah, yes, and Hopalong Cassidy and Flash Gordon, too. But does anyone

[6] Chelwood & District Welfare Association (Chelwood was the name of a local road, where one of the founder members resided).

remember The Taxi Boys?

At Lime Street, however, we tolerated all weathers. A couple of high road bridges[7] spanning the platforms at the throat of the station provided minimal shelter. We stuck it out, through blizzards, too, till our fingers felt frozen to the bones and we could hardly write the engine numbers in our notepads! On such cold days there was little comfort travelling on local stopping trains either. The frequent opening and closing of carriage doors negated the effects of the steam heating system in its attempts to warm the coaches. Steam often found its way inside through ill-sealed doors and gangway connections, and half-shut windows. The single-glazed windows misted over on the inside and engine steam condensed on the outside, particularly when passing through tunnels. On occasions like this I'm sure we used to think, 'What's the point of it all?'

---

[7] The bridges carry St Vincent Street East and Copperas Hill.

4
A long way from home

To us youngsters of the 1950s, almost anywhere outside the boundaries of our home town seemed a 'long way off'. The family car was not yet a common animal and most people travelled everywhere by public transport. When some of us have occasion to do so today, we become very intolerant of queuing, traffic jams, late trains, etc, whereas during the 1950s everyone seemed to accept all this as the norm.

So it was in the summer of 1955 that I embarked on a 10-hour journey by road from Liverpool to Staithes, a little fishing village on the North Yorkshire coast. I'd just completed my final term at primary school, and was about to spend just one more week with some of the Rudston Road senior crowd at the Holiday Fellowship camp, as it was then, which the school patronised. The camp was, and still is, situated at the top of the steep road that climbs out of the village, and comprises a number of green-painted huts. Flanked by high rock faces, the road descends down a ravine to the village and its harbour, beyond which is a beach sheltered by the surrounding cliffs.

But more importantly, for me at least, there was a railway in close proximity, with Staithes station itself about 100 yards from our hut. The line from Middlesbrough followed a tortuous path along the coast down to Whitby, and crossed the ravine at Staithes on a high trestle-type viaduct. The meagre service was handled mostly by three-cylinder 'A8' 4-6-2Ts of North Eastern Railway vintage, and some post-Grouping inside-cylindered 'A5s' of the same wheel arrangement. These latter were built by the LNER under Gresley's direction as a development of Robinson's GCR design. But there were other types as well. I copped 'L1' 2-6-4T No 67742, based at Darlington, and a couple of brand-new Standard Class 3 2-6-0s, No 77004, also from Darlington, and No 77013 from Whitby. One day our party used the train for a trip to Whitby. What stupendous views there were out to sea as the train closely followed the contoured coastline before descending steeply to Sandsend. Sandsend is at sea level, and the train then meandered along the final 3 miles or so to Whitby. We all then enjoyed the delights of the town, and into the bargain I copped a few Ivatt Class 4 'Moguls' that were allocated to the NE Region.

As well as Rudston Road, schools from other parts of the country were present at the camp. There was a certain musical element among some individuals, who sang or whistled some of the popular songs of the time. There was a rendering of 'Unchained Melody', which was high in the 'hit parade', as the 'charts' were then known. It was sung by one Jimmy Young, later of radio DJ fame, who also recorded a different version in 1964. 'Cherry Pink and Apple Blossom White' by Eddie Calvert ('the Man with the Golden Trumpet') and 'Stranger in Paradise' by Tony Bennett were also high-flyers.

So the week passed, and I arrived home, tired and with a banana I'd forgotten to eat squashed into the bottom of my rucksack! I enjoyed the holiday, having been into unexplored territory. I'd seen some unfamiliar locomotive types and took great satisfaction underlining and admiring their numbers in my *ABC*. But oh! If only the school had sent us by train instead of by road. The section of line between Loftus and Whitby, which included Staithes, closed in May 1958.

'We've got a surprise for you,' said Dad, as I prepared for bed one evening during the summer of 1956. 'We're going to Scotland tomorrow.'

This was the stuff of which dreams were made. My parents had purposely kept quiet about it, for they knew if they'd told me earlier I would have kept awake most nights anticipating what engines I might see. Sure enough, my imagination started to run riot as soon as my head hit the pillow! We were going to visit some long-standing friends of my parents, who lived at Cupar on the east coast of Scotland north of Edinburgh. It was obvious I would see some LNER 'big guns' for the first time. The streamlined 'A4s' and other 'Pacifics', as well as the 'V2' 2-6-2s, engines that I had seen only in photographs, were now to become a reality. They must have been in my thoughts time and again before I eventually dozed off, perhaps through nervous exhaustion!

We had to be up and out pretty early to catch our train, scheduled to depart from Liverpool's Exchange station around 9.30 or 9.45am (times varied from year to year). Exchange was a large spacious station having ten straight platforms. It was the LYR terminus for routes to the east via Wigan, to the north through Preston, and for the local third rail electric services to Ormskirk and Southport. Spotters generally never spent much time here; the station had few moments of glamour, although the Glasgow and Edinburgh trains could usually provide something 'big'. After lodging at Bank Hall shed (coded 27A), the locomotive off the previous evening's arrival from Scotland was normally rostered for the northbound working the following morning. Over the years, this took the form of Glasgow Polmadie 'Britannia' and 'Clan' 4-6-2s, or 'Royal Scot' 4-6-0s from Carlisle Upperby (then coded 12A). During the 1960s 'Duchess' 'Pacifics' began to appear on these trains, having been displaced by diesels at Upperby shed and transferred to Kingmoor. Bank Hall itself never possessed anything larger than 'Jubilee' 4-6-0s. Although these worked north on occasion, they were more commonly to be found working eastward into Yorkshire.

Having said all that, I found a 'Jubilee' at the head of our train, the 9.43am departure with sections for Glasgow and Edinburgh. It wasn't one of Bank Hall's trio, though, but No 45701 *Conqueror* from Newton Heath shed in Manchester. This engine would have worked in from the east, and was maybe commandeered by Bank Hall to deputise for the rostered loco for whatever reason. Supposition of course. *Conqueror* got me off to a good start to the holiday, for I copped it. Watching from our train, I noticed that No 40588, a Class 2P 4-4-0, was also in the vicinity. By now a Bank Hall engine, it was once a regular performer down the CLC branch hauling the workmen's trains before the advent of 2-6-4Ts. I felt rather disgusted when it coupled up ahead of *Conqueror* to double-head our train. How could they put a 27A 'stink' on the front? Never mind. I expect the driver of the 'Jubilee' was glad of the 2P, as the train was a heavy one. The Glasgow Central portion was to the fore, with our Edinburgh coaches bringing up the rear.

The immediate exit from Exchange took an elevated path over a series of viaducts, girder bridges and embankments for about 1¾ miles. Looking down to our right from Sandhills station, we could see the marshalling yard for the CLC's Huskisson Dock complex, and at Sandhills Junction the Southport lines diverged to the left. As our train emerged from under Stanley Road Bridge, Bank Hall MPD came briefly into view – only briefly, because it was partly obscured by some carriage sidings. The CLC link to Huskisson ran parallel to the LYR, but at a lower level, as far as Kirkdale. There was some complex railway construction here, as the LNWR Bootle branch from Edge Hill passed underneath both the LYR and CLC tracks at deep level.

After Kirkdale we passed through a cutting, slicing through part of another sandstone ridge similar to that at Olive Mount. Once clear of Aintree, the route to Preston was fairly level and straight, permitting some fast running, even on local services. At Moss Lane Junction our train took the direct spur to join the West Coast Main Line (WCML) tracks from the south at Farrington Curve Junction instead of continuing along the original LYR line to Preston, which crossed the WCML before turning sharp left at Lostock Hall Junction. The line straight on from there still continues to Blackburn today and was to feature prominently in my life during the run-up to the end of BR steam in 1968. The LYR Preston line then formed a triangle with another spur trailing in from Blackburn at Todd Lane Junction, and continued parallel to the WCML across the River Ribble to Preston, where the two lines converged in the station.

Meanwhile, our train continued along the WCML from Farrington Curve Junction. There were now six parallel tracks running towards Preston, although the two westerly ones were for freight and avoided passing through the centre of the station. Summer excursions made use of these tracks. Trains from the north destined for Blackpool headed southward down the LYR line out of Preston. Bearing right at Todd Lane Junction and again at Lostock Hall Junction, they joined the spur our train had just used to regain the WCML. Beyond Preston they took the line to Blackpool. Strange to relate, Preston was never to figure in my spotting activities. What I missed doesn't bear thinking about.

One of the frustrating aspects of stopping at a large station like Preston was that you could hear other train movements but you couldn't always see them. There was sometimes a screen or another train obscuring the view! The screens were usually constructed of translucent glass to act as a wind shield, as 'through'-type stations could be notoriously draughty places! The stations at Preston and Lancaster were already familiar to me, as we passed that way when visiting an aunt and uncle who lived at Dalton-in-Furness. This little town is on the Barrow line, which still branches off the WCML at Carnforth, although the WCML platforms there have been taken out of use. Most of the big railway centres provided cops, mainly from the local sheds, and there was nothing of outstanding value on this journey until we reached Carlisle, where a big 'Duchess' was moving slowly by Upperby sheds.

'Cor! Look at that!'

The long straight nameplate read *Sir William A. Stanier, FRS*, and its number, 46256, had an asterisk in my *ABC*. So did No 46257 *City of Salford*. These final two LMS 'Pacifics' were constructed after the war under the direction of Stanier's successor, H. G. Ivatt. They were provided with roller bearings, as opposed to plain bearings, and an 'altered rear end', according to our *ABC* books.

At this time Carlisle marked the boundary between the LMR and the Scottish Region, so that Kingmoor and Canal sheds north of the city were coded 68A and 68E respectively in the ScR. As a result of the regional boundary changes of 1958, these sheds were transferred to the LMR, becoming 12A and 12C. Our train continued north over the former Caledonian Railway route to Glasgow, which we were to follow as far as Carstairs. Shortly we passed the giant sheds at Kingmoor, where I copped No 45713 *Renown* together with a few others. Canal shed, however, was situated some distance to the west. It was a former North British Railway establishment, serving that company's route to Edinburgh and thus bringing LNER locos into the Border City. Known as the 'Waverley Route', this line diverged left from the WCML before looping back to cross over it. The line then continued by way of Newcastleton and Hawick and across the desolate moorlands before descending into Edinburgh's Waverley station. The Waverley Route closed in 1969.

En route to Carstairs our engines had to negotiate the climb up Beattock Bank, 10 miles with gradients of 1 in 68 and 1 in 75. We pulled up just beyond the station to take on rear-end assistance, provided by the nearby MPD. 2-6-4Ts Nos 42205 and 42130 were on duty, as was No 55234, a veteran Caledonian Railway 0-4-4T, but I don't know which of these helped us up the big hill. At Carstairs our train divided, and a 'Black 5' 4-6-0 hooked onto the rear. There was the usual clutch of local cops from the nearby shed, but before we set off for Edinburgh I saw my first 'Clan' 4-6-2, as No 72001 *Clan Cameron* appeared at the head of a southbound train. The approach to Edinburgh Princes Street station brought some interesting cops, notably No 45154 *Lanarkshire Yeomanry*, one of only four named 'Black 5s'. By now the CR shed at Dalry Road had some LNER locos on its books, and I copped 'J37' 0-6-0 No 64536 and named 'B1' 4-6-0 No 61246 *Lord Balfour of Burleigh*.

So it was that we arrived in Edinburgh Princes Street station, some 5½ hours after departing from Liverpool. All I can recall about this station is its spaciousness and quietness. After all, this was the middle of the afternoon, and no doubt it had its busy periods. There were still a further 40 miles to our destination, however, entailing a train journey from Waverley station, about a mile away along the famous Princes Street itself. What a contrast at Waverley! I soon saw my first LNER 'Pacific', 'A3' No 60096 *Papyrus*, but, being hard to please, I wished it had been a 'blinkered' 'A1' or 'A2'. A streamlined 'A4' 'streak' would have done nicely, though! I couldn't find out what was on the front of our Dundee train, but pulling out of Waverley I copped another 'A3', No 60079 *Bayardo*, then 'A1' No 60154 *Bon Accord*, illuminated by shafts of light penetrating the hanging smoke. A blinkered 'Pacific'! Brilliant! Its number was marked with a dagger in my *ABC* book, signifying that it was one of five 'A1s' fitted with roller bearings. A couple of 'V2' 2-6-2s, a 'V3' 2-6-2T and a 'J83' 0-6-0T (an equivalent of the LMS 'Jinty'), and that was that for the day, 59 cops in all.

We detrained at Cupar, and our friends met us with their car. They had a large house out of the town and not far from the railway. But alas I could see only the trails of smoke, as the trains passed obscured by unfavourable topography at the rear of the house.

One day during our stay was taken up by a trip to Dundee with Dad.

A spotting jaunt, in fact. Although we travelled by train, the only part
of the journey I can recall is of passing over the Tay Bridge, and looking
down at the old piers of the ill-fated first bridge. We took up position
alongside the 1 in 77 climb out of the station leading up to the bridge.
Needless to say, just about everything I saw north of the border was a
cop, but a most unexpected one materialised in the form of 'Jubilee'
4-6-0 No 45627 *Sierra Leone*, which was from London's Kentish Town
depot. How on earth did it find its way up here? As is already apparent,
I had a soft spot for 4-4-0s, and of this type I saw three 'D30s' (known
unofficially as 'Scotts', as they carried names from Sir Walter Scott's
novels) and two 'D49s'. Of the latter, there was No 62719 *Peebles-shire*
with Walschaerts gear and piston valves, and No 62744 *The Holderness*,
which had Lentz rotary gear and poppet valves. I saw my first Standard
2-6-4T in the shape of No 80123, and a lovely surprise, one of the
two lightweight 'V4' 2-6-2s, No 61700 *Bantam Cock*, working south
from Aberdeen. I never saw its sister loco, the unnamed No 61701
(unofficially known as 'Bantam Hen').

Gresley introduced the 'V4s' for principal services over lines from
which their heavier 'V2' cousins were barred. After Gresley's untimely
death in 1941 his successor, Edward Thompson, ordered no more 'V4s',
and proceeded to introduce his own brand of mixed-traffic design,
the 'B1' 4-6-0. It has to be admitted that from both initial cost and
maintenance points of view, the simpler 'B1s' proved more economical,
even if they didn't pack quite the same punch. Nor did they possess as
much charisma!

Back at Dundee, I copped numerous 'B1s', LNER 0-6-0s, 'V2s' and
an 'A1' 4-6-2, No 60161 *North British*. There was also the odd 'Black
5' (you couldn't get away from them!) and CR 0-6-0 No 57324. The
latter was a Stirling (63B) engine, incidentally. Then it was time to go,
but what was lurking in the station? 'A2/1' 4-6-2 No 60507 *Highland
Chieftain* was one of four hybrid 'A2s' for which Mr Thompson was
once again responsible. He cancelled the building of the last four 'V2s'
that were on order, and used their boilers to build these four 'Pacifics',
necessitating the fitting of a rather long smokebox. Anyway, a good cop
to finish the day.

Before we departed for home, our hosts took us to Glasgow, where
I presume Mum went on a shopping spree, as she didn't come with
Dad and myself mooching around the city's four main-line termini.
Time must have been short, however, for I can't recall venturing up
the platforms at any of these establishments. Nevertheless, I achieved
15 cops, the most noteworthy being 'Jubilees' Nos 45715 *Invincible*
and 45732 *Sanspareil* at St Enoch, terminus for the Glasgow & South
Western Railway. Class 2P 4-4-0 No 40594 was also at St Enoch. At

a very quiet Central station, the northern terminus of the WCML, I copped my second Standard 2-6-4T, No 80112, and Class 3 'Mogul' No 77005. At the NBR's Queen Street station, terminus of the West Highland line to Fort William and Mallaig, was 'D30' 4-4-0 No 62438 *Peter Poundtext*, and three 'N15/2' 0-6-2Ts, used for banking heavy trains up the steep incline to Cowlairs. I'm getting a little tired of writing about asterisked numbers in the *ABC* books! These engines were built specially for the Cowlairs incline. They had larger coal bunkers than the 'N15/1' members of the class, as they burned more coal as a result of the hard work that was required of them, not to mention all the idle moments they spent waiting for a piece of the action.

Waiting on Cupar station at the start of our journey home, I thrilled at the appearance of 'A2' 'Pacific' No 60529 *Pearl Diver* pulling up with our Edinburgh train. According to the trusty *ABC* book, this engine had a tractive effort in excess of 40,000lb, one of the highest in the country. So we should experience a pretty lively run, I thought, but disappointment prevailed. Much store used to be placed on the seemingly magical figures calculated as 'tractive effort', ie the combined forces exerted by the driving wheels on the track. Tractive effort used to be regarded as a measure of the power of a steam locomotive, but the true power lies in the ability of its boiler to continuously provide sufficient steam to meet the needs of the cylinders in producing tractive effort. The tractive effort figure is really only nominal and is thus subjective, depending as it does on the condition of both locomotive and the track it runs on.

Back on board our train, I was also a little puzzled at the sound of *Pearl Diver*'s exhaust. The engine was fitted with a Kylchap blastpipe and double chimney, and this was the first time I'd had a chance to sample the sound of one of these exhausts. You could hardly hear it. Instead of the expected deep bark, there was a sound perhaps more akin to Wilson, Keppel and Betty performing their sand dance[8]! No wonder I was disillusioned!

After all this, we now approached Edinburgh and some engines were seen. Here was Haymarket shed, and one very interesting loco hove into view. Ah, *yes*! No 60027 *Merlin*. An 'A4' 'streak' at last. Oh, joy! I probably missed a few other loco numbers just by gazing at this one. I wasn't bothered – *Merlin* was worth six of any other cops! My head still in the clouds, we eventually alighted at Waverley station. There was some time to kill before our Liverpool train was due out of Princes Street station, so we decided to visit the famous gardens of the same name. It follows that I spent about 45 minutes in what to me

[8] A popular variety act of the 1950s.

seemed like Paradise. No, not the beautiful gardens, but the footbridge from same that still spans the main line today, and under which we had so recently passed. This spot lay between two tunnels west of Waverley station. In addition to northbound trains, others ran to Glasgow, and there were also numerous light-engine movements to and from Haymarket shed just beyond the tunnel to the west. Mum and Dad retired to the gardens, leaving me to my hobby.

Well, I didn't see any more 'A4s', but there were plenty of other 'Pacifics'. Of six 'A2s' seen, two were 'A2/1s': Nos 60509 *Waverley* and 60510 *Robert the Bruce*. These and No 60507 seen at Dundee were all allocated to Haymarket. What a pity the fourth member of this quartet, No 60509 *Duke of Rothesay*, was shedded at New England in Lincolnshire! In addition, there were two 'A1s', three 'A3s', a 'V2', two 'B1s' (including namer No 61221 *Sir Alexander Erskine-Hill*), together with a few minnows. Then Dad showed up, and it was time to go.

'There's another coming,' I called, as a big box tender loomed out of the tunnel from Waverley. As the engine reversed towards us I could see it had the curved nameplate of an 'A3' 'Pacific', but it also sported 'A1/A2'-type 'blinkers'. Then the cabside number became legible – 60097. And the name?

'Oh, *Humorist*! So that's *Humorist*!'

Yet another asterisk in the *ABC* told me that this 'A3' was the only one fitted with a Kylchap exhaust similar to *Pearl Diver*, but there was no mention of the straight smoke deflectors. In the years that followed, all of the class received Kylchap exhausts, but instead of the straight type of smoke deflector plates, some were equipped with so-called German trough-type deflectors, suspended directly from the smokebox sides. Why 'German' in particular, I don't know, as this type of smoke deflector was common in many European countries.

And so to Princes Street station. In another nine years this station was to close, and services from Carstairs would run into Waverley station, using a connection installed by BR from a junction on the Leith line between Slateford and Haymarket. The last, and long, lap home produced just two noteworthy sightings: a trio of consecutive 2-6-4Ts at Beattock, Nos 42213, 42214 and 42215, and Standard Class 3 2-6-2T No 82029 at Penrith, my first sighting of one of these engines. This one was from Darlington, and had worked from there over the high and desolate Stainmore line via Kirkby Stephen.

As a postscript, following my visit to Scotland the December issue of the journal *Trains Illustrated* included a photo-feature of Edinburgh. Many of my treasured cops were depicted, including *Pearl Diver*, *Humorist*, *Call Boy*, *Colorado* and *Waverley*. No *Merlin*, though.

Prelude to the Wigan saga

Scott's grandparents lived at Platt Bridge in Wigan. 'Duchesses' were a common sight through Wigan, Scott informed me. Oh yes, it would be great to see a 'Semi' from somewhere other than Camden, so my first experience of Wigan materialised with a run to Platt Bridge with Scott and his parents in their car. Alas, we saw no 'Semis'. There were so many railway lines about this area that I think Scott may have taken me to the wrong place! However, a locomotive came into view that at first we thought was a 'Britannia' 4-6-2. In fact, No 92053 was our first sighting of a BR Standard Class 9F heavy freight 2-10-0. Like the 'Brits', they had side smoke deflector plates ('blinkers' to us spotters) and a wide firebox. This 'first' maybe compensated a little for not seeing any 'Duchesses'!

5
And now for the cheese butties...

It was following my return from Scotland that Spike made it known that he was now seriously into trains. He'd been to London with his parents, and we each took great satisfaction in exchanging our respective lists of cops for scrutiny. Although I still favoured the 'Duchesses' at heart, I had become very pro-LNER since my Scotland escapade. There were so many more large high-powered locomotives to see, totalling 406, although the 'A1s' and some of the 'A2s' had been constructed under the auspices of BR after nationalisation. The LMR, on the other hand, had inherited just 38 'Duchesses', 12 'Princess Royals', and 91 Class 7P 4-6-0s. Spike, though, staunchly favoured the LMS camp. More visits to Lime Street followed with Spike. Then, fed up with seeing only Camden 'Semis', the question 'What about Wigan?' came up again.

'Well, what about Wigan?' I thought, recounting my abortive 'Semi'-less visit with Scott. But going by train, surely we couldn't go wrong if we remained on Wigan station? There was a train from Broad Green at 1.30pm, and our first afternoon at Wigan produced 24 cops. Among them was our first non-Camden 'Semi', No 46249 *City of Sheffield*, whose home shed was Crewe North (5A). Other namer cops that day were 'Jubilees' Nos 45625 *Sarawak* and 45635 *Tobago*, original 6P 'Patriot' No 45537 *Private E. Sykes, V.C.*, and rebuilt 7P 'Patriot' No 45523 *Bangor*. Spike agreed with my opinion that the 6P 'Patriots' were very handsome if maybe rather old-fashioned-looking engines.

It immediately became obvious that the 1.30pm got us to Wigan too late to see both up and down 'Royal Scot' expresses. The preceding train departed from Broad Green at 12.39pm, but that was a little early for a midday meal before setting off from home. Schoolkids could be late risers at weekends, so it was better to take a few sandwiches to eat at Wigan than to have lunch on top of a late breakfast. I had been a very poor eater during my younger years, but by now had been weaned onto more substantial sandwich fillings than syrup (of the Lyle's Golden variety) and jam! Mum had discovered that I liked cheese spreads or cheese slices, and thus encouraged me to have these in my sandwiches, or 'butties', on my outings.

The 12.39 was almost invariably hauled by an LMS 2-6-4T, and, like most trains on the Wigan line, called at all stations. Bearing left at Huyton away from the Manchester tracks, stops were made at Prescot and Eccleston Park before we descended steeply through a cutting and a short tunnel into Thatto Heath station. There next followed a long fast descent through the then intensely industrialised area on the approach to St Helens. The line is elevated, and we crossed a myriad of industrial lines, many of which belonged to Pilkingtons, the glass manufacturers, on which BR engines could be seen working alongside privately owned company locomotives. The BR examples were mostly LYR 0-6-0STs from Sutton Oak shed. This shed was situated a couple of miles away along the old St Helens Railway, which headed due south from St Helens to Widnes. We met this line trailing in sharply from our right as we hit the bottom of the hill and entered the station. St Helens Shaw Street was a three-platform affair; in the past the third platform had accommodated trains from St Helens Junction, Earlestown (on the L&M line), and Warrington, which used the Sutton Oak line. Shaw Street was still five years off being rebuilt, and I remember it as a rather dark establishment. Wigan-bound trains had to stop well short of the platform end, owing to a crossover situated within the station and protected by a single-aspect multi-coloured-lens signal. Shaw Street station was renamed St Helens Central in the early 1990s.

Invariably waiting for the 12.39 at St Helens was a 'Jinty' 0-6-0T with a goods van, which it would attach to the rear. With the van in place, we departed past Pocket Nook, where there were some sorting sidings, and shortly passed under a branch from the old Wigan Junction Railway, which terminated at the original St Helens Central station near the Town Hall. Next, our train diverged right at Gerard's Bridge Junction, and climbed away from the old St Helens Railway, the latter continuing on towards Rainford Junction. (Passenger services to Rainford had ceased in 1951.) At the end of the climb was Carr Mill Junction, where another line trailed in from the south. This line also connected with the St Helens Railway at Sutton Oak, going via Blackbrook and thus avoiding St Helens itself. During its history, the Blackbrook link served several local collieries, and the coalfields extended as far as our destination at Wigan. Consequently, the course of our line could be described as an elongated roller-coaster. Four tracks commenced from Carr Mill, although two were for freight, with only the two from St Helens having platforms at Garswood and Bryn stations.

Not long after leaving Bryn, our anticipation heightened on the long run up to Springs Branch on the outskirts of Wigan. There were numerous sidings containing thousands of coal wagons, with a selection of mainly 'Super D' 0-8-0s in attendance, of which Springs Branch shed had an abundance. Towards the latter part of the 1950s examples of the Standard version of the 350hp 0-6-0 diesel shunter came to Springs Branch. The new machines appeared with a 'D' prefixing a four-figure number, instead of being numbered in the 13000 series. The 'D' substituted the digit '1' as earlier examples were renumbered.

Springs Branch MPD was situated on the far side of the WCML as we swung round to join the latter for the run northward to Wigan's North Western station. Spike called out what numbers he could see, and I jotted them down. The 'Super Ds' apart, Springs Branch had a quantity of LNER 0-6-0s of Class 'J10', which migrated from the former GCR shed at Lower Ince when that closed earlier in the 1950s. The GCR had taken over the Wigan Junction Railway, a branch from Glazebrook on the CLC's Liverpool-Manchester route, together with the line to St Helens Central, which branched from it at Lowton St Mary's. The GCR branch terminated at Wigan Central and closed as late as 1964, but was in no competition to gain the attention of us spotters. The 'J10s' seemed to be particularly favoured by the local LMR sheds. We have already noted that Walton and Brunswick had some; so did Trafford Park, Heaton Mersey, Northwich and Chester Northgate. Occasionally, one of Wigan's 'J10s' could be seen on station pilot duties at the town's North Western station. Coincidentally, the last two surviving 'J10s', Nos 65157 and 65198, were withdrawn from Springs Branch in 1961. To complete the shed's rather cosmopolitan allocation, there was a handful of LYR 0-6-0s there.

Wigan North Western comprised five through platforms. The two main ones ran straight through the centre as now, two more curved around the west side, and the fifth ran around the east side overlooking the LYR lines and goods yard at Wallgate. There was also a couple of bay platforms at the south end and a single bay at the north, the latter mostly used by parcels traffic.

Our 12.39 was always directed into one of the west-side loops (tracks since lifted), where it terminated some 54 minutes after leaving Broad Green. A great crowd of spotters greeted us as our train entered the station. How could so many kids have heard about Wigan? Lime Street was never like this! They were congregated at the south end of the down main platform, a good vantage point from which to view the northbound expresses approaching around the curve from the south.

There was always someone keeping an eye on the colour-light signals.

'Line pegged!'

The down (northbound) signal had turned green. Soon the train came into view, and excited cries filled the air.

'Blinks! Blinks!' Then maybe, 'Semi! Semi!'

Imagine a big 'Duchess', with 14 or 15 coaches trailing, rounding
the curve from the direction of Springs Branch. The engine sways owing
to the turbulence of the water in its boiler, and this swaying appears
exaggerated by the motion of the tender, with perhaps two or three
thousand more gallons slurping about inside. If the train isn't booked to
stop at Wigan, the 'Duchess' is opened up, roaring through the station
to get a run at the bank that commences immediately at the north end.
What a sight! What a sound! But whatever the engine, there are more
jeers and cheers depending on who copped it and who didn't. The
climb from the north end is at 1 in 108 past Boar's Head and Standish
Junctions (alas, junctions no more).

Generally, behaviour was good, with plenty of good-natured banter
between spotters. At times, though, our numbers on the platform
swelled to the extent that authority thought it best to step in by trying
to persuade us to either leave the station, or to catch the next train
home. At the time, we didn't appreciate the need that maybe safety
was being compromised in such circumstances, particularly at busy
periods. Thus there were moans and groans as we were herded away,
drifting down the subway towards the ticket barrier. Having given up
the 'outward' halves of our tickets, we promptly had the 'return' halves
clipped, and headed back along the subway. A nonchalant visit to the
public conveniences might now be a good idea before heading back
onto the platform, and casually reaching the south end again.

A bonus at Wigan, there were also the activities on the LYR line to
watch. This line climbed steeply from the depths under Wallgate to level
with the WCML, and immediately veered south-eastward for Bolton
and Manchester. The LYR traffic supplemented the cop takings to a
degree. Wigan's LYR engine shed was situated north of Wallgate station
in the vee formed by the lines to Southport and Liverpool Exchange.
Among its allocation were some Fowler 7F 0-8-0s and the final five
Standard Class 2 2-6-0s to be built, Nos 78060 to 78064. During quiet
periods at North Western station these types occasionally entertained
us by shunting the Wallgate goods yard (the site of which now forms a
car park). The 'Standard 2s' appeared with front number plates having
a red background as opposed to the usual black. This seems to have
been in response to the Scottish Region's ploy of providing some of its
engines with light blue backgrounds to their plates. Occasionally we'd
see one of Bank Hall's three 'Jubilee' 4-6-0s heading a train between
Liverpool and Leeds or York. Nos 45698 *Mars*, 45717 *Dauntless* and
45719 *Glorious* would be the only namers we'd see on the LYR tracks.

On the WCML, Glasgow Polmadie's big engines regularly worked
as far south as Crewe and we'd see at least one Scottish example during
a session at Wigan. The 'Brits' and 'Clans' ran with blue front number

plates, and possibly the 'Royal Scot' 4-6-0s and 'Duchesses'. Anyway, during the ensuing weeks cops from Polmadie included 'Brits' Nos 70051 *Firth of Forth* and 70054 *Dornoch Firth*, 'Scot' No 46104 *Scottish Borderer*, 'Clans' Nos 72002 *Clan Campbell* and 72004 *Clan Macdonald*, and four 'Semis'. By way of a bonus, I copped Carlisle Kingmoor's No 72008 *Clan Macleod* on the same day as No 72004.

There were ten 'Clan' 'Pacifics', smaller cousins of the 'Britannias', and they spent most of their lives split evenly between Polmadie and Kingmoor sheds. A couple of them sojourned elsewhere early in their lives, but very briefly, as crews in other areas didn't seem to take to them too well. There were reports that the 'Clans' were indifferent steamers, but then every engine had its off days! Changing trains at Lancaster returning from Dalton on a couple of occasions, No 72001 *Clan Cameron* provided some scintillating runs down to Liverpool Exchange.

Well, as things turned out, we discovered that the 'Royal Scot' expresses were Camden turns south of Carlisle, so the 'Semi' 'stinks' we'd seen at Liverpool we saw again on these trains. However, in 1957 the quintet of prototype main-line diesels were back at Camden, and so were likely to be seen hauling the 'Royal Scots'. The locomotives, Nos 10000, 10001, 10201, 10202 and 10203, alternated between working on the London Midland and Southern Regions since their introduction between 1947 and 1954. Nos 10000 and 10001 happened to turn up on the only occasion that Spike and I spent a whole day at Wigan, having caught a train from Broad Green at 9.30am. The LMS twins roared through with the down 'Royal Scot', adorned with the same straight tartan headboard that the 'Duchesses wore'. Presumably the up train that day had a Camden 'Semi' in charge and, as I wouldn't have needed it, I hadn't noted its number.

The twins were probably the best-known diesels of the day, for they were the first main-liners to operate in this country. No 10000 had been completed at the LMS's Derby Works just prior to nationalisation, so bore LMS black livery early in its career. By now, both were painted Brunswick green, with orange and black horizontal lining all around the waist and base of the body. Each was rated at 1,600bhp, so when double-heading as a pair that roughly equated to a 'Duchess' 'Pacific'.

I made 43 cops during that full day's grind, including No 46227 *Duchess of Devonshire* from Polmadie and No 46238 *City of Carlisle* from Kingmoor. No fewer than three 'Royal Scots', two unrebuilt 'Patriots', two 'Jubilees', and 'Brit' *Dornoch Firth* were also underlined in my books that day.

I was on my own for my next visit. The trusty 12.39 got me to Wigan in time to see diesel No 10203 heading the northbound 'Royal Scot'. Shortly afterwards I completed the class, for Nos 10201 and

10202 double-headed the up train. These two were rated at 1,750bhp, while No 10203 was designated as 2,000bhp. Despite being rated at approximately two-thirds the power of a 'Duchess', No 10203 always handled the 'Royal Scot' expresses single-handedly to my knowledge. The superior tractive adhesion of these early diesel locos compensated to some degree for what they lacked in power. Thus, it seems, they were able to do no more than maintain the schedules mapped out for 'Duchess' haulage. A similar situation developed when the 2,000bhp Type 4 (Class 40) diesels (developed from No 10203) were introduced onto the LMR in 1959, and took over many a 'Duchess' roster. The train schedules between Liverpool/Manchester and London did not significantly improve until the advent of electric traction in the 1960s.

Being in the wrong place at the wrong time happened to most loco-spotters, as it did to me on one significant occasion in August 1957. Caught in the middle of Wigan North Western station, I heard the then unfamiliar sound of a two-note horn from the north end. Then came the roar of some sort of diesel accelerating through on the up line, obliterated from my view by a train standing at the down platform. What could that be? The 'Royal Scot' expresses had already passed through. Some info met me as I made my way along the platform.

'38004!'

'38004? No such number!'

The verbal telegraph had become a little distorted on its way along the platform. The diesel's number was actually D8004, a Type 1 of 1,000bhp (later Class 20) from English Electric. These were the first main-line diesels to emerge under the Modernisation Plan, and I guess No D8004 was passing through on a proving run. We didn't catch any more of these Type 1s on such trains, and none were allocated to our patch after acceptance either, being based at Devons Road MPD in London for use on cross-city freights.

Spotting No D8004 was certainly something of a surprise, but I had another on a subsequent visit. On leaving Bryan aboard the 12.39, what should pass by heading westward but a named 'Mickey', No 45156 *Ayrshire Yeomanry*. As reported in *Trains Illustrated* a couple of months later, it had been transferred from the ScR to Manchester's Newton Heath shed. (Sister locomotive *Lanarkshire Yeomanry* had also been transferred, but I didn't need that, having already copped it in Scotland.) This was a brilliant start to another successful afternoon's spotting. Cops on this day included three 'Semis', Nos 46223 *Princess Alice*, 46248 *City of Leeds*, and 46226 *Duchess of Norfolk*. Then 'Scot' No 46141 *The North Staffordshire Regiment* and 'Jubilee' No 45678 *De Robeck* completed the bag of namers.

And so the afternoons wore on and, although rather tired, I/we reluctantly headed for the train home. This was due out at 5.08pm, but if the 'down' 'Midday Scot' was on time, we'd see it pounding through at about 5.00pm. At the time, Crewe North 'Princess Royal' 'Pacifics' were the regular locos on this train, but it was never *Queen Maud*, which I needed to complete the class. As related earlier, I copped this engine back at Lime Street after it returned to Edge Hill shed.

The 5.08pm originated at Preston and usually arrived at Wigan a little before 5.00pm, being routed into the west-side up loop platform. This train was often formed of an odd assortment of rolling stock, for example a mixture of corridor and suburban (non-corridor) coaches, and the locomotive could be anything from a 2-6-4T to a 'Royal Scot' 4-6-0. One day an ex-works 'Jubilee' 4-6-0 appeared, No 45661 *Vernon*, with, for a change, a uniform set of three suburban coaches in tow. Despite the light load, our driver experienced great difficulty in restarting the engine from Bryn on the adverse gradient. Being fresh from shops, *Vernon*'s bearings must have been still quite 'stiff', requiring just a little more steam to turn its wheels than would normally be the case with a 'run-in' engine. Too much steam caused the wheels to lose their grip on the rails, and they would start to spin before being checked by the driver. Our driver kept reversing the train back a little, trying to find a patch of rail on which his engine could maintain grip. Eventually he found one, and off we went. There were no problems departing Thatto Heath, however, the engine restarting successfully on something like a 1 in 85 gradient.

I made innumerable visits to Wigan North Western. On one occasion with Scott, I copped No 46233 *Duchess of Sutherland*, one of the 'Semis' that Spike had already seen. Bumping into Scott one day when I was away on holiday, he wasn't too pleased to learn of my luck. The Wigan days were happy days. But happy days always end at some time. They ended for me when the day's haul of cops started to dwindle. But by then I'd already begun to move further afield – to Manchester. But not just yet!

6
Gossip, and some further escapades

The unique No 71000 *Duke of Gloucester* was a rare bird for many spotters. The LMR envisaged rostering it regularly for the heavy 'Midday Scot' express, but the *Duke* didn't show up for us during our visits to Wigan. Most unexpectedly, I copped it at 'Limehouse' in April 1959. What a scoop! I found it mundanely shunting parcels vans on the south side of the station. A Crewe North engine throughout its short eight years of service on BR, this turn must surely have been a roster for one of that shed's 'Black 5' 4-6-0s. The fact that the *Duke* was used on this occasion may be an indication of the low esteem in which this unfortunate engine was held by Crewe North men.

Unfortunate? No 71000 was built in 1954, officially as a replacement for the ill-fated No 46202 *Princess Anne*, the missing member of the 'Princess Royal' Class damaged beyond repair in the Harrow accident of 1952. Caprotti valve gear was installed on No 71000, and the loco was the only one of the Standard family to have three cylinders. With these innovations and a few other refinements, it had been intended that No 71000 would be a world-beater; but it never consistently lived up to expectation.

The *Duke of Gloucester* story is now quite well known to many enthusiasts, but a brief synopsis here wouldn't be inappropriate. The Caprotti valves and gear provided a very efficient front end, but the engine's fire could sometimes have a ferocious appetite for coal, and at other times wouldn't burn the stuff quickly enough to meet the boiler's demand for steam. It was during official testing of No 71000 in 1955 that the BR Modernisation Plan was launched, in which it was announced that diesel and electric traction would replace steam. High powers then dictated that no more testing or development work would be permitted for steam locomotives, so *Duke of Gloucester* remained with its impediment for its entire working life.

E. S. Cox was the design executive responsible for the BR Standards. In his book on the subject, he expressed disappointment at not being allowed to pursue an answer to the cause of No 71000's shortcomings, but suspected that they were connected with the draughting for the fire. It is a pity that Mr Cox didn't live quite long enough to see his suspicions vindicated. The loco was eventually preserved and restored to working order under the custodianship of the 71000 Duke of Gloucester Steam Locomotive Trust. Expressed simply, it was discovered during restoration that the ashpan fitted to the loco when new had been made incorrectly, and effectively restricted the airflow to the fire. It is outside the parameters of this book to dwell further on this subject (please refer to the Bibliography for reading concerning the story of No 71000). I saw *Duke of Gloucester* just three more times, albeit not in my home city. Apparently it became a fairly frequent visitor to Liverpool from 1959 until its withdrawal three years later.

As an alternative to Wigan, Spike and I tried Warrington Bank Quay, but many of the 'stinks' we'd seen at Wigan on the principal expresses also passed through Warrington. However, we did witness a most unexpected occurrence one day. As we watched activities from a road close to the south end of the station, an 8F 2-8-0 came trundling down the curved embankment from the Manchester Ship Canal bridge. It had a long train of passenger coaches in tow, and as the cavalcade drew into the station we read the roof-mounted destination boards: 'THE ROYAL SCOT' and 'GLASGOW-LONDON'. Trailing in at the rear came diesels Nos 10201 and 10202. This was in fact the up 'Royal Scot', and it transpired that the leading vehicle, a baggage car, had a defective bogie. Rather than let the train continue to Crewe, the 8F had been sent to haul the complete ensemble back to Warrington, where another baggage car was readily available. The contents were then transferred to the other vehicle, which was parked at the adjacent bay platform. The diesels then performed the necessary shunting movements to swap cars, and set off for the south, very late.

Spike wasn't impressed with the noise from the diesels.

'Don't think much of those,' he said. 'People will want to sleep at night!'

I cycled to Warrington myself on one occasion. One day I saw a 'Black 5' heading north with diesel-hydraulic Type 2 No D6305 in tow. All diesel-hydraulics built by the North British Locomotive Co of Glasgow made their way to the WR under their own power. There must have been some serious fault with this one, and it was obviously heading back to its makers for repair, 'under guarantee' presumably.

Although spotting at 'Limehouse' took a low priority when the Wigan phase began, Spike and myself continued to pop into the station when 'in town' shopping or whatever. The 'Camden only' rule at Lime Street seemed to have come to an end, too, for in May 1958 I copped No 46234 *Duchess of Abercorn* from Crewe North, and the following year

No 46232 *Duchess of Montrose* from Polmadie, of all places. I guess that Crewe probably used these locos on fill-in turns to Liverpool between other duties.

I was 'made up' at seeing *Duchess of Montrose*, for this particular example was chosen by Meccano Ltd for its three-rail Hornby Dublo model, which my parents had bought me for Christmas in 1955. Over the following three years I had expanded the 'allocation' to include Standard 2-6-4T No 80054, GWR 'Castle' 4-6-0 No 7013 *Bristol Castle*, LMS 8F 2-8-0 No 48151, and LNER 'N2' 0-6-2T No 69564. Spike brought his 'Duchess' and 2-6-4T, some track and some rolling stock to my house, which enabled us to construct a double-track circuit, on which we re-enacted, among others, Liverpool-London Euston expresses, Birkenhead-London Paddington trains and, inevitably, the 12.39 to Wigan. We ran the 12.39 with the Standard tank[9], the 'N2' substituting for the 'Jinty' at St Helens Shaw Street. (We shall encounter the real-world Birkenhead-Paddington trains a little later.) In turn, I reciprocated by taking some of my stock to his abode.

Speaking of 'Duchesses', during January 1958 the LMR decided to paint No 46245 *City of London* in a variant of LMS red instead of the standard Brunswick green. More examples were similarly treated, but in more of a maroon hue. Some 'Duchesses' remained in green throughout their lives, as did six 'Princess Royal' 'Pacifics' when the rest received the maroon livery.

I didn't consider 'bunking' Edge Hill shed while knocking around with Spike. For one thing, we thought it would be rather difficult to get by without being seen. For another, we'd copped just about all of its allocation by 1957, including the 'Jinty' 0-6-0Ts that were seen either at Lime Street or from the top deck of a No 79 bus crossing the viaduct. It didn't seem to take long to cop any newcomers reallocated from other sheds either. Spike used to ride the No 79 buses en route to his school in the city. He told me about the Caprotti Standard Class 5 4-6-0s he'd seen from his morning ride. The first ten of these were then based at the WR shed of Shrewsbury, and one of them regularly worked to Liverpool in the early morning. Sometimes one of Shrewsbury's 'Black 5s' turned up, but Spike managed to amass nine out of the ten Caprottis. I couldn't let him get away with this, could I?

I nearly always cycled the 1½ miles to school, roughly half the distance to Edge Hill. The solution was obvious. Get out of bed earlier and cycle

---

[9] The Standard Class 4 tanks never appeared on the service. In fact, the only Liverpool shed to receive Standards of any description was Bank Hall, with a handful of Class 4 4-6-0s and Class 2 2-6-0s.

down to the viaduct before heading for school! I managed to pick up seven of these Caprottis, but I was also 'spotted' myself.

'Don't tell me. You've been to Edge Hill and copped blah, blah…,' was how Spike greeted me on the phone. Then the unthinkable happened. Spike was poorly one week, and stayed off school. I copped No 73125, the one Shrewsbury Caprotti he needed, and I couldn't wait to call and tell him on my way home from school.

'Oh, was it?' Spike retorted, or words to that effect. I don't recall if he ever did see No 73125.

On top of all that, a big bonus came my way one of those early mornings. I copped 'Royal Scot' 4-6-0 No 46102 *Black Watch*. This engine was normally based at Glasgow Polmadie, but news came via the grapevine that, after overhaul at Crewe Works, it had been transferred to Edge Hill. In fact, it spent about four weeks at Edge Hill MPD (unofficially, I suspect, for I can find no record of an official transfer) before returning to Polmadie. I was in luck to see a very clean green engine reversing through the hole in the wall from the sheds. 'This has to be *Black Watch*,' I thought, and it was. Backing down to Lime Street, it probably took out the 9.00am to Newcastle. What a scoop!

Coinciding with the 1955 announcement of BR's Modernisation Plan, and just one year after the birth of *Duke of Gloucester*, came the emergence of the prototype main-line 'Deltic' diesel. This was a private venture by the then English Electric Co, and BR agreed to provide facilities for testing and proving the locomotive. At the time it was the world's most powerful single-unit diesel, and amply looked the part with a massive-looking nose at each end ahead of the cabs. It was painted a light shade of blue, with lemon-coloured lining (my own interpretation of the official description of 'royal blue with gold lining'). Anyway, the roof was painted aluminium, as were the bogies and underslung fuel tanks. The 'Deltic' was built at EE's Preston works, but received further attention as became necessary at the company's establishment near Kirkby, just outside Liverpool.

The locomotive was newly based at the city's Speke Junction MPD (coded 8C). This shed possessed fuelling facilities for its own stud of diesel shunters, and was thus the obvious choice for stabling 'Deltic'. To access the Kirkby site from Speke, the loco took the CLC Aintree branch, and thus became the first main-line diesel I saw, albeit not a BR one. While based at Speke it took up duty on the Liverpool-London services, notably the 2.00pm up 'Manxman'. The main line to the south passed within a mile of my school in Wavertree. In summer the unmistakable din from the loco's two Napier engines filtered through the open classroom windows.

'Will you shut up about that "Deltic", Mellor?'

Another interesting interloper arrived on our scene from English Electric during 1957. No D226 was an 0-6-0 diesel-electric shunter of 500bhp. It was also a private venture in an attempt to assess the merits of electric versus hydraulic transmission for diesel locomotives. No D227, from the same manufacturer, was fitted with the alternative hydraulic transmission.

A diesel-electric loco is virtually a mobile electricity power station. The engine drives a generator, which feeds current to the traction motors driving the road wheels. A hydraulic transmission passes power to the road wheels through an oil-filled gearbox, in which an impeller forces oil through a series of turbine wheels and fixed blades. The number of wheels and blades in series approximates to the number of gears in a mechanical transmission. Mechanical transmissions were usually incorporated into locomotives of less than 250bhp, and were thus cheaply and economically utilised in the smaller shunters such as the Hudswell-Clarke examples at Birkenhead. The gearboxes were of the pre-selector type, similarly found in buses.

Well, No D226 came to Speke shed in 1957, and during its time there was sent to Edge Hill to work empty coaching between the storage sidings there and Lime Street station. In 1959 the loco was renumbered D0226, because its original number was allotted to one of the new English Electric Type 4 diesels (which later became the Class 40s) then being delivered. After a sojourn on the WR, No D0226 returned to its maker, which in 1966 donated it to the Keighley & Worth Valley Light Railway for preservation. I didn't manage to see No D0227.

Reference to No D226, the Type 4, brings us back to the subject of BR's Modernisation Plan, which was really gathering momentum by 1959 with the appearance of several types of main-line diesel. It is interesting to note that, at the formation of BR in 1948, it was anticipated that widespread electrification would in the long term replace steam as the prime source of power for main-line work. Hence the decision was taken to build the series of 12 Standard classes of steam locomotives as an interim measure. (This itself seemed to fly in the face of the decision to build hundreds of steam locos to existing 'Big Four' designs that were ordered before nationalisation.) The 'rights and wrongs' of all this have been discussed far and wide, but suffice to say here that, like the diesels now appearing, the Standards were manna to the spotter. We welcomed them, blissfully unaware at the time of the political undertones that would eventually come to light.

BR's pilot scheme produced several different types of diesel in trial batches of three, five, 10 and 20. Most were built by private contractors, but some emerged from BR's own workshops. However, under pressure once again from political circles, BR decided to multiply some of these types in an effort to accelerate the demise of steam, seemingly at all costs. Deficiencies had already manifested themselves in some of the pilot scheme types, thus these were not perpetuated. Of the types that were multiplied, some proved to be unsatisfactory in the longer term, and suffered early retirement for scrapping or sale to private businesses. I encountered many of the doomed diesel types during visits to London a little later on. The BR Type 2s built at Derby (Class 24 and the later Class 25), however, were one of the more successful types. I copped a fair number of these around Liverpool, as the LMR 'ran them in' prior to transfer to the ER. The first 15 were, in fact, intended for the LMR, but were loaned to the Southern Region until delivery commenced of its own Type 3 Bo-Bos (Class 33).

Since the sighting of No D8004 at Wigan, no new main-line diesels appeared on our scene until 1959, when production of EE Type 4s resumed, commencing with No D210. (Nos D200 to D209 appeared in 1958, all of them allocated to the ER.) These new 2,000bhp machines were based on the prototypes, Nos 10201-3, and had the same 1Co-Co1 wheel arrangement. This continental wheel notation indicated that there were two bogies of three driving axles each, with a supporting idler axle at each end of the loco. The D200s needed these idlers to keep within the civil engineer's specification of axle loading. At 133 tons, they were also rather heavy in relation to their power rating, and comparison was made with some diesel-hydraulic Type 4s that had begun to operate on the WR. These were the 'Warship' Class 2,200bhp locos, which weighed in at only 78 tons, making it possible to mount them on two four-wheeled bogies (making their wheel arrangement B-B). We shall encounter the 'Warship' diesels later on. The EE Type 4s, lumbering giants as they were, proved to be very reliable machines, helping BR to 'keep face' with its dieselisation policy when other types were not living up to expectation. Most of the 40s gave three decades of service to BR, making them one of the success stories to emerge from the Modernisation Plan.

Edge Hill, Camden and Crewe received allocations and, after crew training, the Type 4s took over some of the Liverpool-London trains, and soon began to make inroads further north over the WCML. The new locos meant new cops, providing an excuse to visit Lime Street station again to see one take out the up 'Red Rose'. When viewed for the first time in the station, the new diesels seemed extraordinarily long. They certainly looked powerful machines and sounded very impressive in full cry, their four exhaust ducts pointing skyward in a double-vee formation. Yet we were rather surprised to learn that their power was equivalent only to a 'Jubilee' or 'Patriot' 4-6-0. Perhaps this explains why the new diesels couldn't improve on the existing timings set for the Class 7 and 8 steam locos.

7
On unofficial business

Spike's parents had a little Standard 8 car, and they kindly asked me along on some of their outings. A favourite run of theirs was along the North Wales coast to Penmaenmawr or Llanfairfechan, usually on a Sunday. Outward, we travelled via the old and narrow Queensferry Bridge across the Dee. Traffic tailbacks? Today's motorway queues don't compare with the hold-ups created by this bridge at busy times. (And what was the BR slogan at the time? 'No worry, no strain – much better by train' was emblazoned below a photograph of such a queue.) Anyway, after collecting a few pebbles from the beach at Llanfairfechan, and maybe one or two cops courtesy of the Holyhead line, we headed for home. Well, not quite. Instead of taking the Queensferry road, Spike's Dad took us to Chester, where we could visit the station.

Chester was the northern limit of WR territory, and its General station was jointly owned by the LMS and GWR prior to nationalisation (although its history is not as straightforward as that). The WR shed was on the other side of Brook Street bridge at the west end of the station. On Sundays, when there were fewer trains, engine sheds were generally full of locomotives. By evening, engines were being prepared and shunted into their correct positions ready for Monday's rosters. Shunting was performed by the shed pilot, or any other locomotive that was conveniently in steam.

It was just so at Chester, where shunting movements extended from the shed under the bridge and into the station environs. GWR 'Castle' Class 4-6-0 No 5091 *Cleeve Abbey* was being shunted in company with 2-6-0 No 4326 by an 0-6-0PT. What a handsome loco! *Cleeve Abbey* was complete with the traditional GWR embellishments that the 'Castles' retained after nationalisation. The GWR was renowned for its individualism, which the Western Region of BR upheld for a long time after 1948, and this was reflected in the appearance of its locomotives. Except for the 0-6-0PTs and the diminutive 0-4-2Ts, GWR locos were designed without the steam collection dome seen on the boiler-tops of engines of other origins. Instead, the safety valves were placed in that position within a brass shroud, flanked by a pair of clack valves feeding water into the boiler. Refinements were completed with the fitting of a copper-capped chimney and, on named engines, the application of some brass beading. The safety valves were known as 'sizzlers', because they lifted slightly some way below maximum steam pressure, the lift increasing gradually until they were blowing off fully at maximum pressure.

The Swindon 'sizzlers' contrasted starkly with the Ross 'pop' safety valves fitted to most other companies' engines. After emitting a feathering of steam as the boiler pressure rose, 'pop' safety valves suddenly erupted with the full force of steam. All quiet one moment, then total noise! The actual 'pop' sound came when the valve closed, just as suddenly. The 'sizzlers' could be noisy, too, as the brass shroud acted like a megaphone, amplifying the roar of escaping steam.

What puzzled me at the time was why the GWR should build four-cylinder machines, as there were engines of similar power like 'Royal Scots' and 'A3s' making do with just three! 'What a waste of four cylinders,' I naively thought. The fact that the predecessors of the 'Castles', the four-cylinder 'Star' 4-6-0s, were even less powerful just fuelled my indignation. It was GWR policy to design its locomotives with either two or four cylinders, and I would eventually appreciate the development of the four-cylinder family of GWR 4-6-0s, which culminated in the construction of the magnificent 'King' Class. I didn't see any of the 'Stars'; there were only four left when I started spotting, and these disappeared before the 1950s were out.

I copped my first 'County' 4-6-0, No 1022 *County of Northampton*, in similar circumstances to *Cleeve Abbey*. It was being shunted coupled to 'Super D' 0-8-0 No 49082, which was from the former LMS shed at Swansea (code 87K). As in North Wales, the LMS inherited lines in the south of the province. Following nationalisation, these lines pretty soon came under WR jurisdiction, but many of the sheds in South Wales kept their allocations of LMS engines, including Stanier 8F 2-8-0s, some of which also reached Chester.

So! What about going around the shed? Could we do that? Not officially, but the temptation was there, so Spike and I plucked up courage and had a go. It was dark, and we knew we would need our wits about us as we walked down the access ramp from Brooke Street, not only from a safety aspect, but to keep out of view of the shed foreman. Chester West was a straight, three-road, open-ended shed, and there were more stabling roads outside. This was the first time either of us had been in such a place. Treading cautiously into the shed, the experience was awesome. Standing next to them at ground level, the engines seemed huge, even the pannier tank shunters. We passed the first line of locos, then it happened. The foreman spotted us.

'Out!'

So we calmly walked out of one end of the shed, around the outside towards the access road, then back across the tracks at the opposite end to examine some engines standing on the 'outdoor' shed roads. Fortunately, we were at the 'right' end when we were spotted again, and hurriedly made our way back up the ramp to Brooke Street. The star cop was No 1024 *County of Pembroke*, supported by other lesser 4-6-0s – two 'Halls', a 'Grange' and a 'Manor' – together with a mixed bag that totalled 24 cops for the shed. Nos 5015 *Kingswear Castle* and 45617 *Mauritius* were in the station, as was veteran Midland 2P 4-4-0 No 40420. The 2P was based at Rhyl at the time, so had probably worked to Chester on an all-stations service.

Back home that night, *Sunday Night at the London Palladium* was on the telly. Lonnie Donegan appeared with his skiffle group. He was in the hit parade with 'Cumberland Gap', 'Puttin' on the Style', and 'Gamblin' Man'. Other hits of the day were Paul Anka's 'Diana', and Elvis Presley was 'All Shook Up'. There was another skiffle song called 'Freight Train'. Lonnie Donegan maintains he never recorded this number, but it was recorded by a group of artists who performed under the grand banner of the Chas McDevitt Skiffle Group featuring Nancy Whiskey. Many of these artists appeared on a TV programme produced by the BBC for the youth of the day, *6.5 Special*. The best part of the show, I thought at the time, was the background film to the titles! It showed various sequences of express trains, including footplate shots, and the song of the same title was performed by Don Lang and his Frantic Five. Today, if ever I hear the infectious melody of 'Freight Train', it always reminds me of the 1957/58 era.

Having sampled the engine shed and other activity at Chester, we vowed to return for some serious spotting business! But some time was to elapse before we actually made the effort and caught a train from Birkenhead Woodside for the magic of a summer Saturday at Chester. So let us pause awhile at Birkenhead, and at neighbouring Bidston, to sample their offerings. We discovered that these two sheds could throw up a few oddities.

Birkenhead! The very mention of the name conjures recollections of many happy hours spent at the sheds there. Our route was under the river by way of the 'Underground', the third rail electrified line of the former Mersey Railway from Liverpool Central Low Level. At his time, 1956/57, the old American-style 1903-built rolling stock of the Mersey Railway was being phased out. Its replacements were new units based on an LMS design introduced in 1938, when that company electrified the former Wirral Railway lines from Birkenhead Park to New Brighton and West Kirby. Once or twice we managed a ride on the old units; compared to the later stock, the size of the carriages seemed enormous.

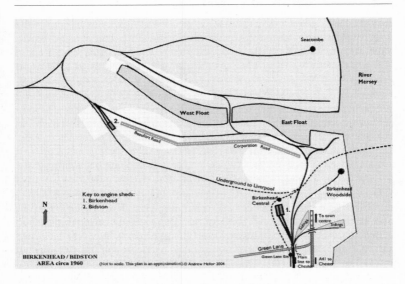

BIRKENHEAD / BIDSTON
AREA circa 1960   (Not to scale. This plan is an approximation) © Andrew Mellor 2004

The official entrance to Birkenhead MPD was from Mollington Street, close to Birkenhead Central station on the 'Underground' line to Rock Ferry. As our business was of an unofficial nature, it would be rather silly to expect to gain entry this way, so we always booked to the next station along the line, Green Lane. Green Lane was a curious station in a cutting below street level, with part of the main line to Chester above supported on girders overhanging the platforms. The electric line then climbed to run parallel with the Chester lines as far as Rock Ferry.

Green Lane station has hardly changed, but the electric trains themselves now run through to Chester. Woodside station closed in 1969, and the line over Green Lane is now just a single track, leading down to what is left of Birkenhead docks. Gone are the sounds of hissing steam and engine movements we heard upon alighting from our electric train, heightening our anticipation as we climbed the steps leading to the street. Across Green Lane itself there was a gate in a wall. Through here and at the top of more steps we found ourselves at the neck of tracks that accessed the sheds from the main line. There were two sheds, one each for the former LNWR-cum-LMS and GWR companies, the former joint owners of the line from Chester. New mechanical coaling plant and ash disposal facilities had not long been added between the yards to each of the sheds, and the tracks on the LMS side were still in the process of being reinstated on our first visit. Close by the steps from Green Lane was a semi-submerged air-raid shelter, a relic from the

Second World War. It was mostly grassed over, and served as an ideal grandstand from which to view various shed and main-line activities. There was also shunting to watch, which took place in the sidings on the opposite side of the main line. The sheds themselves were situated adjacent to the local gas works, and the smell of the manufactured gas of the day didn't blend too well with the sulphurous odours emanating from the engine sheds. We could have identified the place with our eyes shut because of that smell. But we didn't mind that – this was Birkenhead!

As a legacy from joint ownership, there was still a good mix of locomotives of both origins at Birkenhead, although the GWR types were slowly being transferred away. We discovered that a total of ten Class '5100' 2-6-2Ts had not long been dispatched elsewhere, but of these we did see No 4128, which had been moved only as far as Chester. On the other hand, some '4300' 2-6-0s remained for two or three years more, as did four 'Grange' 4-6-0s. Of the 'Granges', No 6878 *Longford Grange* was always noted in pristine condition, in stark contrast to the filthiest of the quartet, No 6831 *Bearley Grange*. For the record, the other two were Nos 6841 *Marlas Grange* and 6859 *Yiewsley Grange*. Until recently the 'Granges' had been used to haul the through expresses to the WR between Birkenhead and Chester. At the start of our visits, though, this work was shared between Stanier and 'Crab' 2-6-0s, and 2-6-4Ts of both LMS and BR Standard varieties. The 'Granges' were relegated to freight work serving the docks, and had left Birkenhead by 1958.

The BR Standard tanks were allocated to both Birkenhead and Chester Midland sheds, having been transferred from the Manchester and London areas. Similarly, another batch of these tanks went to Bangor (6H). During 1957 the Standards and the LMS variants began to dominate the passenger services to Chester.

Despite the departure of some of its own GWR locos, Birkenhead shed continued to play host to a fair number from elsewhere. Docks traffic brought examples of '2800' 2-8-0s and, more rarely, '7200' 2-8-2Ts from South Wales and the West Midlands. London's Old Oak Common (81A) sent 'Hall' 4-6-0s or one of its big '4700' 2-8-0s (much prized by us), of which only nine were built. The latter worked the fast overnight trains conveying meat for Smithfield Market. Other 'Granges' and the lightweight 'Manor' 4-6-0s added to the variety. As for LMS types, there were the usual 'Black 5s', 8Fs and 2-6-0s, and occasionally a 4F 0-6-0. Birkenhead also possessed a stud of seven Stanier Class 3 2-6-2Ts, until recently used extensively on the services to West Kirby, whose branch diverged at Hooton. Most of the Class 3s were put into store following the withdrawal of the passenger services to

West Kirby in September 1956, although freight continued until 1962. As for the oddities, there was a quartet of veteran GWR 0-6-0PTs, Nos 2008, 2012, 2069 and 2134. These had started life around the turn of the century as saddle tanks, being subsequently rebuilt with panniers. Then there was No 41734, a Class 1F 0-6-0T of Midland origin, forerunner of the larger 'Jinties'. It was shortly to be transferred to the ER at Staveley, Chesterfield, for shunting at a steelworks complex. In fact, many veterans around the country survived for similar work where their small size and light weight were essential for working in sidings with tight curves and weight restrictions. There were also three 0-4-0ST locos built by Kitson, Nos 47005, 47006 and 47009, which could be seen pottering around the docks. We missed seeing No 47007, which had not long been transferred away.

However, there were some new diesel shunting locos arriving on the scene, and thus the days were numbered for the Kitsons and the elderly GWR pannier tanks. Initially there were ten shunters, 204bhp 0-6-0s built by Hudswell-Clarke, which had mechanical transmission (ie clutch and gears). The final two had not long arrived new at the time of our first visit, and we shortly copped all ten, numbered 11116-11120 and 11144-11148. (They were all later to be renumbered D2500 to D2509.)

No 11147 was on shed for our first day at Birkenhead, as was No 41734, tending the coaling stage with a string of coal wagons. But of the GWR old-timers, only No 2012 was present. Kitsons Nos 47005 and 47006 were there. We copped two of the four 'Grange' 4-6-0s, Nos 6831 and 6859, together with some of Birkenhead's other GWR residents. Visiting GWR engines included 2-8-0 No 2833 from Oxley and No 6956 *Mottram Hall* from Wolverhampton's Stafford Road shed. Class 9F 2-10-0 No 92047 was an interesting visitor from neighbouring Bidston shed (6F). It was one of three based there at the time for working the heavy ore trains to the John Summers steelworks. Some Stanier Class 3 2-6-2Ts were stored out of use since the recent withdrawal of the passenger services to West Kirby.

Well, having trooped all around the shed, we whiled away the rest of the afternoon perched on our adopted grandstand. It was interesting to compare the two versions of standard shunting engines, the LMS 0-6-0T 'Jinties' and the GWR 0-6-0PTs. GWR engines were claimed to be more sure-footed than most others, and we came to the same conclusion as we watched both examples shunting the sidings on the opposite side of the main line. Having said that, the 'Jinties' never had any problems in completing their tasks.

That brilliant first day had to come to an end. As we awaited our electric train down in the depths of Green Lane station, the sounds of train movements from above sent down signals tempting us to return up the steps. But we thought better of it. We would be late for tea. So off we set in the midst of the evening rush hour, homeward-bound.

But the day wasn't over yet. As our No 79 bus trundled onto the long viaduct at Edge Hill, there was a shiny black object standing in the yard below, obviously ex-works to be in that condition. What was this? Our eyes focused intensely as the bus drew us nearer. Then:

'*Crosti*!'

'*Crosti*!'

'29!'

'29!'

'What's a Crosti?' Did we sense inquisitive thoughts reverberating around a crowded upper deck?

No 92029 was the last of ten Standard 9F 2-10-0s constructed with a Crosti boiler. The concept originated in Italy, where savings of up to 20% on fuel had been claimed. Slung between the frames underneath the boiler proper was a pre-heater. Instead of being ejected through the chimney at the front end, the hot gases from the boiler passed through the pre-heater before being exhausted through a chimney positioned in front of the cab. Cold water from the tender tank was thus 'warmed up' in the pre-heater before being injected into the boiler. The decision to equip ten 9Fs with this boiler stemmed from the fact that there was a coal shortage in the UK during the early 1950s.

This bold experiment was doomed, however. The engines were fed on imported coal, which had a high sulphur content, and the inevitable formation of sulphuric acid caused no end of corrosion problems internally. In poor condition, the Crostis actually burned more fuel than a 'standard' Standard 9F! The crews who manned these engines were not happy either, as the cabs became rather dirty from the close proximity of the chimney on the fireman's side. All ten Crostis had had their pre-heaters removed by the early 1960s, but the locos retained their smaller boilers to the end, which had been necessary when the pre-heater was in situ to keep within the BR loading gauge. They were never to acquire the straight smoke deflectors either, with which the remainder of the class were equipped.

Spike and I were overjoyed at copping our first Crosti, oblivious to a bemused upper deck, which probably couldn't understand why there was so much excitement.

After a couple more forays to Birkenhead, one of which produced Class '4700' 2-8-0 No 4704 and veteran 0-6-0PT No 2134, we decided to pay Bidston shed a visit. This was a little two-road shed close to Birkenhead North station. Here, the electrified line from Liverpool divided to West Kirby and New Brighton. With nothing personal intended, it was a little amusing to discover that the foreman here was a gentleman of rather ample proportions in charge of such a small shed. We encountered him shortly after collecting the first few numbers of some locos stored in a siding alongside the shed. He left us in no doubt that only he could say 'yea' or 'nay' as to our visiting 'his' shed.

'Well, go on, then.'

'Ah! Thanks very much.'

That siding by the shed contained a few surprises, for there were seven GWR locos from Birkenhead shed stored on it. Presumably this was a temporary measure to accommodate them while their home shed was in the process of being rebuilt. There were three '4300' 2-6-0s, Nos 6350, 5398 and 6376, the 'missing' veteran 0-6-0PTs Nos 2008 and 2069, and two diminutive 0-4-2Ts Nos 1457 and 1417. In past years these 0-4-2Ts had been used on the Hooton-West Kirby branch before it was upgraded to accept heavier engines. They were officially withdrawn from service after returning to their home shed following completion of the rebuilding. LMS 0-6-0 Dock Tank No 47166 was also stored, but there was no sign of Bidston's four 'J94' 0-6-0STs, which must have been at work around the docks.

The 'J94s' were MoS locos built for the Second World War, mainly for shipment abroad like the 'WD' 2-8-0s and 2-10-0s. After cessation of hostilities, the LNER snapped up 75 of the 0-6-0STs, classifying them 'J94'. The presence of LNER locos at Bidston was due to ancestral connections with the GCR, which had taken over the line from Bidston to Hawarden Bridge, near Chester. (The MSLR-cum-GCR had reached Chester via the CLC, and also controlled another finger reaching down to Wrexham Rhosddu.) With hindsight, then, there should have been no surprise at finding some familiar LNER types at Bidston, namely Gorton 'O4' 2-8-0s, which I'd seen at home in Childwall. Needless to say, I copped none of these. It was also disappointing to find neither of Bidston's other two 9F 2-10-0s (Nos 92045 and 92046), but we caught up with these on our next escapade across the Mersey.

Spike had the bright idea of 'doing' both Birkenhead and Bidston sheds in one day, by walking the dockland between the two. That was the bit I wasn't keen on. However, there could be some shunting engines at work, including the 'J94s', hopefully. So the cheese butties came in handy again as we headed off to Birkenhead, our first port of call. We copped Birkenhead's No 6841 *Marlas Grange* and 2-6-0 No 6346. Another 'Mogul' was there, No 5361 from Banbury (84C), and, interestingly, a rare sight of a Fowler 2-6-4T, No 42315, the only one based at Chester Midland. I managed a miscellany of six other cops before we headed off to the docks. The morning had been fine, but it developed into a blisteringly hot afternoon.

Our route took us via Corporation Road and Beaufort Road, which basically followed the complex of docks along the East Float and West Float, an inlet of water formerly known as the Wallasey Pool.[10] Spike and I tramped the docks, looking for BR locos, but there were far too many private-owner shunters (referred to as 'industrials') for our liking, which were not listed in our *ABC* books. Nevertheless, we did see a couple of the new diesels, Nos 11116 and 11146, and two 'J94s', Nos 68065 and 68034. Bidston's 9Fs, Nos 92045 and 92046, fell victim to our notebooks, as did some 'Jinty' 0-6-0Ts and a couple of 8F 2-8-0s. Back at Birkenhead, the 'missing' Kitson, No 47009, greeted us, returning after its day's work around the docks. There were also diesels Nos 11120, 11145 and 11144. Cops so far for the day totalled 29, but what was lurking almost out of sight as our homeward-bound electric train emerged into the daylight at Birkenhead Central?

No 68583 was an LNER Class 'J67' 0-6-0T of GER origin. It was used to haul permanent-way maintenance trains on the electrified system, and to shunt 'dead' electric stock at the storage depot alongside Central station. The old Mersey Railway had previously owned two steam shunters. The first, bought from the Metropolitan Railway of London, was replaced by one bought from the LNER, another GER example. This engine was 'worn out' by 1951, and thus heralded the arrival of No 68583, by this time under BR ownership, together with the Mersey Railway itself. It didn't last long after we copped it, being scrapped at Gorton Works in 1958. Diesel-mechanical shunters were then borrowed from Birkenhead whenever the need arose.

Well, visit followed visit to Birkenhead, interspersed with the Wigan trips. We also 'bunked' the local sheds of Speke, Aintree and Walton, mainly on a Sunday to cop the otherwise elusive shunters allocated to these depots.

[10] This used to mirror a corresponding inlet on the opposite bank of the Mersey, the Liver Pool, which stretched inland to where the entrance to the original Mersey Tunnel is now situated. The Liver Pool was filled in during the early part of the 18th century when development of the dock system there commenced.

My parents never owned a car, so all days out were either by the local Home James tour operator, based in Wavertree, or by train. It always came as second nature to invite Spike along with us if Dad was planning a train trip. And so it was for a trip to Llandudno on a summer excursion commencing from Birkenhead.

The train was hauled by one of Birkenhead's Stanier 2-6-0s. Incidentally, these 'Moguls', together with the 'Crabs', had been upgraded from Class 5 to Class 6P5F. Equal to a 'Jubilee' or an original 'Patriot'? Hardly, we thought. The tractive effort figures of the 'Mogul' were similar to those of the 'Jubilee' or original 'Patriot' 4-6-0s, but they had smaller wheels and smaller boilers – OK for short bursts of high speed running, but not for the sustained efforts of which the 4-6-0s were capable.

Anyway, our 2-6-0 had a fairly easy course along the North Wales coast. Our train avoided Chester station by taking the cut-off loop of the triangular junction west of General station. As we passed part of the GWR engine shed, I copped No 1016 *County of Hants* and No 48354, both from Shrewsbury. En route to and from Llandudno there were a few local small fry to cop, including exiled LYR 3F 0-6-0 No 52356 at Rhyl. Interestingly, Nottingham-based MR 3F 0-6-0 No 43378 was also at Rhyl (a long way from home for a small engine), meeting up with home-based classmate No 43396. Also seen at Rhyl were Standard Class 3 2-6-2Ts Nos 82020 and 82021. Many of this class of engine were being moved around between sheds. These two probably worked the Rhyl-Denbigh-Corwen branch, but they were shortly to move to Wrexham Rhosddu (an ex-GCR-cum-LNER shed, but now coded 6E under the LMR). One of Holyhead's Standard 5 Caprottis, No 73136, was also copped that day.

On the return run, our train was held at signals for about 45 minutes on the approach to Mold Junction. Here the line from Denbigh via Mold trailed in from our right. It was most frustrating to watch a couple of trains pass along that line while we were motionless, while on this stretch of quadruple main line three other eastbound trains overtook us. Good fortune prevailed, however. For upon exiting Northgate Tunnels, we came to a stand again, but with our coach sandwiched between two 'Castle' 4-6-0s, Nos 5088 *Llanthony Abbey* and 5033 *Broughton Castle*. Two good cops, and very clean ones, too. Having worked trains into Chester, they would be in the process of using the triangle to turn, prior to going on shed. Other GWR engines in the vicinity were 'Moguls' Nos 5311 and 6380. Some finish to the day!

The 'discovery' of Birkenhead, and the continuing lure of Wigan, had put the Chester idea on the 'back burner' for a while. Eventually the day came, and Spike and I made it to Chester, although over the next three years there were quite a number of occasions when I went solo. We chose to travel from Birkenhead instead of taking the circuitous route from Lime Street via Runcorn and Frodsham. Hamilton Square on the 'Underground' from Liverpool served the Woodside terminus. Dismissing the all-station stoppers, which took an age to get to our destination, we always caught one of the through expresses to the WR.

Woodside station accommodated five platforms under a twin-arched train shed. On entering the station the feeling of spaciousness around the concourse was in complete contrast to the throat of the station, where the tracks converged into two upon entering the tunnel. Our train nearly always departed from Platform 1, which seemed to be the most affected by track curvature; engines had to start their trains on a sharp left-hand curve, to be followed by an equally sharp right-hand bend into the tunnel. By now, 1957, these trains were hauled by Stanier LMS or BR Standard 2-6-4Ts, and the Standards always seemed to create more fuss in getting away. It has been suggested that, for whatever reason, most of the Standard series of engines were more prone to condensation in their cylinders than other types. And so it seemed to us, as the Standard tanks set off with cylinder drain cocks open to blow out the water.

Having passed under the town, we climbed out of the tunnel on a gradient of 1 in 93, sandwiched between some carriage sidings to our left and the line from the docks trailing in on our right. Shortly the sheds came into view. Although the yards were too distant to decipher loco numbers, it was possible to identify a few engines hanging around the coaling stage. Passing our beloved air-raid shelter and across Green Lane, the main line now continued in quadruple on easy gradients along a high embankment towards Chester. There was a panoramic view of the River Mersey and of the Cammell Laird shipyards to our left. The electrified 'Underground' line had now joined us after climbing up from Green Lane, and continued alongside before terminating at

Rock Ferry. As with all expresses, our train stopped at this station to connect with the electric service. Likewise we stopped at Hooton for the Ellesmere Port and Helsby services, which continue to diverge left to this day. The branch to West Kirby diverged to our right. Its passenger service had been withdrawn the previous September (1956), but the line remained open for freight traffic until May 1962. Beyond Ledsham the quadrupling ended, and our train continued along double track. Approaching Chester, the CLC line from the city's Northgate station to Manchester passed overhead, just before we hit the triangular junction west of General station. Our train veered left past the GWR loco shed, and into the station.

Chester General has changed somewhat over the years, but the three through platforms are still in use, running east-west. The longest of these is the down platform on the south side, which formed the original part of the station. There were a number of bay platforms at both ends, those at the west end being used by the WR Birkenhead services, which changed direction after an engine change. Some WR trains were routed into the through platform on the north side. This island platform was added during enlargement of the station in 1890, space being provided down the centre of the station for up and down through tracks. These and the three loop lines around the north side of the station were used by freight trains and summer extras not scheduled to stop in the station. The down platform was subdivided by having separate numbers for its eastern and western halves, and was signalled accordingly. This

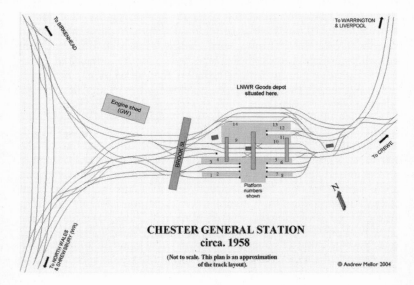

CHESTER GENERAL STATION
circa. 1958

(Not to scale. This plan is an approximation
of the track layout).

© Andrew Mellor 2004

permitted two trains to stand on the same track, and double crossovers linked to the adjacent centre track permitted overtaking. Finally, the outer platform on the north side, referred to above, was signalled for both up and down directions, particularly handy at busy periods.

Maybe the above description gives the impression of a station well able to cope with heavy volumes of traffic, such as during the holiday period. For British Railways, the years 1957 and 1958 proved to be the zenith for holiday traffic, not long before family car ownership really took off. The train was still the prime mover of people at this time, and Chester often became clogged up at times during summer Saturdays. While Exeter St David's was heralded as the 'gateway' to the South West holiday resorts, similarly Chester General was regarded as the 'gateway' to North Wales. It must have rivalled Exeter not only by the intensity of its summer traffic, but also the variety of motive power that passed through as a consequence. The summer extras had to be slotted in between the paths of the regular year-round services, such as the London-Holyhead expresses and the WR Birkenhead services. Trains from Liverpool Lime Street and further north, from Manchester and the ER, converged at a junction east of the station with trains from Crewe, the Potteries and the Midlands.

And so it was into this busy scene that Spike and I landed ourselves one summer Saturday in 1957. We had little problem getting around the GWR shed, friendly acknowledgements being exchanged with both enginemen and shed staff. However, on a busy summer Saturday it was the station and not the engine sheds that proved to be the main attraction. Worthy of note hauling holiday trains that day were brand-new 'Standard 4' 4-6-0 No 75063 from Nottingham and 'Crab' 2-6-0s Nos 42930 from Longsight (Manchester), 42816 from Saltley (Birmingham) and, astonishingly, No 42793 from Carlisle Kingmoor (then still coded 68A in the ScR). Also from Longsight was 'Jubilee' 4-6-0 No 45629 *Straits Settlements*, with another, No 45676 *Codrington*, from London's Camden. I copped three engines from Holyhead: 'Brit' 4-6-2 No 70048 (as yet unnamed, but later christened *The Territorial Army 1908-1958*), Caprotti No 73139 and, interestingly, 'Black 5' 4-6-0 No 45110, unknowingly destined for stardom as one of the last steamers to survive into 1968. Unusually, 2-6-4T No 42665 from Uttoxeter turned up, although I think its train terminated at Chester.

We were never inclined to visit the LMS shed at Chester (6A). It had nothing larger than 'Black 5s' on its books, and it was possible to see most of its allocation on the main line or in the vicinity of the station. However, the WR shed produced 'WD' 2-8-0 No 90010 and 'Black 5' 4-6-0 No 45143, both from Shrewsbury, and four GWR Class '2800' 2-8-0s. Other GWR locos copped on that day were Nos 5061

Earl of Birkenhead, 1003 *County of Wilts*, 1026 *County of Salop*, 7822 *Foxcote Manor* and 7817 *Garsington Manor*, and four 'Hall' 4-6-0s. *Garsington Manor* was the only Western namer allocated to Wrexham's Croes Newydd (84J), nominally a freight shed.

GWR engines were noted for their sharp exhaust beats, and generally made noisy exits when departing from Chester. The 'Counties' took first prize for blowing the decibel meter off its scale! Having backed onto an arrival from Birkenhead, it wasn't long before the safety valves started to sizzle. Came departure time, and with steam now screaming from the brass safety valve bonnet, the 'County' set off with a bark like gunfire, torturing the eardrums as it passed under Brooke Street bridge. From Chester, as with all WR trains, it ran along the former LNWR North Wales tracks as far as Saltney Junction, from where it veered southward down the old GWR line towards Wrexham and Shrewsbury.

Between 1893 and 1903 the LNWR quadrupled much of the North Wales line up to Llandudno Junction. Despite this quadrupling and the seemingly ample facilities at Chester General, the station was still something of a bottleneck as holiday trains queued to pass through, even those not scheduled to call there. Such was my experience when I spent a holiday at Llandudno with my parents in 1957, repeated in 1959. Travelling from Lime Street with another Stanier 2-6-0 at the head, our train was routed onto the freight loop along the north side of General station. Inevitably we drew to a halt alongside the infernal glass screen, through which I could see absolutely nothing of what was going on in the station. Each minute seemed like ten before we eventually got going again.

I didn't cop any GWR engines on this outward run, but was in for a surprise at Connah's Quay. No 68671, an 0-6-0T of LNER Class 'J72', was spotted shunting down among the small number of dock sidings. These sidings once belonged to the Wrexham, Mold & Connah's Quay Railway, which chose this location on the River Dee as an outlet for its goods traffic. Having been backed by the GCR during its struggle to survive, the system eventually came under LNER ownership. Hence the locomotive, which was actually of NE Region origin, and not a GCR example. No 68671 was one of three 'J72s' allocated to Wrexham Rhosddu at the time.

The quadruple track along the coast was not continuous; there were some stretches of double track, one of which lay between Abergele and Colwyn Bay. On the four-track sections I recall overtaking Standard tank No 80040 on a stopper, and running neck and neck for a time with 'Jubilee' No 45555 *Quebec* heading another holiday train. At Llandudno Junction we left the Holyhead line and curved sharply northward, negotiating the level crossing over the busy A55 trunk road.

Trains always took precedence over the crossing, and the hold-ups to road traffic here during the summer are today unimaginable. There was now one intermediate stop at Deganwy before arrival at Llandudno itself. The following day I copped LNER 'B1' 4-6-0 No 61186 in the station; it was from Colwick, so had probably worked through from Nottingham Victoria.

There followed visits to Conwy Castle, the Great Orme (via the rope-hauled trams) and the Pier Pavilion, where Terry Scott, Bill Maynard and the Beverley Sisters were appearing. Much that I appreciated all this, I enjoyed our outing on the Wednesday more so. Dad booked us on the land-cruise train known as the 'Cambrian Radio Cruise'. This train comprised six coaches, some of which had been gutted of their traditional seating fixtures to be replaced by free-standing armchairs, which we could adjust to our liking. In today's world intercom systems are taken for granted, but in 1957 to find one installed on a train was sheer novelty. Commentary was given about points of interest along the route (hence the 'Radio' in the train's title).

My favourite 4-4-0s, the Compounds, were well in evidence along the North Wales coast at this time and one of them, No 41164, headed our land cruise train as far as Rhyl. We saw another, No 41120, upon departing from Llandudno. Both were based at Llandudno Junction shed. Once clear of the junction, No 41164 gave us a scintillating run non-stop to Rhyl. Here, Standard 4-6-0 No 75033 was attached to the other end of the train to retrace our steps to Foryd Junction. From here we headed down the old Vale of Clwyd line, meeting up with the line from Mold at Denbigh. The train then continued down to Corwen to join the GWR line from Ruabon to Barmouth. However, before arriving at Barmouth there was a short run down the coast to visit Aberdovey.

From Barmouth, the train continued northward, passing Harlech Castle, and eventually reached Llandudno Junction via Afon Wen Junction, Caernarfon and Bangor. The run provided some interesting cops. Among them were Nos 5801 and 5809, two 0-4-2Ts similar to the two seen at Bidston and Birkenhead earlier, and No 4555, a lightweight 2-6-2T, which in the mid-1960s became the first of its type to pass into preservation. I copped another 'first' in the form of outside-framed 4-4-0 No 9018, a hybrid dating from 1936, built with parts from two earlier 4-4-0 designs. There was also No 75026, one of a number of 'Standard 4' 4-6-0s to receive double blastpipes and chimneys later on. Little did I know that I was to reacquaint myself with this engine ten years later, when it was transferred to Tebay shed to assist heavy trains up Shap incline.

Friday, the penultimate day of our holiday, saw us at Colwyn Bay, participating in a circular tour aboard an 'open-topper'. These old Guy-engined buses were so slow on the steep hills that abound around the town that no one had grounds for complaining about being so rushed that they couldn't appreciate the scenery! The remainder of that afternoon was spent near the railway station. Where else? My parents sat on the promenade while I was up on the footpath by the trackside. Dad gave me the chance to try my hand at railway photography by lending me his Kodak Sterling II camera. My first attempts had been at Birkenhead photographing 'still' engines using a box camera. Moving trains were a different matter, as I was shortly to discover. I fired the shutter too early on some shots, but achieved some reasonable results with 'Jubilee' No 45649 *Hawkins* (which I copped) double-heading with a 'Standard 4' 4-6-0, as well as a 'Crab' 2-6-0, both on summer specials. No 70047 passed, the only 'Brit' to remain nameless throughout its working life, and a couple more 'Standard 4' 4-6-0s double-headed a Chester-bound stopper.

The journey home from this holiday was a bit special for me, for at the head of our train was another Compound 4-4-0. Although I couldn't discover its identity until arrival in Liverpool, I did manage to count ten coaches as the train rounded the curves en route to Llandudno Junction. Some load for the 4-4-0, but it managed to achieve a reasonable speed along the coast. On one of the four-track sections we passed a 9F 2-10-0, its wheels and rods a blur as it hurtled westward with another holiday extra. The big 9Fs were not uncommon on such trains in the late 1950s, but with only 5-foot-diameter wheels this practice was frowned upon by some in high authority. Also heading west was 'Black 5' No 45154 *Lanarkshire Yeomanry*, which I'd copped the previous year in Scotland. Like its sister *Ayrshire Yeomanry*, seen earlier at Bryn, it had been transferred to the LMR at Newton Heath. Chester provided a handful of GWR cops, including No 1025 *County of Radnor*.

Having successfully progressed through Helsby and Frodsham, our 4-4-0 now had to climb the steep bank up to Halton Junction to join the Crewe-Liverpool line. As trains on this line normally took precedence, we came to the inevitable dead stand on the incline. The signal cleared, but with its heavy load and only four coupled wheels for adhesion, the Compound persistently slipped. From our coach, which was at least halfway down the train, we could hear it struggling as driver and engine fought to get the train on the move. Eventually, after letting the train roll back several times, our driver found a patch of track on which the 4-4-0 managed to gain sufficient momentum to keep us moving in the right direction. Good work! Across the Runcorn bridge and heading along the curved viaduct towards Ditton Junction, another Compound passed us, No 41167, a bonus cop for me.

At Lime Street we walked past our engine towards the ticket barrier. I was quite appalled at what I saw. The engine was red. Not painted red, but rusty red, all over. This suggested that it had been stored in the open air for a long period, then pressed into service to assist with the summer traffic. Its number, 41111, was chalked on the cabside.

The Llandudno holiday of two years later was comparatively uneventful as far as number-spotting was concerned. There was the usual small quota of Western cops at Chester, together with two notable 'Jubilees' en route back to Liverpool, No 45652 *Hawke* from Kentish Town and No 45704 *Leviathan* from Carlisle Kingmoor. This time a 'Standard 4' 4-6-0 headed our train, number not recorded, probably a Chester or Llandudno 'stink'. Inevitably, it proved to be more sure-footed than the Compound.

9
Please whistle at Bonwm

There is not much at Bonwm in the way of civilisation, only the outstanding beauty of the countryside at what is virtually an extension of the Vale of Llangollen. Some neighbours from our close at home part-owned a cottage there, and this was our holiday destination for the year 1958. Situated up the hillside about 1¼ miles east of Corwen, a mountain track led to it from the A5 trunk road from Llangollen. Parallel with the A5 ran the WR line from Ruabon to the Cambrian coast. (Indeed, at the time of writing, the section between Llangollen and Corwen is being restored by the Llangollen Railway.) There was an unstaffed halt at Bonwm, a facility once so commonly found in rural areas served by the old GWR.

My parents asked Spike to come and stay with us, an invitation he accepted. It was arranged that he and I would travel down by train with Dad, while Mum would make the trip with the luggage courtesy of Spike's parents with their Standard 8. For Spike and myself, this entailed another run from Birkenhead Woodside, with the obligatory call at Chester en route. At Chester, the former GWR shed had by now been transferred to the LMR, the result of some regional boundary changes earlier in the year. Consequently, some of Chester West's allocation of GWR locos had been swapped for LMS types. So it wasn't surprising that I copped three Stanier 8F 2-8-0s newly allocated there – Nos 48471, 48424 and 48402 – all three transferred from sheds on the WR. My notes also reveal that No 5031 *Totnes Castle* was on hand, which may have been the engine that took our train forward from Chester. At Ruabon, junction for the Barmouth line, we had to alight and wait for the branch train, which rolled up behind 0-4-2T No 5810. Would this little engine manage four suburban coaches up the steep gradients around Acrefer and Trevor? It did just that, no problem. Meanwhile, at Ruabon, Dad had spoken to the guard about the prospect of setting us down at Bonwm Halt, customary practice for unstaffed stations in those days. The platform at Bonwm was barely the length of one coach, and our driver stopped the train with our compartment having overshot. With waves of assistance from the guard, the driver reversed, causing heads to appear from most of the windows, and we eventually alighted safely onto the platform. Later in the day we saw No 5810 returning with its train to Wrexham.

And what of the cottage? It was well secluded among some trees at the side of the mountain track. Access was by means of a footbridge across a stream, which ran down parallel to the track and entered the Dee after passing under the A5 and the railway. The cottage depended on this stream for its water supply, for there was no water main here with which to connect. A pipe leading to a small hand pump in the kitchen provided filtered water, the kettle probably taking as long to fill as it did to boil.

As it happened, tea brewing took even longer one day, as Spike and I thought we'd have fun building a dam in the stream. Quite a number of stones had been rearranged close to the footbridge before Dad came bounding down the path, enquiring what had happened to the water supply. Oh dear! The water level had dropped below the filter connected to the supply pipe. So here was a real opportunity to prove our skills in dam-building as we fought, and eventually succeeded, in raising the water level sufficiently to submerge the filter.

There was a large wheelbarrow on hand at the cottage. Being miles from any fairground, it seemed that the next best thing to riding on a roller-coaster was to give each other rides in it. Inevitably, we tipped each other into the stream, the barrow zooming off course (purposely) as the pair of us hurtled down the hill! We also took it upon ourselves to turn the place into a 'railway'. 'Please Whistle' signs were affixed to the footbridge and gates and a station nameboard to the cottage itself, and there were 'advertisements' for refreshments to be found within. Despite the seclusion, Dad's worries that someone could take the latter seriously almost proved to be well founded. One morning, a bewildered postman pondered over the notices.

'It's all right. It's the lads' doing,' Dad called from one of the windows, and the postman trundled back down the path, chuckling away to himself as he went.

Our 'pride and joy' was the erection of a lower-quadrant semaphore signal, a piece of wood fixed to a post by a single screw, so that it would swivel as required. Somehow we managed to secure the 'assembly' into the dry-stone wall by the path. Remote control was facilitated by the use of a long length of string. Magic moments!

'Magic Moments', the song, had been a hit for Perry Como earlier in the year. Popular around the time of our Bonwm holiday were the Everly Brothers with 'All I Have To Do Is Dream' and 'Claudette'. Later in the year came Tommy Edwards and 'It's All in the Game', and Lord Rockingham's XI, who belted out 'Hoots Mon'.

These days a car would be considered essential for a place like Bonwm, but for us in 1958 it had to be the bus or Shanks's pony. With Corwen about 1¼ miles distant, I don't know how Mum managed to keep the larder well supplied for the four of us. Crosville Motor Services provided the bus services in these parts, and as far as I can recollect there were only two buses each way per day between Llangollen and Corwen. At least, they ran at a more convenient time of the day than did the trains, as we discovered when Spike and myself decided to go to Wrexham to 'do' the two sheds there. We caught the morning bus to Llangollen to wait for the service to Wrexham. Crosville used 'low-bridge' double-decker buses on this run. The upstairs gangway ran along the right-hand side of the bus, and the seats, four abreast, were accessed by a steep step up. You had to crouch down while shuffling along to the window on the opposite side. New buses were appearing on the scene, constructed with a lower central aisle downstairs, which in turn permitted a lower floor upstairs; thus in these later buses the seating arrangement on the upper deck was of conventional layout. The journey to Llangollen took half an hour, where, after a 20-minute wait, we boarded one of the newer buses bound for Wrexham. Forty-five minutes later we were on General station, where I photographed No 1022 *County of Northampton* heading a Paddington train (Dad had lent me his camera again). The station still has its staggered platforms today, the up platform being to the south of the island platform serving the down main and loop lines. The old GCR line from Connah's Quay and Shotton swept by on the west side with its own Exchange station adjacent to the island platform. This line dived under the GWR line to the south to reach Wrexham Central, and once continued on to Ellesmere and Whitchurch.

Croes Newydd shed was next on our itinerary, where we found outside-framed 4-4-0 No 9004. We also saw our first GWR 0-6-2Ts. There were some Class '2800' 2-8-0s, one of which was a cop, No 3810 from Cardiff Canton. The only namer on shed was No 5971 *Merevale Hall* from Worcester. Rhosddu shed proved interesting. For a start, it was now under WR jurisdiction, having swapped shed codes with Chester West. We copped four LNER locos still outposted here, all with shedplates bearing the WR code of 84K. I completed the shed's trio of 'J72' 0-6-0Ts by copping Nos 68727 and 68714, and the quartet of cops was completed with 'J69' 0-6-0T No 68553, an ex-GER loco, and 'N5' 0-6-2T No 69281. The latter was an ex-GCR engine, and was thus on 'home' territory, but was parked inside the shed marked as withdrawn from service. Also present was a gaggle of Stanier Class 3 2-6-2Ts, but while at General station we saw a Fowler version, No 40058, passing through Exchange with a stopper. Curiously, it was recorded in the *ABC* shed book as being allocated to Shrewsbury, so what was it doing helping out on the GCR line while resident Stanier tanks were available? Apart from those, Standard Class 3s Nos 82020 and 82021 were also now allocated to Rhosddu.

During an interlude at Oswestry we saw some of the rare Class '5400' 0-6-0PTs, together with four WR-allocated Ivatt Class 2 2-6-0s, the forerunners of the 78000-series Standard version. Oswestry was once the headquarters of the former Cambrian Railways, and it was along a section of the Cambrian that we travelled for a trip to Barmouth. As its name implies, the Cambrian ran along the Cambrian Coast, and its branch from Barmouth met the GWR line from Llangollen end-on at Dolgellau to form a through route to Ruabon.

As we waited in anticipation on Corwen station, what should roll in with our train but a grubby No 6346, a GWR 2-6-0 from Birkenhead that we'd seen many times already. On a rather unpleasant day, there wasn't much to do at Barmouth except hang around the shops, or brave the elements on the sea front. There was just a handful of cops including No 2251 of the curiously designated Class '2251' (the first of the type was numbered 2200). Standard 4-6-0 No 75050 also arrived with a special from Chester via Bangor, Afon Wen and the Cambrian coast.

Heading back from the coast, the line to Llangollen climbs moderately as far as Dolgellau, after which the gradient steepens to 1 in 100/91, followed by a section at 1 in 50, all over a distance of about 3½ miles. Plodding up past Dolgellau our train eventually ground to a halt on the single track. Heads out of windows could see a great column of black smoke at the head of the train. No 6346 had run short of steam.

'Well,' we thought, 'what would you expect with a Birkenhead "stink" like that?'

Unfortunately, the holiday was most memorable for 'the wrong reason', as we might say today. On the second Sunday Spike's parents came for lunch. Later his Dad ferried us all to Llangollen, necessitating a double trip with the little Standard 8. The weather was dry and pleasant as we walked over the Chain Bridge and spent some time by the Horseshoe Falls. Then the weather dramatically changed. A raging thunderstorm brought torrential rain, and there was no alternative but for us all to cram into the car to return to the cottage. Spike and I were 'big lads' now, and this was certainly the last time either of us sat on our mothers' knees! The 9 miles back to Bonwm were painfully slow, and the wipers at times couldn't cope with the volume of water. The storm had abated by the time tea was finished, and Spike's parents returned to Liverpool, leaving us contemplating the prospect of a second week.

There was more rain that night, and it started to seep through the roof at the rear of our bedroom wall. So buckets, bowls and towels were placed in position to catch the drips. More rain came on Monday night, and the following morning Dad greeted us with:

'Have you noticed anything?'

From where the roof joined the rear wall, much of the plaster had fallen to the floor, missing my head by a couple of feet! Amazingly, both Spike and I had slept on, undisturbed. Well, after this latest development it was decided we'd had enough, and that we should return home. Our 'railway' signs came down, all, that is, except two 'PLEASE WHISTLE' signs, one on the footbridge across the stream and the other at the cattle grid halfway down the track to the main road. My recollections at this point are unclear, but I guess we journeyed to Corwen by taxi, which Dad would have summoned by phone from a nearby farm. And wasn't the sun 'cracking the flags'? There was no turning back now, though. We didn't fancy the prospects of another wet night at the cottage, and we had to let Jack know what had happened.

Our train was a 'through' service to Birkenhead, and arrived at Corwen headed by a 'Manor' 4-6-0. Its number is not recorded, but it was probably one of Chester's. At Wrexham the signalman routed us into the down loop platform, and shortly another train drew into the down main. It, too, was bound for Birkenhead.

'Can we change to that train, Dad? It's got a "Castle" on the front.'

'What about all this luggage?'

'We can manage that.'

'No!'

Well, it was worth a try. The 'Castle' 4-6-0 was No 4092 *Dunraven Castle* from Reading, and was the star cop of the day. It left Wrexham ahead of us.

Chester stumped up another LMS 2-8-0, No 48415, and two of its newly reallocated Standard 2-6-2Ts, Nos 82032 and 82036. All these Standard tanks arrived on the scene to displace the GWR '5100' types, which were being moved back into WR territory.

The journey time between Corwen and Birkenhead was about 2¼ hours; adding on time between Childwall and Birkenhead brought the total to at least 3 hours. The equivalent journey by today's new roads takes half that time, but it's not half as much fun!

Postscript

I returned to Wrexham with Spike in May the following year. Rhosddu shed now had a stud of GWR types, including Class '2251' 0-6-0s Nos 3204 and 3207, and more Standard Class 3 2-6-2Ts, including the pioneer No 82000, had replaced the Stanier examples. Inevitably, some pannier tanks had also materialised. Class 'J39' 0-6-0 No 64718 was there from Gorton, but although the LNER regime at Rhosddu had come to an end we hadn't seen the last of the trio of 'J72s', Nos 68671, 68714 and 68727. We found them in store at Bidston shed, pending movement to Gorton Works for scrapping. No 68671 bore a cast shedplate bearing the curious code of 97L. This fact has been recorded in the correspondence columns of railway journals, and so far no one has been able to explain the significance of this shed plate.

10
As one era draws
to a close...

It was Hank, my classmate at school, who suggested I went to Manchester with him. (He was referred to as 'Hank' because of a likeness to a certain guitarist of the Shadows.) His interest wasn't in railways, though, but in buses, and it is thanks to him that I gained what little knowledge I have of the buses of the day. It was April 1958 when I took him up on his suggestion. We journeyed to the Cotton Capital via the CLC route between the respective Central stations.

From the ground-level station[11], trains ran to Manchester Central, Stockport Tiviot Dale, Warrington Central and to the Aintree branch. It had six platforms and existed on a cramped site behind the big Lewis's department store. Central was the 'Cinderella' of the three city-centre stations, as no engine from further afield than Manchester appeared there on a regular basis. Not surprisingly, spotters were not seen there unless they were catching a train! There were only a handful of long-distance services, each of them having to reverse direction at Manchester Central. After changing engines in the process, these trains retraced their path as far as Throstle Nest Junction, from where they veered away southward. These long-distance services comprised one train to Harwich, for connections to the continent, one to Nottingham Midland, two to Hull, and one to Sheffield Victoria. On summer Saturdays there were a couple of additional trains to Sheffield, too. All except the Nottingham trains took the Fairfield loop at Chorlton-cum-Hardy to join the electrified line to Sheffield at Guide Bridge.

There was a 'fast' service of trains to Manchester, calling only at Farnworth (later called Widnes North) and Warrington Central on a 45-minute schedule. At that time LMS 2-6-4Ts predominated on these expresses, although by 1960 some 'Black 5' 4-6-0s had been transferred to Brunswick shed to join them. The CLC route was quite undulating,

---

[11] The low-level platforms formed the terminus of the 'Underground' line to the Wirral. Nineteen years were to elapse before it became part of the single-line loop now linking the system to Lime Street station, and to Moorefields, at the former site of Liverpool's Exchange station.

with alternating gradients throughout. For example, in each direction the steepest were at 1 in 185 around Halewood and Hough Green, and at 1 in 135 both sides of the Manchester Ship Canal bridge beyond Irlam. Despite these hindrances, the tanks, with their 5ft 9in driving wheels, performed wonders keeping to the tight schedule, often reaching speeds well into the 70s. The call at Warrington involved a deviation from the otherwise straight course between Sankey and Padgate Junctions, and the necessary slow progress around here contrasted with the high speeds achieved on either side of this 'detour'. The direct line, which avoided Warrington, was used by through freights and summer extras not scheduled to call at the town. The cut-off line crossed the WCML close to that line's Dallam engine shed, and was closed in the late 1960s, while the loop line still spans the WCML nearer to Bank Quay.

Well, I got off to a good start with Hank on arrival at Manchester Central. Standing alone at one of the buffer stops was diesel No 10100, an experimental loco that was the brainchild of one Dr Fell. It was a machine of 2,000bhp, generated by four 500bhp engines driving through specially adapted mechanical transmissions. The loco's wheel arrangement was 2-D-2, ie a rigid eight-coupled driving wheelbase flanked by two four-wheeled bogies, but was later modified to a 2-B-B-2 after the removal of the centre coupling rods. By now I was regularly taking Dad's camera on my spotting adventures, and had it with me on this occasion. Much to my regret, I didn't photograph the unique No 10100. I didn't possess a light meter and I considered that the light was insufficient for a satisfactory photograph. Anyway, I was bound to get another opportunity to photograph it, so I thought. It was not to be, for No 10100 caught fire on a later date and was withdrawn for scrapping after a period in store at Derby Works, its birthplace.

Having arrived at Manchester, I split from Hank for the day until it was time to return home. He scoured the bus terminus at Piccadilly, and I divided my time between London Road and Victoria stations. At London Road I was particularly keen to see some of the electric locomotives employed between Manchester and Sheffield over the Woodhead route. Electrification had been completed in 1954, having been started by the LNER in the 1930s, but held up by the Second World War. I saw two of the seven Co-Co locomotives, Nos 27001 and 27004, both unnamed at the time. An interesting steam cop was No 63579, a Class 'O1' 2-8-0. This engine was shedded at Nottingham's Annesley, and had just been outshopped from overhaul at Gorton Works. There were local engines from Gorton shed in the form of 'L1' 2-6-4Ts and 'A5' 4-6-2Ts, types that Gorton deemed not to send along the CLC into Liverpool. After a long walk to Victoria station, I was rewarded with a further eight cops to add to the ten seen at London

Road. In view of the time spent walking between the stations, I decided in future to visit either London Road or Victoria, but not both on the same day. Buses wouldn't have helped, as all radiated from Piccadilly, and I still had to trudge back to Central to meet Hank and return to Liverpool. Anyway, the CLC journey out and back provided 15 cops, making a total of 33 for the afternoon.

I made a few visits to Manchester with Spike, some by the CLC route, others over the former L&M tracks from Lime Street to Manchester Exchange. From the latter, we accessed the LYR Victoria station by the once famous connecting platform, which vanished when Exchange closed in 1969. The east end of Victoria station proved to be the best vantage point to observe all the action. Trains departing from Exchange for Yorkshire and the North East passed through the centre of Victoria station, immediately beyond which is the steep incline to Miles Platting. The heavy trains accepted assistance from bank engines supplied by Patricroft shed. During my initial visits these bank engines were often Class 2P 4-4-0s, but they were displaced by LMS 2-6-4Ts at the turn of the decade. From the north side of the station trains departed for the LYR route through Newton Heath to places like Rochdale on the myriad of lines that existed north-east of Manchester at the time. The south side of Victoria was used by electric multiple units (EMUs) to Bury (latterly replaced by the Metrolink tram service). We saw some of the original EMUs, built at the LYR's Horwich Works from 1916, before they were replaced in 1959 by new BR-built units. Trains left the west end of Victoria for places like Blackpool, Southport and Liverpool Exchange.

There couldn't have been a more fitting end to one particular day on which we travelled via the CLC both ways. At the head of our train back to Liverpool a Compound 4-4-0 was substituting for the normal 2-6-4T. (Alas, its number is not recorded.) The train, the 'rush hour' 5.30pm, was strengthened by the addition of a seventh coach and, because of the time spent attaching this vehicle, we left Manchester 5 minutes late. What a scintillating run we had! Even with the extra coach, our Class 4P had regained 3 minutes of lost time upon arrival at Liverpool. Needless to say, I was 'dead chuffed' that this had been achieved by a Compound 4-4-0.

An interesting motive power development occurred in Manchester during July 1958. Six 'Britannia' 4-6-2s were transferred from the ER to Trafford Park, which also received further Class 7 power in the form of some 'Royal Scot' 4-6-0s. In both cases the locos in question had been ousted from their former stamping grounds by diesel power, the 'Scots' moving from the WCML. The prospect of seeing one of the 'Brits' at Manchester Central brought the CLC route back into favour for me.

On subsequent visits I duly copped Nos 70021 *Morning Star* and 70017 *Arrow* waiting to leave with Midland line trains while I awaited my train for Liverpool.

Brief mention was made earlier of an aunt and uncle who lived in Dalton-in-Furness. During the 1950s there were excursions from Liverpool Exchange through to Barrow at times such as Easter and Bank Holiday weekends. Climbing away from Preston on one such excursion in the summer of 1960, I was taken aback as a number of engines came into view, stored in the sidings at the former coal yard at Maudlands. The engines were all red-rusty, their paint having been burned off in a fire that had raged through Preston engine shed one day in June. Among the 13 engines that suffered in the fire were a Standard Caprotti 4-6-0 and a Crab 2-6-0, having worked to Preston from elsewhere. Some of Preston's 'Super D' 0-8-0s were also affected.

Proceeding along the Furness line from Carnforth, there was a good view of the loco yard at the engine shed there – that is, once our train had cleared the concrete wall on the down platform, constructed as a defence against cold, wintry weather. I spotted most of the last surviving Furness Railway engines, some Class 3F 0-6-0s ending their days at Carnforth just before they went for scrapping. One day in 1962 there was a surprise on shed in the form of Class 9F 2-10-0 No 92201, from Doncaster on the ER.

Staying at Dalton on my own a few times, I visited Barrow and Carnforth sheds. Carnforth was always a dodgy shed to 'bunk', as the BTC Police were present close to the access footbridge. You stood a slim chance of success by entering the west yard, from where later the entrance was sited to Steamtown Museum[12]. I thought I had succeeded on my second attempt on Carnforth, only to be spotted by a Constable as I tried to sneak back out along the perimeter wall.

'Oi! Come 'ere.'

There followed a lecture about trespassing, and the officer put it to me that I wouldn't venture onto Morecambe Pier without first paying at the gate, would I? I replied that I wouldn't waste my time walking along Morecambe Pier when I could be spotting at Carnforth or similar. (Did we really have to pay in those days to access our famous piers?) Anyway, the officer let me off with a warning, and I returned to the station for the train back to Dalton.

The summer of 1959 was long and hot, and in the August following the family holiday in Llandudno we spent a week at Dalton. One

---

[12] Carnforth MPD became Steamtown during the late 1960s as the preservation era took hold. After being run down as a museum following a take-over early in the 1990s, it closed its doors to the public in 1997.

glorious day we took my aunt and uncle on a tour. This entailed a train to Penrith via Carnforth and a bus over the Kirkstone Pass to Bowness, followed by a boat trip down Windermere to Lakeside. The tour concluded with a crowded three-coach run along the FR's Lakeside branch to Plumpton Junction on the Barrow line, the engine for that final leg being 2-6-4T No 42581. BR commonly advertised such tours in conjunction with the bus and boat operators. However, travel was by public service conveyance, and entry onto the normal service buses was not guaranteed at peak holiday time. This happened to us on this tour, and we didn't particularly enjoy the experience of a crowded branch train either.

There were some vintage Midland Class 2F 0-6-0s based at Barrow. Having copped a couple of these shunting the morning pick-up goods at Dalton station, a visit to the sheds netted five more cops. There were also a couple of 2P 4-4-0s, Nos 40654 and 40695. I didn't see these engines in use on any of my visits to Dalton, as Barrow's 2-6-4Ts were used on local services. A surprise resident at this time was Class 1P 0-4-4T No 41904, the only example I was to see of this type. Alas, it was in store.

The hot weather continued for some time following our return home, interrupted by thunderstorms as expected during such weather. One storm produced a most unexpected sight as I journeyed homeward from town on a No 79 bus one Saturday. Clad in shirt sleeves and without a 'mac', I made my way to the Pier Head to catch my bus. Having crossed the Dock Road, I had to scurry for the bus when large spots of rain began to fall. By the time I boarded it was bucketing down, and thunder was fast approaching. The downpour continued as my bus made its cautious way out of town, until it came to a standstill in traffic approaching a busy junction close to Liverpool University. This particular junction, local readers may recall, was where Crown Street crossed the intersection of Pembroke Place and West Derby Road, and was controlled at busy periods by a policeman on point duty. My bus was held up in Elizabeth Street[13], intending to turn right into West Derby Road. The junction itself, which was completely under water, was laid with wooden setts. Such was the volume of water during the storm that hundreds of them were torn up and floated down Pembroke Place, past the Royal Infirmary, to continue down London Road towards Lime Street. From the Co-operative store in London Road where he worked, Dad vividly remembered seeing the spectacle from a staircase window. With careful guidance by the Police, traffic was eventually able to

---

[13] Which vanished when the university buildings were extended.

negotiate the flooded junction, and my bus continued up West Derby Road and headed for Edge Hill, where, on this frustrating journey home, a temporary diversion awaited it.

In connection with electrification of the Liverpool to Crewe line, it became necessary to raise the central portion of the viaduct across the main-line tracks to allow sufficient clearance for the overhead wires. Road traffic along the viaduct was restricted to one way only, city-bound, but a detour was initiated for outward-bound traffic. So my bus turned off the normal route along Wavertree Road into Tunnel Road, crossing the west end of Edge Hill station in the process. The regular route was regained opposite the small Wavertree goods yard. The detour added something like an extra 15 minutes to the journey home from town, and was in force for more than a year while the viaduct was rebuilt. I felt hard done by at missing the customary view from the buses crossing the viaduct, so the rail service to Broad Green was sometimes preferred.

A couple of visits to Carlisle ensued during further holidays at Dalton. For one of these I decided to try the coastal route via Whitehaven and Workington, with gorgeous views on the journey – the Irish Sea to my left, and the Lakeland mountains to my right. But the journey took 3½ hours, and involved a quarter-hour wait at Workington for a connection onward to Carlisle, as there were no through trains over this route, and both trains called at all stations. For comparison, the journey time via Carnforth was just over 2½ hours, and the Glasgow/Edinburgh expresses from Liverpool took about 3 hours to reach Carlisle from Merseyside.

As well as the 'local talent', I copped Class 'A2' 4-6-4 No 60530 *Sayajarao* from Edinburgh's Haymarket, and a couple of ScR 'Black 5s', Nos 45174 from Carstairs and 45465 from Perth. Interestingly, the 'A2' was spotted at the south end, having arrived from Newcastle. A Haymarket engine would normally have been seen at the north end after traversing the Waverley Route. I returned to Dalton by catching a through train to Warrington and changing at Carnforth. The Warrington train was 'all stations', although the wayside stations on the WCML were few and far between. Now there are none.

For returning to Liverpool, there was a choice of three trains calling at Dalton between 1.00pm and 1.40pm, although all necessitated a change at Preston or Lancaster. I usually caught the first of these, which was a through train to London Euston. It was frequently double-headed by either two 'Jubilees', two 'Scots', or a combination of both. The purpose of double-heading this train was to return the leading engine to Lancaster following an unbalanced working north. This saved track occupation with light-engine movements to get a locomotive to where it was next needed. Particularly for heavy freight trains, Lindal

Summit, between Dalton and Ulverston, was something of an obstacle with gradients on either side of 1 in 95. They took rear-end assistance, westbound from Plumpton Junction near Ulverston, or from Askam[14], north of Barrow, when heading eastward.

The mid-1950s saw BR introduce diesel multiple units (DMUs) on selected services previously worked by steam. (Indeed, by 1958, some of the prototype 'Derby Lightweight' DMUs were operating between Workington and Carlisle.) After the announcement of the Modernisation Plan, DMU production was accelerated, modified designs emerging as technology advanced and experience was gained. BR laid emphasis on the novelty aspect of the DMUs, extolling their virtues as ideal for scenic tours. Quite true. On these first-generation railcars you could see the track ahead through the driver's cab, were you lucky enough to obtain a seat near the front of the train. BR issued hundreds of leaflets to stations, advertising tours to this and that place by 'Special Diesel Train'. These trains normally ran at weekends or on Bank Holidays from spring to autumn.

In 1960 Dad and I took one of these excursions to Harrogate. However, rather than sample the Spa waters we took a bus to York, my first ever visit there. The bus, incidentally, was a Bristol-engined Lowbridge of similar design to Crosville's. In view of the time taken for the bus journeys, we didn't really have sufficient time to appreciate the city, nor what the railway station had to offer. We did visit the 'old' museum at Queen Street. On the East Coast Main Line (ECML) I copped three 'Pacifics': 'A2/3' No 60522 *Straight Deal*, 'A1' No 60131 *Osprey*, and 'Brit' No 70014 *Iron Duke*, one of those transferred to Trafford Park in 1958.

The first Ian Allan *ABC* booklet of diesels appeared in 1958, and sadly I started collecting the DMU numbers listed therein. The York trip in 1960 added a host of such 'cops', and my notebooks became littered with such numbers. I eventually found the practice rather tedious, and thankfully gave it up. In this book no multiple unit numbers are included in cop totals.

I returned to York with Hank in early June 1960, just before we sat our GCE (General Certificate of Education) examinations; we considered that the trip would provide a welcome break from all the studying. Either a 'Scot' or a rebuilt 'Patriot' headed our train out of Lime Street, the 9.00am to Newcastle. Hank and I alighted at Leeds City station, as our train was about to change direction to continue its journey north via Harrogate. Class 'A3' 4-6-2 No 60082 *Neil Gow* was

---

[14] Through freight trains used the Barrow cut-off loop, avoiding the horseshoe route through Barrow station, and rejoined the main line at Dalton Junction.

the new train engine, and for the difficult run to Harrogate Standard Class 4 2-6-4T No 80119 was provided as pilot. A quintet of these tanks, Nos 80116 to 80120, had been transferred to Leeds Neville Hill shed from Whitby the previous year, and I saw four of them on this day. As a compromise with Hank, I agreed to 'bus it' between Leeds and York. At York I made 32 cops, which included my second 'A4', No 60031 *Golden Plover*, seen in the station. Also of note was one of the station pilots, Class 'J72' 0-6-0T No 68736, which sported the NER green livery of the pre-Grouping era, although the BR emblem was emblazoned on the tanksides together with the NER coat of arms. Among the remaining cops at York were five 'A3' and two 'A1' 4-6-2s. Another 'A1', No 60119 *Patrick Stirling*, was seen at Leeds on our return journey.

I had decided to leave school that summer, and was due to start work in September. To make the most of the final long summer break I would get, I decided to go to Doncaster. It was one day in August. Spike wasn't keen on the idea, so I went solo, catching the 9.30am through train to Hull from Liverpool Central. From Manchester, after the customary reversal, another engine took the train to Guide Bridge on the electrified line from Manchester London Road. The route took the train onto the Fairfield Loop, which diverged from the MR route to Derby at Chorlton-cum-Hardy. I used this train a few times in the coming years, and motive power to Guide Bridge could be anything from an LMS 2-6-4T, 'Crab' 2-6-0 or 'Black 5' 4-6-0 to an LNER 'B1' 4-6-0 or 'K3' 2-6-0. It seemed that whatever engine happened to be available was used for this leg of the journey. But no matter what was on the front, the plod around the Loop was in complete contrast to the usual spirited run from Liverpool, and the following speedy run with electric traction between Guide Bridge and Sheffield Victoria. The electric loco, normally one of the seven Co-Co Class EM2s, came off the train at Sheffield, and from there to Doncaster a 'B1' or 'K3' was usually supplied.

I made plenty of local cops on this part of the journey, as might be expected. For the whole day I made the massive total of 141, good going considering that I didn't bother going around the sheds at Doncaster. There was too much going on at the station anyway, as it was a summer Saturday on which many extra trains were run. One of these commenced at Doncaster and was hauled by Class 'D49' 4-4-0 No 62765 *The Goathland*, one of the examples fitted with poppet valves and sub-classified 'D49/2' by the LNER. Destined for Hull, this train comprised an assortment of Gresley and Thompson vintage compartment stock. 1960 was the final year in which steam was rostered for most of the long-distance expresses, and among a host of 'Pacific' cops were six 'A4' 'streaks'. Just as in Edinburgh four years ago, I was so impressed by the quantity of 'big' engines on view, though not so impressive was the noise from their safety valves!

I was also briefly reacquainted with the prototype 'Deltic' locomotive, by then working over the ECML. It was to be withdrawn the following year, when the production series of 'Deltic' locos made their debut, replacing steam on the principal rosters. In 1963 the prototype was towed to London, where it found a home at the Science Museum before moving to the National Railway Museum at York in the 1990s.

Unfortunately, I couldn't photograph any moving trains that day, as the camera I had been borrowing from Dad had been stolen earlier in Liverpool, admittedly through my own carelessness. As a quick fix I'd bought a Brownie camera from Hank for 5 shillings. As it had a fixed shutter speed of about 1/25th second, it was totally incapable of stopping movement. However, I did get some quite acceptable photos of static subjects in the station.

So that was that. Doncaster was my final big fling as an era of innocence drew to a close. The influx of diesels had now dispelled young ideas that steam would remain supreme for some years yet. Soon the production series of 22 'Deltics' would replace 55 steam 'Pacifics' on the principal ECML workings, and the first AC electric services between Manchester and Crewe were about to commence.

Back home, I visited Spike.

'How many "A4s" was it?' he asked.

I didn't see him again. He just seemed to step out my life. I think he was destined for university. But at a time when Cliff Richard and his backing group The Shadows had separate entries in the pop charts with 'Please Don't Tease' and 'Apache', I was about to start work, making new friends and getting used to a new routine in my own life.

11
...so a new era begins

In the meantime, what had been happening at the bottom of our garden? Well, the summer excursion trains to Southport had disappeared, although the Grand National steeplechase continued to attract a few specials over CLC metals until 1962. On the locomotive front, the 'O4' 2-8-0s were becoming rare, while 'WD' and LMS 8F 2-8-0s persisted, having been joined on the scene by the massive Standard 9F 2-10-0s. Even two of the Crosti-boilered version appeared, Nos 92026 and 92027, when still in their original condition. Gorton shed had lost its 'K3s' by 1960, but the last one I recall seeing at home, actually in September 1959, was No 61940, a rare cop from Doncaster. As it appeared to be in ex-works condition, it might have been running in after overhaul[15]. Despite the fact that Gorton shed was now under LMR administration, LNER locos, mainly 'B1s' and 'J39s', remained on its books, including the occasional reallocation; thus it could still throw up a cop or two at home. 'WD' 2-8-0s were replacing the 'O4s', and 'Crab' 2-6-0s had ousted the 'K3s'.

There was no shortage of 'B1s' to be seen at home anyway, as representatives from York continued daily. York did spring a surprise occasionally by sending a couple of 'K1' 2-6-0s (Nos 62057 and 62061), and three 'B16' 4-6-0s made their appearances, too. Two of these were 'B16/1s', examples of Vincent Raven's original NER design.

In November 1960 the three workmen's services between Aintree and Liverpool, Warrington and Manchester ceased. Latterly the first morning train to Manchester and the evening service from Liverpool were operated by a pair of two-car DMUs. These didn't reside overnight at Aintree, however. Early in the morning they ran empty from Liverpool to Aintree to form the early train to Manchester. After returning in the evening, they returned from Aintree as a service train back to Liverpool Central. I can't recall ever seeing many patrons on it, though! On Saturdays there were just two services returning to Aintree at lunchtime from Manchester and Warrington. Passengers from

[15] At which works, Gorton or Doncaster? Maybe the latter. I am unaware that Gorton overhauled 'K3s'.

Liverpool connected with either of these via the regular DMU service from Central to Gateacre.[16]

By now the entire LMR allocation of Standard 2-6-4Ts had been swapped for LMS examples from the Southern and Scottish Regions. The purpose was to rationalise the provision of spare parts for the respective types to specific areas, in order to reduce engine movement costs when major overhauls were due. The incomers to the LMR were in fact post-war engines designed by Charles Fairburn, some of which had actually been built at the SR's Brighton Works after nationalisation. It was from this variant that the Standard 2-6-4Ts were derived. Other Standards on the move were Shrewsbury's Caprottis, Nos 73125 to 73134. They were swapped for Patricroft's stud of piston-valved engines, Nos 73090 to 73098 (note an imbalance of one).

On the diesel front, apart from the appearance of locomotives some local services were now operated by DMUs. In January 1959 the Lime Street to Wigan service was provided with some Cravens-built units with hydraulic transmissions. However, after problems were experienced with these, some 'old' Derby Lightweights were brought in as temporary replacements. Some four-car diesel-mechanical sets were operating out of Liverpool Central on the CLC expresses to Manchester, supplemented by two-car units for the local all-stations services to Warrington and Gateacre.

Such was the scene as I left school, and started work as an engineering apprentice at a Speke factory in the south of Liverpool. My place of work was situated close to the Liverpool-Crewe main line, and coincidentally close to where I used to cycle during my schooldays to make some early attempts at railway photography. Speke station once adjoined Woodend Avenue just here, evidenced by the fact that the slow lines still veer away from the fast lines where the island platform had been accommodated. The station closed in 1931, before the spread of the Speke Industrial Estate – what price now for a station at this site? As the lines were in a cutting, I couldn't even see what trains were passing the premises during my lunch breaks. Instead, I played football with my workmates.

There was no one with a like-minded interest in railways in my new environment; most of the younger element were mainly interested in pop music. With only a passive interest in pop, I didn't frequent the 'beat' clubs, as they were called, as often as some. But speaking of the

[16] Services over the CLC route to Manchester were transferred in 1966 to Liverpool Lime Street, using the spur at Allerton connecting the CLC to the LNWR main line. However, through a point of law, the Gateacre service from Liverpool Central survived until 1972, when the latter terminal finally closed and was demolished.

music scene, there was one newcomer who turned many an ear by the name of Roy Orbison, who entered the pop charts for the first time with 'Only the Lonely'.

Perhaps fittingly, then, my enthusiasm to wander far and wide waned a little. Over the winter months I made just two trips, one to Manchester, the other to Crewe. The number of cops available at Manchester was now dwindling, but No 61008 *Kudu* was a surprise. It was one of several 'B1s' that were curiously transferred to Agecroft, in former LYR territory, from the Leicester area's GCR sheds. As the Manchester to Crewe electric services had just commenced, I decided to sample the new traction from Piccadilly, as London Road station had now become. I caught an EMU outward and a loco-hauled train back. Apart from the obvious new electric locos, the only cop worthy of note was Type 4 'Peak' (later Class 44) No D10 *Tryfan*, then allocated to Camden. Electric services between Liverpool and Crewe commenced in 1961.

I continued to pop into Lime Street station when 'in town', which was fairly frequently. Here the presence of LMR Class 40s was now supplemented by the appearance of examples from the NE Region's Gateshead MPD, having taken over from steam on the Newcastle services. Instead of changing engines at Leeds, as was the previous practice during the steam era, the diesels worked right through to Liverpool. Edge Hill provided reciprocal workings, which worked through to Newcastle. In complete contrast, the Hull 'exies' had radically changed. A batch of handsome six-car DMUs built at BR's Swindon Works were provided for this service, each comprising four powered cars, an open trailer, and a buffet trailer. The provision of four powered cars was considered necessary in view of the steep gradients on either side of the Pennines, not forgetting the 1 in 93 climb from Lime Street to Edge Hill. The Trans-Pennine units, as they became known, clipped 40 minutes off the overall journey time between the Liverpool and Hull.

The following March (1961) saw me at Aintree, not for the races but to see the Race Day special trains arriving. There was the added bonus of watching some of the engines being turned and serviced at the former LYR shed. My first Race Day visit was in 1959, when I copped 'Standard 5' No 73003 of Bristol, and 'B1' No 61305 from Hull. There were also two 'Jubilee' 4-6-0s from London, Nos 45680 *St Vincent* and 45740 *Munster*, and a handful of other cops mainly from the Midlands.

Aintree used to boast three stations. Racecourse station, as the name implies, was used only on race meeting days. It was sited close to the racecourse itself on a line linking railways in the Bootle and Seaforth areas to the LYR Liverpool to Wigan line, which it joined at Fazakerley Junction. Trains from London and the south-west gained the LYR metals at Wigan, crossing from the WCML and diving down through Wallgate. 1961 was the final year in which Racecourse station was used. Three trains from London arrived, headed by 'Scot' No 46146 *The Rifle Brigade* and rebuilt 'Patriots' Nos 45530 *Sir Frank Ree* and 45534 *E. Tootal Broadhurst*. The last-mentioned took one of the few remaining Class 2P 4-4-0s, No 40684, as pilot from Wigan, while the other two had Standard Class 2 'Moguls', Nos 78061 and 78063. Wigan supplied 'Crab' No 42864 to assist 'Jubilee' No 45586 *Mysore* on a train from Birmingham, but 'Scot' No 46126 *Royal Army Service Corps* arrived at Racecourse station single-handed with a train from Watford. (In view of the fact that this engine was local, ie allocated to Edge Hill, it would have been interesting to note whether or not it was used on the return working to Watford.) Last into Racecourse station was ex-works 'Jubilee' No 45706 *Express* with an excursion from Manchester via Wigan Wallgate. There was an interesting pairing in the form of Ivatt Class 4 'Mogul' No 43124 with 'Black 5' No 45273, both from Farnley Junction shed near Leeds. They arrived with a combined train from Newcastle and Hull, the two portions joining at Mirfield.

A train from Cleethorpes regularly travelled to Aintree Central with an ECML Pullman car and an ex-Southern Pullman observation car attached to the rear. (The latter was one of those used on the 'Devon Belle' express of earlier years between London and the West Country.) In stark contrast, at the front end in 1961 was a rather grubby 'Crab' 2-6-0 (number not recorded). In previous years I had seen this train at home headed by a pair of Class 4F 0-6-0s. The only other train using the CLC that year originated from St Albans, and arrived behind 'Black 5s' Nos 44918 and 44667. Rebuilt 'Patriot' No 45512 *Bunsen* crossed to Aintree Central from the LYR with a train from Glasgow, then the loco retired to Walton shed for turning and servicing.

The following year no trains used the CLC, and with the closure of Racecourse station the progressively diminishing number of specials then used the LYR's Sefton Arms station. Adjacent to Central, Sefton Arms was on the Liverpool to Preston line, its two main platforms accommodating the third-rail EMU services between Liverpool and Ormskirk. Except for the Glasgow train, all race specials now approached Aintree via the Bootle connection, veering off the Fazakerley line to pass around the back of Aintree MPD into either of the two excursion platforms at Sefton Arms. To get to Bootle, trains from the south gained the L&M tracks from the WCML via Winwick Junction and Earlestown, proceeding thence as far as Olive Mount Junction, and so onto the Bootle branch.

My visit to Aintree of 1961 sparked off a new friendship. I had encountered Mike there the previous year, but this time we decided to team up. Mike was five years older than me, and turned out to be well experienced in the practice of 'bunking' sheds, particularly the more 'difficult' ones. However, on race days tight security made Aintree shed a 'no go' area, so when all the specials were 'in' Mike and myself headed away. Our first port of call was Walton shed, where *Bunsen* was being prepared for its return north. On shed I copped Ivatt 'Mogul' No 43146 from Millhouses[17]. Mike then introduced me to Edge Hill shed, after which I did likewise for him with Birkenhead. I was surprised to make six cops at Edge Hill; among them was Standard Caprotti Class 5 No 73127, now of Patricroft shed. Stored out of service were 'Princess Royal' 'Pacifics' Nos 46204 and 46208, parked on two adjacent dead-end roads. Edge Hill depot originally comprised 20 such dead-end roads, and in the early part of the 20th century 12 of these were extended to form the 'new' shed, open at both ends. The remaining dead-end tracks were then used to store or repair locomotives as necessary, and thus here we found the 'Prinny Royals'. There was a stillness in this part of the shed, which gave us an eerie experience during a further visit in the early summer. We could hear water bubbling in the boiler of No 46204, as the engine was being prepared for a return to traffic for the summer timetable. No 46208 was similarly treated the following week. Great! We may have despised these engines as 'stinks' in bygone years, but now we loved them. Others that had been in store elsewhere were also returned to traffic for the summer season.

Rugby was not the most inspirational of destinations for an Easter Sunday, one may think. However, BR advertised a cheap trip, and Dad suggested going. I wasn't going to decline. So on a rather grey day we set off from Lime Street behind a mere 'Black 5' 4-6-0. At Rugby we bantered with the shedmaster to let us tour his establishment, and duly proceeded through the main entrance, something I was not used to doing. Of significance on shed was 'Royal Scot' No 46145 *The Duke of Wellington's Regiment*. This engine was in fact the pioneer of the class, LMS No 6100 *Royal Scot*, but identities were swapped in 1933 with the original No 6152. The latter was a newer engine, so the LMS chose it to represent the company's latest development of express passenger power for a publicity visit to the USA that year. The Americans presented a plaque that was affixed to the engine, and it seems that for this reason

---

[17] Sheffield Millhouses was another example of an LMS shed finding itself geographically out of position after nationalisation. It was by now administered by the ER, although it retained its LMS-type motive power, which included some 'Jubilee' 4-6-0s.

identities were never reversed when the engine returned to the UK. While at Rugby, we noticed four unrebuilt 'Patriot' 4-6-0s in store outside the shed, doomed for the cutter's torch. Inroads into express passenger steam power for scrapping had begun.

I was overjoyed when a 'Duchess' rolled into Rugby with our return train. It was No 46229 *Duchess of Hamilton*. As with *Pearl Diver* in 1956, I felt there was something of an anticlimax once we got on the move. The train comprised only eight coaches, a mere token load for such an engine. After a few brief barks from the chimney on starting away, there was nothing except occasional bursts of steam from the safety valves or the exhaust from the tender's steam coal-pusher. Anyway, this turned out to be the one and only time I had the pleasure of riding behind one of these majestic machines in the steam age.

Another BR handbill appeared advertising a trip to Hull by diesel train. I naively thought this would be an opportunity to travel on a Trans-Pennine unit, but I was to be disappointed. The Trans-Pennine units were ER stock, whereas the LMR was running this trip. So, on an April Sunday I boarded a six-car train comprising three two-car DMUs – six coaches, and I was one of very few people on board! Having got over the initial disappointment, I was delighted with the bagful of cops I made on the day. Out of a total of 101, there were three 'B1' namers, together with 'A3' 4-6-2 No 60045 *Lemberg*, which was spotted at Selby.[18]

At home on the evening prior to my Hull visit I was taken aback by the sound of an approaching diesel. A Brush Type 2 (later Class 31), No D5688, emerged from under the bridge, heading south with a freight; the loco was from Sheffield Darnall MPD. It transpired that there was now a regular working for these locos into Liverpool via the CLC, which continued at least until I finally gave up collecting engine numbers in 1966. Having travelled from Yorkshire overnight, the diesel usually reached Liverpool around breakfast time, sometimes passing home before I left for work.

One of these Class 31s slipped to a standstill one morning, coming to a halt close to the nearby access bridge. After a pause of about 10 minutes, it managed to get moving again. The same phenomenon beset two steam locos, too. A Stanier 'Mogul' and a Caprotti-fitted Standard Class 5 4-6-0 suffered the same indignity, but they both managed to restart without requiring assistance. These three incidents occurred fairly close together in time, and I don't recall seeing the like ever again.

[18] The ECML used to pass through Selby. The route was realigned in the 1980s to avoid the Selby swing bridge and associated curves, all of which imposed speed restrictions.

However, there was one more unusual incident. An 8F 2-8-0 came hammering up from the south one Saturday, with just one open wagon in tow. The rest of the train was following about 25 yards behind! Obviously a coupling link had broken. The engine driver had to keep on the move, for attempting to stop a loose-coupled freewheeling train on a rising gradient could have caused a rollback. Anyway, both engine crew and guard at the rear of the train must have had things under control, for the breakaways fortunately didn't reappear.

Further adventures with Mike got off to a good start on Easter Monday. A trip to Shrewsbury produced my first sight of a GWR 'King' 4-6-0, No 6016 *King Edward V*. There was the usual cross-section of other GWR types, together with some LMS examples that swelled the total of cops to 43 for the day. There was still a fair quantity of LMS types still allocated to the WR. Shrewsbury shed itself had been a joint affair between the GWR and LMS, and still possessed a stud of 'Jubilee' 4-6-0s, which worked down the former joint line to Hereford and beyond.

The art of serious unofficial shed-bashing then really took a hold. Visits to Birkenhead, Chester and Wrexham followed. I was carrying on from where I had left off, but with one difference. The days of standing on platforms waiting for trains were now replaced by seeking out potential cops at the sheds. Obviously, though, we needed to ensure that we were not 'copped' ourselves!

The month of May saw us stomping around the West Midlands, bunking sheds in the Birmingham and Wolverhampton areas. There were more 'King' 4-6-0s, seven of them, on Wolverhampton's Stafford Road shed, and I copped an eighth, No 6011 *King James I*, viewed from our return train to Liverpool as it passed above the shed yard. We even managed to bunk the locomotive works at Stafford Road, where No 1011 *County of Chester* was residing. As I was to discover, you could find some rare birds at loco works; engines from various parts of the country, not normally seen far from their home territory, converged on the works when major overhauls were required. Among others on this visit, I saw 0-6-0PT No 1503 of Old Oak Common, London, and 0-4-2T No 1442 from Oxford. We caught our homeward-bound train at Birmingham's New Street station, having taken a train ride from Wolverhampton. No 45690 *Leander* was there, one of Bristol Barrow Road's stud of 'Jubilee' 4-6-0s. Alternating with similar engines based at Leeds, these engines worked trains from the West Country to the North East, normally between Bristol and Leeds or York. Thus they were rarely seen anywhere near our home territory in the North West. Cops on this West Midlands trip totalled 134.

There was no slackening of pace when Mike was around. He

insisted on visiting the local sheds because 'you never know what could be there from other places'. Further afield, the sheds of Sheffield, Crewe and Derby had fallen victim by July 1961. At Crewe and Derby, as at Wolverhampton, you were guaranteed to see rare specimens as they awaited attention at the locomotive works. At Crewe I copped Polmadie 'Duchess' No 46230 *Duchess of Buccleuch* and 'Scot' No 46145 *The Duke of Wellington's Regt (West Riding)* from Leeds Holbeck. Also from Holbeck was 'Jubilee' No 45589 *Gwalior*, and another, No 45615 *Malay States*, was from Leicester Midland.

Travelling to Derby by rail, Mike and I used the 9.30am Hull train to get us to Manchester Central to connect with one of the Midland line expresses to London St Pancras. The brief reign of 'Britannia' 4-6-2s at Trafford Park had ended, as by now these trains were in the hands of Type 4 'Peak' (Class 45) diesels. (The 'Pacifics' were transferred to Birmingham's Aston depot, where they met up with other 'Brits' displaced from elsewhere.) The 'Peak' diesels looked very attractive in Brunswick green, with very pale green radiator grills and a stripe along the lower edge of each bodyside. Initially they were notorious for starting their trains with a severe jerk. The matter was eventually rectified, but I wonder how many standing passengers in the meantime found themselves nursing a few bruises or whiplash as a consequence of those rough starts.

By the time we arrived at Derby, the weather had taken a turn for the worse, and rain teemed down for the whole of our visit. The works yard proved to be very interesting. There was much Midland 'junk', as we irreverently dubbed the elderly 0-6-0s and 0-6-0Ts. Of special interest was, in fact, veteran Class 1F 0-6-0T No 41835. Except for this example, the few remaining survivors had been rebuilt at some time with boilers of the Belpaire type, with a flat-topped firebox. As No 41835 still retained its round-topped firebox, we expected it was at Derby for scrapping. Not so! It emerged from the works later with a Belpaire boiler. These Class 1Fs were retained for working over lines within the steelworks complex at Chesterfield, as were a handful of Class 0F 0-4-0T survivors, also of MR origin. However, we found one of the latter at Derby, No 41532, already withdrawn from service. It was weight considerations that prolonged the retention of these veterans for a while yet. Apparently, no suitable diesel shunter was available to replace them, particularly one that could negotiate the sharp curves that abounded on the steelworks' systems.

Back at Derby there was another oddball gem in the works yard in the shape of North London Railway 0-6-0T No 58850. The engine had in fact ended its career working on the Cromford & High Peak line in Derbyshire. Following withdrawal, it was preserved and found sanctuary on the Bluebell Railway in Sussex, which reopened in 1960. Also on view were four of Stanier's three-cylinder 2-6-4Ts, including the since preserved pioneer, No 42500. Having three cylinders instead of two reduced the 'hammer blow' effect on the track when the engine was being worked hard. This condition satisfied the then Civil Engineer's requirements for the London-Southend line for which these engines were specially built in 1934. Subsequently, after track improvements, some of the two-cylindered version worked the line, together with some BR Standard 2-6-4Ts drafted in following nationalisation.

It seemed that the end had arrived for four of the five surviving prototype diesels. In the works yard were Nos 10000, 10203, 10201 and 10202. The last two had recently moved from Crewe, where we had seen them a fortnight earlier. All four, however, languished at Derby for a further two years, not being officially withdrawn until December 1963. Surprisingly, No 10001 continued in service until mid-1965, mainly working out of Willesden. It was finally withdrawn in March 1966.

Of interest on Derby shed was 'B1' 4-6-0 No 61096 from March MPD, and there were seven of the novel Co-Bo diesel-electrics, one-third of the total of 20. All were based at Derby at the time. They possessed two-stroke engines, which never achieved a satisfactory level of reliability throughout the locos' career. After reconditioning of the power units, the Co-Bos spent their final years in the Furness area, working along the Cumbrian coast until withdrawal in the late 1960s.

Next, Mike came up with the idea of a major shed-bashing adventure using a BR Rail-Rover ticket. We paid £6 for one week's unlimited travel on the LMR between 5 and 11 August 1961. However, as a prelude to 'the big travel', I decided to spend the first week of my two weeks of annual leave staying with my aunt and uncle at Dalton. At Carnforth I was elated to cop No 45513, the last 'Patriot' I needed to complete the class. It passed southward along the WCML, heading a fitted freight. On this occasion I successfully negotiated Carnforth shed! Nothing worthy of report, though.

I knew I would visit Carlisle with Mike the following week, but couldn't resist a preview trip from Dalton. By now I possessed a copy of the *British Locomotive Shed Directory*, the well-known booklet 'compiled by (the now late) Aidan L. F. Fuller, F.C.A.'. This booklet gave such information as walking time to sheds from railway stations, and bus routes when these were available. In Carlisle I was able to use it to good advantage to find Canal and Kingmoor sheds. Many a spotter became familiar with the name Etterby Road. It happened to cross the WCML close by the River Eden, and from the railway bridge another road led down to Kingmoor shed. However, officialdom appeared rather menacing that day, so I just made do with viewing the yard from the end of the road. Among others I copped resident 'Jubilee' No 45723 *Furious* and some visiting engines: 'Standard 5' 4-6-0 No 73062 from Glasgow Polmadie and 'Black 5s' No 45087 from Carstairs, 45151 from Motherwell, and 45194 from Ayr. At Canal I hoped to see something LNER, and I wasn't disappointed. Considering that this shed was now under LMR administration, there was an appreciable quantity of LNER stock still allocated there. Canal's allocation included a couple of oddities, 'N15' 0-6-2T No 69155 of NBR vintage, which was in use, and 'N2' 0-6-2T No 69564, a Gresley LNER design, which was in the shed, having been withdrawn. (The 'N2' Class was the basis for my Hornby Dublo model, which bore the number 69567 and was now itself 'in store'.) Visiting from other sheds were 'Pacifics' Nos 60037 *Hyperion*, 60152 *Holyrood*, 60012 *Commonwealth of Australia* and 60090 *Grand Parade*. 'B1' 4-6-0 No 61324 was there from Aberdeen, as was 'K1' 2-6-0 No 62010 from Blaydon on the NE Region. Back at the station, I took what has become my most prized photograph. 'Pacific' No 46200 *The Princess Royal* departed, having relieved a Class 40 diesel on a Perth-Euston train. Alongside was 'Duchess' No 46250 *City of Lichfield*, waiting on one of the centre roads to take over a Glasgow-Birmingham train.

Mike and I agreed that we should return home each night during our rail-roving. After all, as a first-year apprentice I was earning only about £3 10s a week, and I couldn't really afford bed and breakfast and additional meals. Our Rail-Rover schedule was as follows:

Saturday	Carlisle
Sunday	Manchester, Crewe and Chester
Monday	Blackpool and Fleetwood
Tuesday	London
Wednesday	Leicester, Wellingborough, Nottingham and Derby
Thursday	Doncaster
Friday	Wolverhampton and Birmingham

So, having returned from Dalton on the Friday, it was back to Carlisle with Mike the following day. We caught the 9.15am from Liverpool Exchange, a summer Saturday relief to the regular 9.30am. We departed from Exchange with nine coaches behind a 'Black 5' 4-6-0, but picked up five more at Burscough Junction, brought from Southport by a 2-6-4T.

Fourteen coaches was some load for a moderately powered locomotive such as a 'Black 5', but was not an uncommon occurrence during those heady summers of steam. Needless to say, our train stopped at Tebay to take on rear-end assistance for the climb to Shap, 4 miles of which is on a 1 in 75 gradient. How could I forget? We stood in the vestibule, heads out of windows to watch the bank engine, another 2-6-4T, buffer up. A sudden jerk knocked us both off balance, as the banker's driver opened up his engine. Had he forgotten he was assisting a passenger train and not a freight? We'd just managed to peel ourselves from the teak panelling when our 'Black 5' pulled hard, and the same thing happened again!

Arrival at Carlisle was more or less to time. About half an hour later came the regular train from Liverpool, hauled by a 'Royal Scot' 4-6-0. I copped the pioneer 'Clan' 'Pacific' No 72000 *Clan Buchanan*, together with two more during the day, Nos 72006 *Clan Mackenzie* and 72007 *Clan Mackintosh*. On Canal shed we found 'A2' 'Pacific' No 60532 *Blue Peter*, eventually destined to become the only 'A2' in preservation. But there was a sad sight on Kingmoor shed. 'Princess Royals' Nos 46201 *Princess Elizabeth* and 46210 *Lady Patricia* were both stored in the open out of use. *Lady Patricia* would not run again, but *Princess Elizabeth* and five others of her class were to be reinstated in January 1962 to help cover for diesel failures. She, too, would eventually enjoy a life in preservation. Regrettably, though, I wasn't inclined to photograph the 'Pacifics', preferring instead to snap CR 0-6-0 No 57653. It, too, was withdrawn from service, having been the sole survivor of its class on Kingmoor's books. Our train back to Liverpool was double-headed by two 'Black 5s', one of which was No 44731 of Blackpool, the other an unrecorded Caprotti.

We thought we had got off to a bad start at Longsight on the Sunday, when some high-ranking shed staff scared the pants off us. They detained us, albeit temporarily, while discussing whether or not to hand us over to the British Transport Police. Maybe it was all 'part of the act', because eventually they let us go after a 'ticking off'. There was nothing out of the ordinary at Longsight anyway from what we were able to see. We managed to cop the pioneer 'Peak' diesel No D1 *Scafell Pike*, as well as inevitably some electric locos. Over on LYR territory, I copped two more of Agecroft's recently acquired 'B1' 4-6-0s, Nos 61201 and 61369. On Monday we found two more 'B1s' at Blackpool, visitors on summer excursions from the Wakefield area. Further up the coast at Fleetwood were Dock Tank 0-6-0 No 47165 and four Standard Class 2 2-6-2Ts, Nos 84010, 84011, 84017 and 84018. Standard Class 5 4-6-0 No 73160 was visiting from Normanton shed.

The day arrived for our first visit to the capital. Electrically hauled as far as Crewe, the 1 in 93 climb to Edge Hill was a doddle for the locomotive. Gliding under the rebuilt Wavertree Road viaduct, we then swung sharply to the right, burrowing under lines connecting Wapping with the 'gridiron' reception sidings, and climbed past the engine sheds on another 1 in 93 gradient. Passing over Wavertree Road this time, we were now heading southward above the terraces of red-bricked houses in Wavertree itself, and shortly ran along a high embankment with the wide open space that is Wavertree Park to our left. About a mile distant on the far side of the park is the distinctive red-bricked clock tower of my former school, the Blue Coat. (Oh, how welcome were the chimes of 4 o'clock, finishing time!) To our right we could see the city's Anglican cathedral (the Roman Catholic counterpart was yet to be completed). Onward through Mossley Hill and Allerton, we crossed over the CLC lines to Manchester before next swinging eastward through Speke. From there our train was running along an alignment of the St Helens Canal & Railway, forged in that company's endeavours to reach Garston Docks. Speke Junction engine sheds were situated in the triangle of lines linking with what was now the Garston Dock branch. There wasn't much chance to observe what was on shed as we sped past on the cambered curve. Heading onward past my place of work and through Halebank, the CLC Manchester line came into view again on its high embankment near Halewood. At Ditton Junction the route of the St Helens Canal & Railway[19] continued straight on amidst a myriad of industrial sidings around Widnes, as our train now climbed the 1 in 114 embankment to Runcorn Bridge, and southward once again to Crewe. In Crewe station No 71000 *Duke of Gloucester* was standing on one of the through roads, waiting to take over a southbound express.

The London visit was 'mega', producing 237 cops. On the way down (or should that be 'up' to London?) we noted some LNER locos around the Rugby area. These were 'B1s' No 61283, from London's Stratford, and locally based No 61368 from Woodford Halse, while from Cambridge were No 61301 and 'K3' 2-6-0 No 61817. At Willesden Southern 2-6-4T No 31919 had arrived at one of the marshalling yards with a transfer freight from its home territory. This was my first ever cop of an SR locomotive.

Once in London it soon became obvious that the Underground railway system was the surest way to get from A to B. The route maps plastered on station walls were easy to follow, and it was up to us to ensure that we didn't board a wrong train. The disadvantage of this

[19] The company's line continued to Warrington, forming an inverted 'T' with the original St Helens Railway line at Widnes. The whole undertaking eventually came under control of the LNWR.

mode of travel, though, was that we couldn't see any of the city sights above ground, although Mike wasn't particularly bothered about this aspect. We 'did' Willesden shed first, then the Western's Old Oak Common, which was practically next door. What a big shed! Inside were four turntables, from which radiated the locomotive stabling roads, and there were more engines idling outside. Old Oak provided us both with our biggest haul of cops, about 90 in my case, including five 'King' 4-6-0s. I photographed one of the recently introduced 'Hymek' diesel-hydraulics, No D7003, which happened to be there. Later I copped another 'King', No 6028 *King George VI*, in Paddington station, together with some D800 series diesel-hydraulics. 'Brit' No 70016 *Ariel* was also in the station. The 'Brits' were never very popular with WR men, and many of them were congregated at Cardiff Canton until transferred away to other regions. Maybe most of the men were quite happy when No 70016, together with the remainder of its sisters still on the WR, were transferred to the LMR within the next 12 months.

I look back to these scenes with my mind's eye. What a great shame I wasn't inclined to take more photographs than I did. Many enthusiasts mutter the same sentiments today. For many of us, there were financial constraints. To buy a film, then pay for processing cost about one-third of my week's wages. Another two years were to elapse before I took up photography as a hobby, and discovered that processing my own films and prints was to prove considerably cheaper than letting a professional laboratory do the work. At the start of our Rail-Rover week, I had just acquired an Ilford Sportsman 35mm camera, the results from which were quite acceptable to me for the time being.

At King's Cross station four 'Baby Deltics' were humming about. These Type 2 Bo-Bos were just as noisy as their Type 5 cousins, the production series of Co-Co locomotives developed from the prototype 'Deltic' locomotive. The production series began to appear in 1961, and one of them, No D9006, as yet unnamed, was in the station. 'A4' No 60003 *Andrew K. McCosh* was there, together with two 'A3s' and an 'A2/3' (Thompson variety). The remaining cops comprised diesels of Brush Type 2 and BTH Type 1. The only other steamer was 'L1' 2-6-4T No 67770.

Digressing from the rail-roving for a moment, I had another bash at London with Mike the following April. This time we decided to return home by a late train, which enabled us to visit the sheds at Willesden, Old Oak Common, Neasden, Cricklewood, Kentish Town and King's Cross, as well as King's Cross, Liverpool Street and Waterloo stations. On that visit we saw nothing of note at Willesden, but there was another glut of GWR cops at Old Oak, together with some 9F 2-10-0s. Of particular interest was No D601 *Ark Royal*, a 2,000bhp diesel-hydraulic built by the North British Locomotive Co with an A1A-A1A wheel arrangement. They were a little overweight for the WR Civil Engineer's liking, hence the unpowered supporting axle in the centre of each bogie. For this reason only six were built. Later examples from NBL were constructed as B-Bs, similar to the Swindon design, and were similarly placed in the D800 number series. We didn't know what to make of their appearance at first. Based on a German design, they reminded me of the upper half of the British Railways 'Flying Sausage' logo of the day.[20] One of Swindon's version was on view, No D803 *Albion*, but we also caught sight of our first 'Western' Type 4, No D1002 *Western Explorer* (later Class 52). What a handsome design! A total of 74 were built at both Swindon and Crewe, and they remained arguably the most distinguished-looking diesels ever produced for British Railways.

The ex-Great Central shed at Neasden produced just one LNER engine, 'B1' No 61078, the rest being LMS and Standard designs. This was not surprising, as the southern half of the old GCR line was now under LMR rule. Darkness had fallen by the time we reached King's Cross MPD. Steam still had nine months to go at Top Shed, as it was known amongst railwaymen. Typically for a Sunday night, the place was brimful of engines being prepared for their Monday rosters. I copped five namers, 'A4' No 60028 *Walter K. Whigham*, 'A3s' Nos 60063 *Isinglass* and 60109 *Hermit*, and 'A1' No 60158 *Aberdonian*. 'Deltic' No D9001 *St Paddy* was the fifth. There were no fewer than nine 'WD' 2-8-0s, including top-of-the-list No 90000. They were mainly from New England depot, as were three 9F 2-10-0s. We also saw five of the now dwindling number of 'N2' 0-6-2Ts. Unlike No 69564 at Carlisle, these 'N2s' possessed condensing apparatus to direct exhaust steam back into the engines' water tanks; this was to minimise condensation in the tunnels around London's Moorgate, through which these locos. worked. Some LMS Fowler 2-6-2Ts and GWR 0-6-0PTs were similarly equipped for the same purpose.

No 'Baby Deltics' appear in my notes for this 1962 visit. They were known to be problematic, and may all have been temporarily withdrawn at this time for attention. They did not enjoy the same level of success as their illustrious cousins, the Type 5s, and all ten were to be withdrawn by 1971.

There was nothing of note in Liverpool Street station, which was by now steam-free. But before we returned to Euston and our train home, we popped into the SR's Waterloo station, where I saw my first 'big' Southern engines. These materialised in the form of 'Pacifics'

[20] The 'Flying Sausage' logo appeared on timetable literature, leaflets and as station nameboards, all of which appeared in the colour of the respective region.

Nos 34038 *Lynton* and 34071 *601 Squadron*. The former was still in
its original 'air-smoothed' condition, as conceived by the Southern's
CME O. V. S. Bulleid, while the latter was one of those rebuilt in the
late 1950s into a more conventional form. Bulleid had been Gresley's
understudy on the LNER at Doncaster. He moved to the SR in 1942
after Gresley's premature death, and perpetuated his former mentor's
innovative streak. Some would say that Bulleid 'went over the top',
because whereas Gresley enjoyed considerable success from his ideas,
some of the innovations that Bulleid built into his 'Pacifics' proved
to be rather troublesome. Most notably, apart from the air-smoothed
casing, the piston valves for all three cylinders were driven from a single
eccentric crank assembly via a system of gears and chains enclosed in an
oil bath. The latter was supposed to be oiltight, but inevitably leakage
occurred, and, when hot ashes were blown forward from the ashpan,
the lagging under the lower part of the boiler occasionally became
ignited. Bulleid hit on a winner, though, with his boilers, for they had
no trouble providing ample steam for whatever task the engines were
asked to perform.

Between 1956 and 1960 all 30 of Bulleid's 'heavyweight' 'Pacifics',
the 'Merchant Navy' Class, were rebuilt without their air-smoothed
casing and with three sets of valve gear. An improvement of locomotive
availability was demanded, and post-rebuilding statistics did in fact
indicate that the reconstructed locomotives paid for themselves via
fuel economy and reduced maintenance costs. Only 60 of the 110
'light' 'Pacifics' were similarly treated from 1957. Rebuilding was
stopped when it was realised that the engines would not have much life
expectancy left, as the quest to eliminate steam gathered momentum. In
retrospect, the decision to start rebuilding the 'light' 'Pacifics' is perhaps
a little surprising in view of the prohibition of any more development
for steam following the onset of the Modernisation Plan referred to
earlier. Besides that, arguments have since raged as to whether or not so
many should have been built in the first place!

End of digression. Back to our rail-roving of 1961.

The day following our demanding one in London, we tackled the East
Midlands. I copped 'Scot' No 46112 *Sherwood Forester*, appropriately
at Nottingham, to which it was allocated, and bagged a total of four
'Jubilee' 4-6-0s. On Wellingborough shed Crosti-boilered 9F 2-10-0
No 92021 was in store. It was the last to remain in its original condition,
and was awaiting movement to Crewe for removal of its pre-heater.

Next day it was Doncaster once again, by way of the Woodhead
route. Our LMR Rover tickets permitted travel to Sheffield, which
was in the ER, but travel onward to Doncaster would require an ER
ticket. Through the mists of time I'm not sure now how we overcame

On Grand National Day, 26 March 1960, Class 2P 4-4-0 No 40681, a Wigan (LYR) loco is serviced at Aintree MPD. It had piloted a 7P 4-6-0 forward from Wigan, where the race specials crossed from LNWR to LYR tracks. This was the last occasion on which a 2P 4-4-0 was used, as Standard Class 2 'Moguls' were provided in the following years.

On the same day 'Crab' 'Mogul' No 42886 and 'Black 5' 4-6-0 No 44964 are returning to Central station after servicing at Walton shed. They will be separated before returning their respective race specials back along the CLC tracks. In the background, stock for another race special crosses on the LYR link from Bootle to Sefton Arms station, from where trains departed via Bootle for the LNWR lines to the south.

'Black 5' 4-6-0s Nos 44734 and 44927 double-head the Royal Train into Liverpool along the Manchester tracks at Broad Green on 24 May 1961. The coal yard is on the right, and the CLC branch from Halewood to Aintree passes underneath approximately where the bracket signal is seen.

This picture was my second attempt at photographing a moving train (on my first attempt I cut off the engine's tender!). Rebuilt 'Patriot' Class 4-6-0 No 45531 *Sir Frank Ree* passes under the then main road to Ditton with an up express in the summer of 1957. Little did I know at the time, but in September 1960 I was to start work at a firm further down the line at Speke as an engineering apprentice.

'Jubilee' 4-6-0 No 45643 *Rodney* arrives at Aintree Sefton Arms with a train from the Eastern Region in March 1965. At the main-line platform stands Class 5 No 45171, having arrived with the annual special from Glasgow.

Pighue Lane (pronounced 'Piggy'), situated between Olive Mount and Edge Hill, became a popular location in 1968 for watching the dwindling steam activities. Officially, steam finished in Liverpool on 3 May, but this view was taken on the following day. Photographed from the Lane, two Class 8F 2-8-0s (No 48476 leading) have brought a train of track sections off the Bootle branch. They are about to burrow under the embankment, hitherto used for gravity shunting wagons into the Edge Hill 'gridiron' sidings. Emerging at the other side, the train will gain the LNWR's line to Manchester at Olive Mount Junction. Note the overhead catenary on the embankment; it was hardly used, indicating BR's conception of the 1960s as to how freight would be handled in the future. The area between here and Edge Hill is now an business estate.

Having arrived with a freight off the Manchester line, Edge Hill's Class 7F 0-8-0 No 49416 awaits the signal to proceed with its next movement in 1959. It will likely draw forward before propelling its train up the tracks seen above the coach to the hump at Olive Mount. From there, the wagons will run by gravity into the 'gridiron' sidings for sorting.

York's Class 'B1' 4-6-0 No 61039 *Steinbok* rests at Walton CLC shed, Liverpool, awaiting its evening departure back to its home county on 24 June 1961. The branch passing by the shed led to that company's Huskisson Dock on the River Mersey. Note the 'Whistle' board for trains heading into the tunnels that burrowed under this northern part of the city.

Standard Class 5 4-6-0 No 73069 heads the LCGB's 'Two Cities Limited' through Kirkby, north of Liverpool, heading for Manchester along the LYR route via Wigan Wallgate in May 1968.

This photograph was taken from Pighue Lane during the last week of steam operation in Liverpool, which ended on 4 May 1968. Having arrived with a freight at the reception sidings at Edge Hill, a Class 5 4-6-0 pushes it train up the hump towards Olive Mount, from where wagons will be uncoupled and allowed to run by gravity into the sorting sidings down at Edge Hill.

It's Grand National Day at Aintree in 1964, and two ECML Pullman cars, together with the 'Devon Belle' observation car, are bringing up the rear of a train from Cleethorpes. The engine at the head of the train is rebuilt 'Patriot' 4-6-0 No 45522 *Prestatyn*. On the extreme left can be seen steam activity at Aintree Central station.

This photo shows the CLC branch from Halewood to Aintree as it passed the back bedroom window of my home in Liverpool. The view is looking north towards Walton and Aintree. The tracks were lifted after closure of the line in 1978, and the trackbed was eventually converted into a linear park, stretching the whole length to Aintree. I revisited the location in 2002, discovering that the bridge could not now be seen from the house through the mass of trees, and the one-time school playing field beyond the railway is now a residential housing estate.

Photographed from the Roch Valley railtour of July 1968 is Gateacre station on the CLC branch from Halewood to Aintree. It was from here that my parents took me to Southport for a day at the seaside, which would have been in 1948 when a passenger service was still operating. The train accessed Lord Street station at Southport via the CLC Extension Railway from Aintree. Passenger services to the resort via this route ceased in 1951.

GWR Class '3800' 2-8-0 No 3865 enjoys the convenience of the mechanical coaling plant at Birkenhead MPD. An LMS cousin in the form of a Class 8F 2-8-0 stands over the ash pits in the background.

Preserved 'Castle' Class 4-6-0 No 7029 *Clun Castle* speeds through Bromborough en route to Birkenhead. The train was sponsored by the Stephenson Locomotive Society and ran on 5 March 1967 to mark the end of through services between Birkenhead/ Chester and London Paddington. The previous day *Clun Castle* had been in action hauling the Ian Allan specials between Oxford/Banbury and Chester.

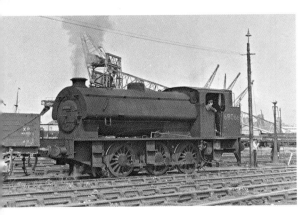

Top: On a summer's day in 1959 Class 2F 0-6-0 Dock Tank No 47160 tends to coal wagons feeding the mechanical coaling tower at Birkenhead sheds, while Class 3 2-6-2T No 40144 clambers up from the former LNWR shed. To the right of the Dock Tank can be seen the goods lines leading to the docks and to the terminus at Birkenhead Woodside. The LMS Dock Tank was a rare breed, as only ten were built. Birkenhead also had No 47164 on its books, while No 47166 was at neighbouring Bidston.

Middle: The crew of 'Jinty' 0-6-0T No 47677 enjoy a break from shunting at Birkenhead, close to the MPD seen in the background, in 1959. Behind me was the former air-raid shelter I used as a grandstand, together with the steps leading down to the unofficial entrance from Green Lane.

Bottom: Class 'J94' 0-6-0ST No 68066 shunts in the sidings around the West Float docks near Birkenhead on 27 July 1959. Its home shed, Bidston, was situated close to Birkenhead North station, on the western outskirts of Birkenhead.

At Bidston shed on a fine day in 1961, LNER Class 'O4' 2-8-0s were then still visiting from Gorton via the former Cheshire Lines system. Of the two examples seen here, No 63848, nearest the camera, is of the Class 'O4/7' variant with round-top firebox, while the other, with a Belpaire firebox, may well be of Class 'O4/1' or 'O4/3'. The 'O4s' were the first engines I noted at the start of my spotting era. They were one of a number of LNER classes that passed my home, mingling with the LMS types. The 9F 2-10-0 is No 92054, visiting from Wellingborough.

In this unusual scene at Bidston shed on 24 July 1959, three Class 'J72' 0-6-0Ts of NER vintage, Nos 68671 (nearest), 68727 and 68714, stand withdrawn together with Bidston's own Class 2F 0-6-0 Dock Tank No 47166. The 'J72s' had been allocated to the former GCR shed at Wrexham Rhosddu and were stopping off at Bidston en route to Gorton Works for scrapping.

Chester, Wrexham, Shrewsbury and Bescot

Over the weekend of 4/5 March 1967, four special trains were run to mark the cessation of through passenger services between London Paddington and Chester/Birkenhead. Here on the 4th preserved 'Castle' 4-6-0 No 4079 *Pendennis Castle* is returning from Chester Midland MPD after servicing, and will head the return 'Zulu' special southward.

Clun Castle heads into the sunset as it leaves Chester with the Stephenson Locomotive Society special on 5 March 1967. The previous day the loco had been in action hauling the Ian Allan specials between Oxford/Banbury and Chester.

This was my first sighting of a GWR 'King' Class 4-6-0. No 6016 *King Edward V* is on Shrewsbury shed for servicing on 3 April 1961.

The Great Western influence was still in evidence at Chester in June 1960, as 'Modified Hall' Class 4-6-0 No 6963 *Throwley Hall* poses at Platform 2 at General station, having arrived with a train from Cardiff. Alongside is '4300' Class 2-6-0 No 6357 of Croes Newydd shed, Wrexham, which has arrived with a train from the Barmouth/Llangollen line.

In April 1967 the RCTS ran a railtour encompassing local lines around Wrexham and part of the Wirral peninsula. Having arrived at Wrexham General from Llangollen behind 8F 2-8-0 No 48697, two 2-6-4T locomotives, Nos 42616 and 42647, took over the train for the next stage of the tour. Here the train is seen departing from the GWR station, and is about to cross to the GCR tracks to head for Bidston and New Brighton.

Standard Class 5 4-6-0 No 73011 heads a stopping train for North Wales away from Chester in July 1961. It is overtaking a train of cattle wagons headed by LMS Class 5 4-6-0 No 45343. The pair will shortly reach Saltney Junction, where the former GWR route still diverges southward.

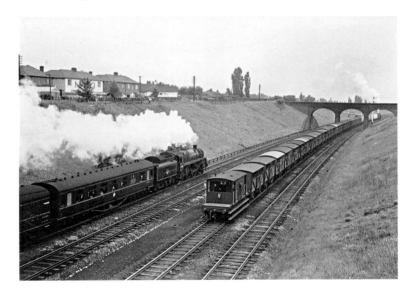

Scenes like this were commonplace at the west end of Chester General station. The former GWR shed, beyond Brooke Street bridge seen in the picture, didn't seem to possess a regular shed pilot, and shunting of engines was carried out by anything close at hand that was conveniently in steam. In this view taken on 27 February 1960, Standard Class 5 4-6-0 No 73038 has moved out to allow 'Mogul' No 6380 to shunt a 'Hall' Class 4-6-0, while 'Grange' 4-6-0 No 6872 *Crawley Grange* manoeuvres sister loco No 6812 *Chesford Grange*. On the extreme left, a 'County' Class 4-6-0 waits in one of the bay platforms.

One of the handful of 'Super D' 0-8-0s, No 48895, basks in the fog at Bescot MPD in the autumn of 1964 on the day we had travelled south in 'The Ark on Wheels' (see Chapter 13).

Manchester

After a lengthy struggle to get on the move, 'Black 5' 4-6-0 No 45110 backs the empty stock of the Roch Valley Railway Society tour out of Manchester Central on 21 July 1968. Persistently slipping, the engine eventually primed, showering most of its spectators with sooty water.

On Sunday 4 August 1968, the Stephenson Locomotive Society ran two 'farewell to steam' special trains. Each commenced from Birmingham New Street with electric and diesel haulage to Manchester Victoria, from where steam took over. Each train then made a circular tour of Lancashire, briefly crossing the border into Yorkshire in the process, before returning to Manchester. Aboard No 1 special, we see the train approaching Manchester Victoria, with two 'Black 5s', Nos 44871 and 44894, waiting to back onto our coach.

London

Top: One of Churchward's nine magnificent mixed-traffic 2-8-0s, No 4706, receives attention over the ash pits at Old Oak Common MPD on 15 December 1963.

Middle: 'Merchant Navy' Class 4-6-2 No 35017 *Belgian Marine* heads a down express through Clapham Junction on 28 March 1964.

Left: Neat-looking Standard Class 3 2-6-2T No 82022 is on an empty stock working at Clapham Junction in the summer of 1964.

Crewe and the West Coast Main Line

At the end of an historic and eventful day, 'A4' 4-6-2 No 4498 *Sir Nigel Gresley* rests at Crewe on 1 April 1967, having completed its inaugural main-line run under the auspices of the A4 Locomotive Preservation Society. The railtour commenced at Crewe, and a brilliant run in fine weather to Carlisle via Shap was thrown into sharp contrast by the return run over Ais Gill. There was persistent wheel-slip in falling snow on the climb to the summit, and bouts of slipping were also experienced restarting at Hellifield and on the climb up Wilpshire bank near Blackburn. After this photo was taken the 'A4' removed its own empty stock.

Heading a northbound freight in 1966, Class 5 4-6-0 No 45368 has taken the direct line from Winwick Junction to bypass Earlestown and Newton-le-Willows. The train will eventually pass under the Liverpool to Manchester line between the two towns on the climb to Golborne.

'Jubilee' Class 4-6-0 No 45698 *Mars* glides up the 1 in 135 rise through Moore, south of Warrington, heading a northbound freight on 21 March 1964. It will shortly be crossing the high-level bridge spanning the Manchester Ship Canal. Note the trackbed of the former Grand Junction route, used before construction of the canal.

A vista for the historian: 'WD' 2-8-0 No 90295 approaches Acton Grange Junction from the Frodsham direction on the same day. On joining the WCML, the tracks continue climbing to cross the high-level bridge spanning the Manchester Ship Canal, seen in the background with a train about to cross. Construction of the canal and bridge necessitated deviation of both the Crewe and Chester lines. Note on the left, just before the junction, the short tunnel used to carry the deviated Chester line over the original GJR tracks from Crewe. To the right of the photograph, the path of the old Birkenhead, Lancashire & Cheshire Junction Railway is discernible; this joined the Crewe line at Walton Old Junction and a short section of it was latterly used as a refuge siding and for storage of condemned rolling stock. The deviations as seen here were opened in 1893.

The refuge siding provided by the old Birkenhead Railway near Moore provided accommodation for a tanker train from Stanlow, double-headed here in June 1967 by two 9F 2-10-0s. After the passage of other traffic, the two engines, Nos 92020, a Crosti-boilered conversion, and 92110 back their train out onto the main line from Chester before proceeding northward towards Warrington Arpley. From there they would most likely continue heading eastward to Yorkshire.

Looking south from Springs Branch, near Wigan, an eastbound freight headed by a Class 8F 2-8-0 crosses the WCML in April 1966. Passing underneath on the relief lines is Standard Class 5 4-6-0 No 73097 with a northbound freight.

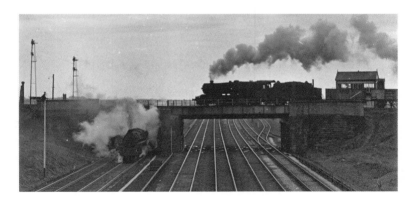

One of the Standard Class 5 4-6-0s fitted with Caprotti valve gear, No 73144, heads a Chester-bound empty stock/parcels train at Walton Old Junction, near Warrington, in April 1967. The train is about to cross the Grand Junction Railway bridge of 1837 vintage, which spans the River Mersey. Originally a link in the WCML prior to the building of the Manchester Ship Canal, this line now forms a loop to the present main line, out of sight to the left of the photograph.

Standard Class 4 2-6-0 No 76083 runs off the same bridge in the summer of 1967. The embankment carrying the WCML is glimpsed on the left, under which the engine will burrow to gain the main line near Bank Quay station. On the right, an ex-Crosti-boilered Class 9F 2-10-0 waits with a freight on the spur from Arpley.

Having just crossed the GJR bridge spanning the River Mersey, Class 9F 2-10-0 No 92029 accelerates a freight past Walton Hall Junction, just south of Warrington. The 'Black 5' 4-6-0 is returning to Arpley, having assisted the previous train up the 1 in 69

incline as far as the Ship Canal bridge. The original lines of the WCML and the line to Chester divided at Walton Hall Junction, prior to the building of the Ship Canal. No 92029 was one of ten 9Fs originally fitted with a Crosti pre-heater beneath the main boiler. When rebuilt into conventional form, the original boiler was retained, as evidenced in this photograph, taken in April 1967.

Around Shap and the S&C

On a dull 30 August 1967, Class 5 4-6-0 No 45212 eases past Tebay station and engine shed, having called for a banking engine. The banker, Standard Class 4 4-6-0 No 75037, is about to leave the shed seen in the background to buffer up at the rear of the freight. The locos will then exchange whistles before heading for Shap summit.

Making an unassisted attack on Shap on a calm day in August 1967, Class 9F 2-10-0 No 92054 hammers up towards Scout Green with a northbound freight.

In appallingly wet and windy conditions in September 1967, a Class 9F 2-10-0 fitted with a double chimney plods towards Scout Green on the climb to Shap, assisted at the rear by another double-chimneyed loco, Standard Class 4 4-6-0 No 75026.

The last passenger train rostered for steam haulage over Shap ran on 6 September 1967. Here is 'Britannia' 'Pacific' No 70025 *Western Star* slogging up the famous bank with eight coaches in tow, forming a London to Carlisle train.

Preserved 'A3' 4-6-2 No 4472 *Flying Scotsman* storms past Scout Green as it attacks Shap incline with a ten-coach enthusiasts' special in June 1969. (The second tender, added as a water carrier, weighed at least as much as about two coaches.) This was one of the last public runs the 'A3' made prior to its departure to tour the USA.

Just yards from Ais Gill summit, Nos 44871 and 44781 speed into history with train No 1T57, the 'Fifteen Guinea Special'.

Top: Two locomotives to escape the cutter's torch and enter preservation are seen here at Lostock Hall MPD on 31 July 1968. Class 5 4-6-0 No 45305 is on the right, with Ivatt Class 4 2-6-0 No 43106 just outside the shed to the left.

Middle: The driver of No 70013 *Oliver Cromwell* checks round his locomotive as it pauses at Rose Grove with the Roch Valley railtour on 28 July 1968. Meanwhile, the occupants of the train have disgorged to the MPD.

Bottom: On 2 August 1968 Class 8F 2-8-0 No 48727 drifts past Rose Grove MPD with a freight. The coaling tower would become redundant in two days' time. Note two of the surviving 'Black 5s' stored alongside the engine shed.

On a snowy 10 February 1968, Class 8F 2-8-0 No 48476 drags a coal train up to Hoghton Towers, the summit of the 1 in 99/101 climb from Bamber Bridge on the Preston-Blackburn line.

Class 4F 0-6-0 No 43931 heads through Grange-over-Sands with an eastbound freight on 27 August 1959. That summer was particularly hot, hence the absence of visible exhaust from the loco. The 4Fs were some of the first locos with which I became familiar at the start of my spotting era. To the engine's left is one of the camping coaches that were sited here.

Carlisle and Scotland

One of the two 'Patriot' 4-6-0 prototypes, No 45501 *St Dunstans*, has threaded its way around Carlisle with a freight on 1 August 1961. It has just passed beneath the WCML (off camera), which it will gain at Upperby Junction after rounding Upperby MPD. Citadel station is discernible in the left background, and the line entering the picture from the left leads to Crown Street goods yard, where Ivatt Class 2 2-6-0 No 46455 is shunting. Crown Street was the one-time terminus of the Maryport & Carlisle Railway, whose trains had to reverse out onto Newcastle & Carlisle metals (seen above *St Dunstans*) and change direction to gain their own line.

Star turn at Carlisle: on the same day 'Princess Royal' 'Pacific' No 46200 *The Princess Royal* sets off with a Perth-London train, on which it has just relieved a Type 4 (Class 40) diesel. 'Duchess' 'Pacific' No 46250 *City of Lichfield* waits to take over a Glasgow-Birmingham train.

Entering the north end of Carlisle Citadel station in the summer of 1964, Standard Class 5 4-6-0 No 73005 pilots 'Jubilee' 4-6-0 No 45698 *Mars* with a Glasgow to Blackpool excursion. The Standard 4-6-0 will be detached here, leaving **Mars** to continue single-handed.

A Glasgow to London Euston relief has arrived at Carlisle on a busy Saturday in August 1964. The pilot, Standard Class 5 4-6-0 No 73075, has been detached, and is about to leave 'Britannia' 4-6-2 No 70007 *Coeur-de-Lion* to continue its journey single-handed. On one of the centre roads is 'Jubilee' 4-6-0 No 45573 *Newfoundland*, waiting to take over another express, while EE Type 4 (Class 40) No D337 pauses with an express from Glasgow and Edinburgh to Birmingham.

This photo, taken during the four-day tour of Scotland at Easter 1963, shows 'Coronation' 4-6-2 No 46256 *Sir William A. Stanier, F.R.S.* at Perth MPD on the Saturday. The sight took me back to the occasion when I had looked in awe at this engine from a train on my way to stay with friends in Fife seven years earlier.

A pair of Standard Class 2 2-6-0s repose in Bathgate MPD in September 1965.

The North Eastern Region and Haworth

A visit to Holbeck MPD, Leeds, in August 1967 saw 'Jubilee' 4-6-0 No 45593 *Kolhapur* and Class 'K1' 2-6-0 No 62005 around the turntable. Both were destined for preservation.

The old racecourse platform by the Holgate bridge at York was a favourite location from which to photograph the trains. Here Class 'A3' 4-6-2 No 60044 *Melton* departs from York for the south with an express comprising a mixture of LNER and BR stock on 4 August 1962.

Class 'A4' 4-6-2 No 60006 *Sir Ralph Wedgwood* leaves York with an express for London King's Cross in May 1963.

On 14 September 1963 Class 'V2' 2-6-2 No 60858 passes West Hartlepool shed with a southbound train of mixed stock. Out of a total of 184 'V2s', this loco was one of only eight to receive a double chimney during the late 1950s.

'Royal Scot' 4-6-0 No 46115 *Scots Guardsman* was stabled on the KWVR at Haworth for a time at the start of its much-chequered career in preservation. Here the author and his friend Chris are seen in the cab during an early visit to this line in its embryonic stage of preservation.

this slight problem. Engine changes at Sheffield Victoria could be quite slick, say 3 or 4 minutes, not much time to nip down to the booking hall for the tickets. I guess we rode our luck to Doncaster. If challenged, we could honestly claim lack of time to rebook.

En route we saw the prototype Bo-Bo electric locomotive No 26000, built in 1941 at the LNER's Gorton Works for the embryo Woodhead electrification scheme. The scheme was shelved during the Second World War, being eventually completed by BR in 1954. As it couldn't be used, No 6000 (as the loco was then numbered) was loaned to the Netherlands State Railways. The Dutch referred to it as 'Tommy' (after the archetypal British soldier), and the name became official when the locomotive returned to Britain. BR built 57 more Bo-Bos mainly for freight work, particularly over the steeply graded line to Wath. They were classified as EM1 and later as Class 76. Seven more powerful Co-Co locomotives, which we have encountered earlier at Manchester London Road (Class EM2), were also constructed for passenger work.

At Doncaster we saw No D6708, one of the brand new Type 3 (Class 37) Co-Cos that emerged from English Electric in 1961. As was expected by now, there were plenty of Brush Type 2s (Class 31) around. The up 'Elizabethan' passed through headed by 'A4' No 60014 *Silver Link*, this being the only time I saw this train. Other big-name cops were 'A4' No 60005 *Sir Charles Newton*, 'A1' No 60118 *Archibald Sturrock*, 'A2/3' No 60523 *Sun Castle*, and 'A3' No 60112 *St Simon*, while pioneer Standard loco No 70000 *Britannia* headed through with a freight. Returning home, I copped 'Jubilees' Nos 45607 *Fiji* and 45573 *Newfoundland*. The total cop haulage for the day amounted to 111.

The final day of our rail-roving saw us back in the West Midlands, when I copped three more 'Kings' together with a miscellany of other GWR and LMS locos. There was just one engine of special interest seen on this day. Somerset & Dorset Joint Railway 2-8-0 No 53801 was on Saltley shed awaiting movement to Derby Works for scrapping. It was one of the original batch of six engines built at Derby specifically for the S&DJR, and all succumbed to the cutter's torch before any of the second batch of five, built by Robert Stephenson & Co.

So ended seven hectic days, which yielded a grand total of 752 cops. There are no entries in my notebook for a whole week after that! After recuperation, the local sheds took another bashing. Then five weeks later, Mike and I were tramping around Leeds and York sheds in the pouring rain. Among the resulting haul of cops was 'Brit' No 70008 *Black Prince* from March, which was on York MPD. No 'A4s' on this day, though.

At home, the Gresley three-cylinder beat had been absent since the removal from Gorton of the 'K3' 2-6-0s. Then, during September

1961, the Cheshire Lines sprang yet another surprise, or rather York MPD did, more to the point. Before leaving for work one morning I heard that distinctive six-beat exhaust approaching from the south. My eyes glued to the window, I disbelievingly saw a 'V2' 2-6-2, No 60963, which York had sent in place of the usual 'B1' 4-6-0. I went on to cop seven 'V2s' in the following two months, although they continued to appear in Liverpool until about March 1962. After that the 'B1s' made a brief return until they too finally disappeared.

Saturday 30 September was a Gresley sort of day in North West England. To begin with, I awoke to a curious cacophony of sound emanating from a train approaching from the south. The rhythm was reminiscent of a 'V2', perhaps one that had shed part of its valve gear? There was a 'V2' all right, No 60810, but with Walton's 2-6-4T No 42540 as pilot. The Gresley theme continued later that morning, as I travelled to Preston to see World Speed Record Holder *Mallard*, No 60022. I hadn't seen it on any of my visits so far to the ECML, so the 'A4' proved a most unlikely cop to make on the WCML. It was hauling an Illuminations special between Doncaster and Blackpool, another of Alan Pegler's ventures.

What a turnout there was at Preston to witness *Mallard*'s passage through the station. The crowded platform anticipated scenes at many stations a few years later as the age of steam on our railway network drew to a close. While at Preston I learned that the preserved Midland Compound 4-4-0, No 1000, had passed through light-engine before I arrived. It too was heading for Blackpool and was scheduled to double-head *Mallard* back to Doncaster that night. Although disappointed at having missed the 4-4-0, I wasn't sufficiently dedicated to return to Preston around midnight to see the pair heading back east. Anyway, before I departed from Preston for home, I copped No 72009 *Clan Stewart*. A nice little bonus.

Towards the end of 1961 I went with Dad to a branch meeting of the Stephenson Locomotive Society, held in the Chambers at the old Central station in Liverpool. During the course of the evening we found ourselves in conversation with a prominent member of the Society, with the result that I was enrolled as a member. The gentleman we spoke to, I must say, reminded me considerably of the shed foreman Spike and myself had encountered at Bidston five years previously. Was it...? I didn't ask!

Consequently, I found myself on a Society railtour in October, with Dad as a 'guest'. The itinerary, by DMU, included the Mold to Denbigh line, which was to lose its passenger service the following April. At the same time the section of line between Rhydymwyn and Denbigh was to close completely. The day was particularly drab, both weather-wise and for the fact that I made only four cops. There was No 6931 *Aldborough Hall* and a diesel shunter at Chester, and at Rhyl shed were 2-6-2T No 40185 from Llandudno Junction and, interestingly, 4F 0-6-0 No 44259 from Cricklewood. (The engine shed at Denbigh was closed in 1955, but was still standing at this date.) After Rhyl, our DMU proceeded up the branch to Dyserth from Prestatyn, which had not seen a passenger train since September 1930. The tortured squeal from the wheel flanges as our train climbed the steeply graded, sharply curved line brought out inquisitive local residents to witness our passage.

I now have to say with much regret that, after this run, I decided that railtours were not for me. I was still intent on spotting as many locomotives as I could, preferring not to travel along some doomed railway line that would bear very little fruit in the way of cops. Another five years were to pass before I partook in another railtour. I did continue my membership of the Stephenson Locomotive Society, though, as I found the monthly Journal most beneficial. It published locomotive stock alterations, ie lists of new, reallocated and condemned locomotives. Its news reporting was usually one month ahead of *The Railway Magazine* and *Modern Railways* (as *Trains Illustrated* had been renamed in January 1961). The Journal also listed locomotives visiting the various works for overhaul or for scrapping, so I took advantage of the works and shed visits organised by the Society.

The first of these was to Crewe on New Year's Day 1962, and I took Mike as a 'guest'. Approaching Crewe by rail from Liverpool, the train passed part of the works on the right. No idea of the size of the works could be gained from the train, from which we could see the boiler shop, some machine shops and various storage spaces. Our train then negotiated the triple junction with the lines from Chester and Manchester before entering the station. After meeting up with the SLS delegation, Crewe North shed was 'done' first. Joy, oh joy! I copped my final 'Duchess', the elusive No 46222 *Queen Mary*, to complete the class. Then off we trooped towards the works.

We soon began to appreciate the sheer size of the establishment. Crewe Works at the time had the distinction of being the largest railway-owned works in the world, and it felt like it as we walked and walked! Our party entered the premises from Mill Street near the locomotive offices, and proceeded alongside the access tracks towards the main body of the works. I copped veteran LYR 0-6-0ST No 51444, which Crewe had bagged to use as a works shunter. Then, not content with completing the 'Duchess' class, further on in the works yard was 'Royal Scot' No 46109 *Royal Engineer*. Two classes completed in one day! It was actually withdrawn for scrapping, so I saw it in the nick of time. Nothing much mattered after that, but I did make another 58 cops that day. There were some LMS types from the NE Region and ScR, and of interest among some from the Midlands was No 70026 *Polar Star*, one of the 'Brits' transferred to Aston MPD. I had already copped three Aston 'Brits' at Lime Street station during the closing months of 1961, Nos 70024 *Vulcan*, 70025 *Western Star* and 70028 *Royal Star*. No 70022 *Tornado* from Kingmoor was also present at Crewe.

New 'Peak' Class diesels were under construction, Nos D58 to D67. Cheating or not, even though only the main frames of some were recognisable, we still counted the allocated numbers as cops. Anyway, we probably saw most of them a few times in service later on. Nos D134 to D137 were in the works yard, brand new. (When construction was shared between different works, the fleet numbers allocated were not always in sequence.) They were the last numerically of what became Class 45, and Nos D138 to D193 became Class 46, having different electrical equipment from the 45s. Crewe South, the freight shed, was omitted from our attention on that day.

The following Saturday saw us at Oswestry, which gave me an interesting variety of 26 cops. The old Cambrian Railways made Oswestry its headquarters, and it established a railway works in the town, which was still in use for overhauls of the smaller engines at the time of our visit. There we saw hybrid 'Dukedog' 4-4-0 No 9017, which was eventually restored as No 3217 and named *Earl of Berkeley* when it later moved to the preserved Bluebell Railway in Sussex. Keeping company with the 4-4-0 was No 823, an 0-6-0T of the narrow-gauge Welshpool & Llanfair Light Railway. Formerly in BR stock, this loco, too, was eventually restored to run again over that line, which, after purchase from BR, was reopened by a band of dedicated enthusiasts. On shed or in the vicinity, I copped three more 0-4-2Ts, Nos 1458, 1447 and 1438, which found use on the short shuttle service between Oswestry and Gobowen. These trains connected at Gobowen with services on the Shrewsbury-Chester main line.

Yet another visit to the Derby area followed on Saturday 21 January. This time we decided to 'do' Burton shed to see if we could spot any of the five Crab 2-6-0s that possessed Reidinger poppet valve gear. Although I had seen two of them back home, Mike wanted the lot. So we duly caught a train at Derby, the motive power for which proved to be 'Royal Scot' 4-6-0 No 46103 *Royal Scots Fusilier*. We felt quite privileged, for, as we discovered at Crewe, inroads were now being made into this famous 4-6-0 class for scrapping. The engine was based at Birmingham's Saltley depot at the time, but later that year was moved to Carlisle Upperby to replace one of its sisters withdrawn from there.

At Burton, as luck would have it for Mike, all five Reidinger 'Crabs' were on view, Nos 42818, 42822, 42824, 42825 and 42829. They were stored out in the open, withdrawn from service. I made 16 cops at Burton, which also included 'B1' 4-6-0 No 61370 from the ER's Canklow depot near Sheffield. We caught a DMU back to Derby, where I copped a host of steam freight engines and diesel shunters from Toton depot, most of which were awaiting works attention. Was Toton depot practically empty this day, I wonder? It was during this Derby visit that we learned that continued use was now uncertain for the remaining veteran Midland 0-6-0Ts and 0-4-0Ts still operating around Chesterfield's steelworks. We felt we must now visit Chesterfield to catch sight of these engines before they fell victim to the cutter's torch.

It was a bitterly cold February Sunday that saw two mad bods setting off on their quest to see a handful of old workhorses. We alighted from our warm, electric-hauled train at Sheffield Victoria and consultation of my *Shed Directory* advised us of the buses we could catch to our chosen destinations. The first port of call, though, was Sheffield Darnall shed. Coded 41A, it was the main shed in the area. Here we found mostly 'B1' 4-6-0s, 2-8-0s of classes 'O1', 'O4' and the three-cylinder 'O2s', together with 'K3' 2-6-0 No 61820. Inevitably, a few Class 31 diesels were about the place.

Next, a bus across the county border into Derbyshire landed us at Staveley in Chesterfield. There were two sheds here, the GCR shed coded 41H, and the Midland Barrow Hill shed. The latter was now administered under the ER and coded 41E, but it still retained an allocation of mostly LMS engines. 'Jubilee' No 45725 *Repulse* was there, late of Millhouses MPD, which had recently closed. Although the veterans we had come to see were officially allocated to Barrow Hill, they were in fact hired out to the steelworks for use on its railway systems. They were usually kept on the works premises for periods at a time, being coaled and watered on site, returning to their parent depot only for attention when light repairs became necessary. Perhaps because the day was a Sunday, we found four of the 0-6-0Ts on Barrow Hill shed, Nos 41739, 41804, 41708 and 41763. Apart from the three missing 0-4-0Ts, Mike still needed to see No 41734, the Class 1F I had seen at Birkenhead six years ago. Thus he insisted we did a tour of the steelworks. Reluctantly I tagged along, fretting about the cold. We soon caught sight of No 41734, and a little later saw two of the 0-4-0Ts, Nos 41533 and 41528. This left No 41531 outstanding, so on and on we plodded. We'd exhausted our supplies of grub and the hot contents of our flasks, so were beginning to flag in the bitter cold. After what seemed like an hour, but was probably only about a quarter, something resembling a small steam engine was spotted in the distance. We studied it through a pair of binoculars (actually, an old pair of theatre glasses given to me by a dear family friend), and sure enough the outline of a Midland 0-4-0T of Class 0F could be discerned. We couldn't read its number – we didn't need to. It could only be No 41531. What relief!

The trek back to civilisation and the return bus to Sheffield didn't seem quite so bad now. We knew where we were going: to Victoria station to grab some much-needed sustenance and a train home, in that order.

Grand National Day fell on the last day of March in 1962, but an SLS visit to the former GCR works and running sheds at Gorton was advertised for the same day in the Society's Journal of the preceding month. A visit to Gorton appealed to me, as I anticipated I would see some rare LNER birds there from distant ER sheds. So I forsook my usual visit to Aintree and set off, without Mike this time, for Gorton.

En route to Manchester via the CLC, Bo-Bo electric No E3304 was spotted at Allerton. This was, at the time, one of five designated Type B locomotives that were equipped with lower traction gearing for the purpose of moving heavy freight trains. They didn't last long in this form, as the standard version of those first-generation electrics proved quite capable of meeting such requirements. The five were subsequently converted to standard specification, No E3304 being renumbered E3099. I was not to be outdone through cutting out my visit to Aintree, either. For as my train entered the outskirts of Manchester, 'Jubilee' 4-6-0 No 45622 *Nyasaland* passed with an Aintree-bound race special from the London area. The engine was from Kentish Town depot, and the train would have traversed the Midland main line to gain the CLC system south of Manchester. It would have joined the line to Liverpool at Throstle Nest Junction.

In and around the works 'WD' 2-8-0s predominated, mainly from South Yorkshire, but No 90442 was far away from its home, visiting from Tilbury. There were inevitably several 'O4' 2-8-0s on view, also from Yorkshire, as well as three 'O1s' (rebuilt from 'O4s' by Edward Thompson). These were Nos 63591, 63689 and 63806, all ex-works after overhaul. I was astonished to read in the railway journals published subsequently that all three had been withdrawn for scrapping without returning to their home shed of Annesley (in the Nottingham area). Annesley had been transferred from the ER to the LMR in 1958, together with all other sheds south of Chesterfield on the former GCR main line to London. The last trunk route to be built in Britain, the GCR ran through three regional territories: from the ER at Sheffield, through the LMR via Nottingham, Leicester and Rugby, and the WR between Princes Risborough, High Wycombe and Northolt Junction[21], south of Ruislip. It then proceeded to its own terminus at Marylebone. After transfer of the London extension to the LMR, the

---

[21] Prior to nationalisation, the section between Princes Risborough and Northolt Junction was operated jointly with the GWR.

Great Central had become a withered artery (subsequently losing its status as a 'through' route from the north in 1966). By 1962 it seemed that Annesley was one shed determined to rid itself of all things LNER rather more quickly than others on the line. But what a waste of money to scrap newly overhauled engines, and comparatively recent rebuilds at that. The same fate befell all other 'O1s' based at Annesley, a total of about 17 locomotives succumbing to the cutter's torch.

I copped a handful of residents at Gorton shed. Interestingly, these included five LMS engines, one of which was No 41702, a Midland 0-6-0T of Class 1F. This one had seemingly escaped the clutches of the steelworks in Chesterfield! Like Bidston, Gorton also possessed a few 'J94' 0-6-0STs, of which only No 68012 was on show this day. However, all were to be transferred away before too long. I also copped 'B1' 4-6-0 No 61077, newly reallocated to Gorton from London's Neasden shed. Cops for the trip totalled 46.

In the meantime, visits to Birkenhead shed produced a couple of extraordinary cops. 'B1' 4-6-0 No 61252 from Norwich was lodging on 17 February, and 'County' 4-6-0 No 1002 *County of Berks* was there on 10 March. Both types were pretty uncommon at Birkenhead, but a 'B1' from so far afield was very rare indeed. The 'County' was from Didcot, and was probably deputising for a 'Hall' 4-6-0.

12
The 'South Lancashire' years – Part I

I had now been a member of the Stephenson Locomotive Society for six months. The fact that members had to make their own way to shed and works visits enabled me to keep my independence, which I preferred. But Mike pointed out that by joining an enthusiasts' club that organised tours to various parts of the country, we could reach sheds in far-off places that otherwise we could only dream of visiting. So it was that we joined the South Lancashire Locomotive Club, based in Manchester.

Club tours were either day trips or overnight runs, depending on how far the selected areas were from Manchester. The tours were mainly wholly by road, although the occasional rail/road tour was thrown in. The long-distance overnight runs normally commenced on the Saturday night, so that most of Sunday could be spent shed-bashing before returning to Manchester. It so happened that our first trip with the Club was indeed a rail/road affair, commencing from Piccadilly station, Manchester, on Saturday night, 7 April 1962. Memory is uncertain as to how far we travelled by train. Timetable research suggests we boarded an 11.20pm departure and alighted at Stoke at a scheduled time of 23 minutes past midnight. Travel to the Midlands from there was by coach, and we reached Burton-on-Trent at around 3.30am.

The party trouped out of a nice warm coach into the cold air of that dark April morning. I groaned inwardly. What on earth was I doing here at this hour on a Sunday? I should have been sleeping soundly, dreaming of the prospect of a lie-in until nearly dinnertime! There were not many shed lights burning and an eerie calm existed all around the place. One of Burton's 'Jubilee' 4-6-0s, No 45618 *New Hebrides*, was present, and copping this provided a highlight in the darkness. Following my visit to Burton with Mike in January, it isn't really surprising that I made only one other cop, 4F 0-6-0 No 44332, also slumbering at its home shed.

By the time we arrived at Oxley shed, situated near to Wolverhampton racecourse, daylight was breaking. Oxley provided a good variety of mixed-traffic and freight locos., mainly GWR types. Wolverhampton's

Stafford Road was next on our itinerary; coded 84A, it was the main shed in the area. The shed foreman wasn't too pleased to see us. Even though the Club possessed a group permit, he chose to be awkward and wouldn't let us in for half an hour. Had he known of our presence at Oxley, he would have stopped us there, too, he informed us!

'Why – do you run Oxley from here?'

'Yes!'

I copped four more 'King' 4-6-0s on Stafford Road – Nos 6001 *King Edward VII*, 6020 *King Henry IV*, 6021 *King Richard II* and 6027 *King Richard I*. Stourbridge was next, and at Wellington there were three diesel railcars of GWR origin, Nos W21W, W25W and W31W. This was the only occasion I caught sight of any of these railcars until the age of preservation. Bromsgrove shed was on the former MR main line between Birmingham and Gloucester, and was specially built to supply locomotives for the purpose of assisting northbound trains up the 1 in 37½ incline to Blackwell. Coming under LMR administration at nationalisation, the shed was coded 21C, but was transferred to the WR in the 1950s and recoded 85B. Despite this, it retained a few LMS 'Jinty' 0-6-0Ts such as No 47276, which I copped, but the WR authorities replaced some with their big Hawksworth 0-6-0PTs of the '9400' Class. Of these I copped Nos 8400, 8401, 8402, 8403, 8480 and 9493. Class 9F 2-10-0 No 92079 was also there. It is well related in history that in 1955 this engine replaced the famous MR 0-10-0 No 58100, specially built for use on the bank in 1919. As may be gathered by the number of locos present, there wasn't much requirement for assistance up the hill on this Sunday. In fact, we saw nothing on the main line except a 'Peak' diesel descending with a passenger train, much to everyone's disgust, so we continued on our way.

Worcester, Stratford-upon-Avon and Leamington Spa were next, before we found ourselves at Rugby. On shed here were two engines from the former ER shed, Woodford Halse, 'WD' 2-8-0 No 90524 and named 'B1' 4-6-0 No 61028 *Umseke*. Nuneaton and Coalville concluded the tour, before we headed back to Derby for our return train to Manchester. Coalville provided us with some veteran Midland Class 2F 0-6-0s, Nos 58136, 58137, 58163 and 58166. At Derby I duly copped a few 'Peak' diesels and four more steamers to round off the day.

Next came the April visit to London referred to in the previous chapter, and some local shed bashes followed. An interesting visitor to Edge Hill at this time was diesel No DP2. This locomotive was English Electric's contender for Type 4 diesels in the 2,700-2,800bhp range. (DP1 was the prototype 'Deltic', which never actually bore the number.) The venture led to BR striking a contract with EE to provide 50 Type 4s, which later became the Class 50s, originally numbered in the D400 series. There were two other prototypes in this power range: No D0260 *Lion* (nicknamed 'The White Lion') came from the Birmingham Locomotive, Carriage & Wagon Co, and employed a Sulzer engine of 2,750bhp, while two Maybach engines, each of 1,400bhp, were installed in No D0280 *Falcon*, built by Brush Traction. In the event Brush won the contract to build what became the Class 47s, using the Sulzer 2,750bhp engine instead of the two Maybachs, something that puzzled us at the time.[22] In 1970 BR took *Falcon* into its stock, numbering it D1200, but withdrew this non-standard locomotive in 1975.

It was Doncaster's turn again now. This time both works and shed were visited, courtesy of the SLS, with Mike as guest once more. Doncaster Works was just less than half the size of the works at Crewe, and occupied a site alongside the station. As usual there were buckets-full of cops, which included some electric Bo-Bo locos (Class 85s) under construction for the LMR's electrification. A notable cop among the 'Pacifics' in the works was 'A3' No 60103 *Flying Scotsman*, which was receiving its final overhaul while working for BR. In another 12 months the loco would be withdrawn for private preservation by Alan Pegler. As yet, no one could have forecast that *Flying Scotsman* would become a legend – destined for immortality, if you like. There was just one 'A4' in for attention, No 60011 *Empire of India*, but three 'Brits' were there, Nos 70002 *Geoffrey Chaucer*, 70011 *Hotspur* and 70040 *Clive of India*, all still allocated to the ER. After a 20-minute walk from the works, the shed produced two more 'Brits', Nos 70036 *Boadicea* and 70013 *Oliver Cromwell*, the latter another engine destined for stardom a few years hence. Also on shed was No 60500 *Edward Thompson*, named after its designer, successor to Gresley as CME of the LNER. It was the first of Thompson's production series of 'Pacifics', classed as 'A2/3'.

In June my parents decided to visit a cousin of Dad's, who lived just outside Shrewsbury. Upon arrival at the station, Norman picked up my parents with his car, while I headed for the engine sheds. An interesting cop here was Class '2251' 0-6-0 No 3205, which in six years' time would become one of the first engines to operate in private preservation on the Severn Valley Railway.[23] WR diesel-hydraulics were now making forays north of Birmingham, and I caught three of them at Shrewsbury that day. On shed was 'Warship' Type 4 No D834 *Pathfinder*, while

---

[22] The reason became apparent later. Separate high-speed diesel engine/generator sets were lighter in weight than medium-speed sets, and two engines provided better weight distribution. With advancement of technology, weight savings became possible using a single medium-speed engine, hence the choice of the Sulzer engine for the Class 47s.

[23] This line was to open between Bridgnorth and Hampton Loade in 1970.

Hymek/Beyer Peacock Type 3 No D7010 was in the station. However, the biggest surprise of all came when the pioneer 'Western' Type 4 No D1000 *Western Enterprise* rolled in from the south with our homeward-bound train. The loco was still painted in its original sand colour, and I was delighted to discover that it was to continue hauling our train as far as Chester. This turned out to be the only experience I had of 'Western' haulage. Incidentally, most of the class were painted maroon, but some received Brunswick green.

Shortly after my D1000 experience I saw the first 12 of the Crewe-built 'Westerns', Nos D1035 to D1046, under construction during another visit to the works with Mike. Crewe was still building 'Peak' Type 4s, of which Nos D53, D55, D56 and D57 were on view. We did all the sheds that day, too, including the former GWR shed at Gresty Lane, where I copped No 6971 *Athelhampton Hall*, No 5983 *Henley Hall* and 0-6-0PT No 9636. 'Warship' diesels were much in evidence at Crewe this day. Nos D808 *Centaur* and D867 *Zenith* hovered in the vicinity of the station, while Nos D850 *Swift* and D854 *Tiger* were on North shed. Locomotives destined for scrap were also accumulating. Inroads into Stanier's classes were now being made, and an example was on Crewe South shed in the form of 2-6-4T No 42678. This wasn't the first Stanier engine to go, however, as that unfortunate distinction belonged to 'Black 5' No 45401.

On the night of Saturday 30 June I headed for Manchester with Mike to join a South Lancs Sunday trip to Glasgow. We were especially looking forward to seeing engines of Caledonian and North British vintages; inroads had already been made into the Caledonian Railway classes for scrapping, but many of the NBR examples seemed to be soldiering on regardless. Also there were some Type 2 diesels built by the North British Locomotive Co, all of which were allocated to the ScR.

The overnight long-distance runs usually departed from outside Manchester's Victoria station between 11pm and midnight. There was no convenient train from Lime Street to Manchester Exchange, from where it was possible to make a convenience of the connecting platform as a short cut to Victoria. As it was, we used a fast train between the two Central stations. Arriving in Manchester at 10.15pm, we hoofed it across the city, but there was still some time to while away before our departure. It was our custom to gain entry to the platforms at Victoria to see the night-time activity. Although there was not much passenger traffic at this time of night, the place was abuzz with newspaper traffic. This was when Manchester was 'the Fleet Street of the north'. Strings of platform trolleys loaded with sacks of newspapers were dragged around to their appropriate trains by electric tractors. These trains would later be heading for destinations in Wales and the North West and North East of England. Motive power was usually a Standard or a 'Black 5' 4-6-0 from Patricroft shed.

There was a head count, and relief all round when we knew that everyone who had booked was now on board. So our coach set off, heading out of town up the A6. Soon we left behind the suburbs of Manchester and the street lights. The main interior lights were extinguished and a couple of ultraviolet lamps switched on. With the coach now effectively in darkness, everyone could relax without the glare of normal light bulbs, and this was a help to those who could sleep. I tried to sleep, but was not normally one for slumbering while travelling. It was going to be a long drag for insomniacs; there were only two stretches of motorway then open on our route – the part of the M6 that became known as the 'Preston Bypass' from Bamber Bridge to north of Preston, and from Lancaster to Carnforth. We then had to follow the A6 all the way to Carlisle, negotiate the city, then follow the A74 onward into Scotland. There wasn't much conversation. Sometimes I tried reading number books, magazines and whatever else. Some guys dozed off, their heads rolling about with the motion of the coach. Even a thump on the window pane wasn't enough to wake them! Sometimes I just shut my eyes and listened to a transistor radio someone else had brought on board.

'Bunnnnnnnng,' sang the radio station's signature signal. Then a voice said, 'This is Radio Luxembourg broadcasting on 208 metres, medium wave...'

Current hit records were played by disc jockeys until about 2.00am, pre-empting those of the pirate radio stations, and subsequently of Radio One. Volume was turned down to a sufficient level, and thus the monotony of night travel was relieved somewhat. During daylight hours, given the chance, some revellers at the rear of the coach struck up a few choruses of current pop songs. There was also The Poet, who honoured us with his company on most trips. He was 'way out', as we said in those days (today he would be 'from another planet'). Encouraged by the revellers, The Poet recited his own compositions, which, I thought at the time, resembled the style of Homer's Iliad (something I had endured at school). Few could understand The Poet, but I wonder who was 'taking the mickey' out of whom; he joined in the mirth by continuing to oblige with a few lines upon demand, to the accompaniment of laughter from the rabble.

Travel in the summer months on trips like this one to Scotland was not too bad. At around 3.30am there was usually a faint glimmer of light in the sky. So it was on this particular trip, but it was still extremely dark at ground level as we stopped at Beattock shed. There were mostly banking engines here, used for helping trains up the 10-mile climb northward. Anyway, it provided a welcome break for all, including our driver. There were five 2-6-4Ts lurking around, including No 80002, since preserved on the Keighley & Worth Valley Railway. There was also a curious visitor, veteran CR 4-4-0 No 54507. Its number was not included in the summer edition of the *ABC* shed book, so it had obviously been withdrawn for some time. Maybe it was temporaly parked en route to a scrapyard. 'Black 5' No 45177 of Grangemouth passed on the main line.

After the break we headed onward towards Glasgow, calling at Motherwell and Hamilton on the way. Glasgow itself was sprawling with railways. Most of them were constructed by the Caledonian (later part of the LMS), as was the WCML north of Carlisle to Glasgow Central. The CR built lines both north and south of the River Clyde, but the LNER's presence was at Queen Street, having absorbed the NBR with routes to Edinburgh, as well as the West Highland line to Fort William and Mallaig, which was operated by the NBR in the pre-Grouping age. By now, 14 years since nationalisation, some integration had taken place, and many Scottish sheds had both LMS and LNER types on their books. As the day unfolded, our notebooks became filled with numbers of mainly freight and mixed-traffic types from both railways. There was also a fair quantity of Scottish Standard types, and a few Class 'WD' 2-8-0s and 2-10-0s. On the diesel front, many different designs of shunter were in evidence, as supplied by various manufacturers. The depots at Parkhead, St Rollox, Eastfield, Corkerhill and Polmadie provided a host of main-line diesel numbers, mostly comprising two classes, English Electric Type 1s (later Class 20s) and North British Loco Type 2s. Some of the former were brand new, as the type was perpetuated. Probably many of the steam locos we saw were shortly to be withdrawn, to be replaced by the diesels once these had passed their acceptance trials. There was a handful of 'Peak' diesels around, too, having ventured north of the Border via the GSWR route from Carlisle.

Notably I copped the two remaining named 'Black 5s' still in Scotland, Nos 45158 *Glasgow Yeomanry* on St Rollox shed and 45157 *The Glasgow Highlander* on Corkerhill. Like most of my fellow travellers, I needed five 'Jubilee' 4-6-0s, which, according to our shed books, were allocated to Corkerhill. So we were properly disappointed to find only one of them on shed that day, No 45677 *Beatty*. Moving on, Class 'A2' 4-6-2 No 60525 *A. H. Peppercorn* was also on St Rollox, but Dawsholm shed yielded some rather special celebrities. Accommodated here were four preserved veterans in the form of GNSR 4-4-0 No 49 *Gordon Highlander*, NBR 4-4-0 No 256 *Glen Douglas*, CR 4-2-2 No 123, and

HR 4-6-0 No 103. They were four pre-Grouping engines that the Scottish Region had restored to running order to work special trains. However, 4-4-0 No 54398 *Ben Alder*, also a former Highland Railway engine, was stored in the condition in which it had been withdrawn from service. Still in BR livery, it was awaiting a decision whether or not to preserve it. Tragically, this locomotive was eventually scrapped. There were only two diminutive CR 'Pug' 0-4-0ST engines left, one of which, No 56039, we saw at Dawsholm. We found the other 'Pug', No 56029, at Kipps. This shed was actually a former NBR establishment, but at this time was also providing storage accommodation for 21 CR locomotives of various types. One interesting NBR loco present was No 65216 *Byng*, one of a few Class 'J36' 0-6-0s that carried names (commemorating military personnel from the First World War). Standard 2-6-4Ts were very much in evidence at the various Glasgow sheds, including the pioneer No 80000 on Eastfield depot and, on Polmadie, No 80054, which was the example represented by my Hornby Dublo model. However, despite BR's rationalisation of the allocation of the 2-6-4T types, there was still a plentiful supply of the Fairburn variant around Glasgow.

The first five 'Clan' 'Pacifics' were still allocated to Glasgow Polmadie. I needed to see No 72003 *Clan Fraser* to complete the class of ten, but was disappointed not to see it on shed. Instead, I had to make do with hoards of 'Black 5s', Type 1 diesels, diesel shunters, Standard and LMS 2-6-4Ts, some old CR locos, and a handful of other types. Of note among the CR vintages were 4-4-0s Nos 54502 and 54463, and of special interest was Class 8F 2-8-0 No 48774. Before the advent of the Class 'WD' 2-8-0s this engine was one of many built to Stanier's design for the Ministry of Supply's early requirements for the Second World War, and had remained the property of the Military after hostilities ceased. In 1957, together with two of its sisters, it was handed over to BR, which allocated the trio numbers 48773, 48774 and 48775. All three were sent to Polmadie shed, and became the only 8Fs allocated to the Scottish Region. In another strange quirk of railway history, the ScR withdrew these 8Fs from service in 1962, but they were reinstated when it was decided that the LMR could make use of them. On our way home from Scotland we called at Carlisle Kingmoor and Upperby sheds. What should we see but 8F No 48774! I also copped Kingmoor's own 'Jubilees', Nos 45657 *Tyrwhitt* and 45716 *Swiftsure*.

Once back in Manchester, Mike and I had to catch a train back to Liverpool. We were fortunate in that, on most occasions, the coach arrived sufficiently early for us to catch a Newcastle-Liverpool train, due to leave Exchange at 9.42pm. A later arrival entailed crossing the city again to Central for a train that left at 10.30pm. Unfortunately, it took an hour to reach Liverpool after calling at all stations out of Manchester.

In the intervening period between this and the next South Lancs trip, I took a holiday in Bridlington with my parents. Here was a chance to sample the delights of travelling on a Trans-Pennine DMU all the way to Hull. The open saloon trailer in the centre of the train provided a very comfortable ride. From Hull we caught a local DMU, a 'boneshaker' by comparison, which took us up to Bridlington.

It was during my stay here that I discovered I was no sailor. There was a big swell out in the North Sea the day I decided to sample one of the pleasure cruises on offer, and the waves were easily as high as the craft I was aboard. Our captain decided to go and investigate a ship lurking a couple of miles off shore. It turned out to be Russian, so our captain shouted through the Tannoy, 'Does anyone speak English?'

The Russians were not giving anything away, as one of them, without as much as a modicum of originality, simply replied, 'Does anyone speak Russian?' His ship continually disappeared from view as the waves tossed our little boat up and down at a greater frequency than a roller-coaster ride! I didn't feel very well for a while after that trip, nor did some of the other passengers!

There were some more pleasant experiences than that (apart from number-spotting), like walking along the cliffs to Flamborough Head, visiting Burton Agnes Hall, and sampling the delights of the ballroom. It wasn't that I was into dancing – I liked listening to the live bands and watching others dancing. The 'twist' craze was now well and truly 'in', with dancers twisting themselves silly to 'Nut Rocker', a number recorded by B. Bumble and the Stingers, no less. I rather liked the 'B' side to this one, 'Nautilus'. Frank Ifield was No 1 with 'I Remember You', the strains of which were often heard at our 'lodging', a guest house, as the young and tasty staff went about their chores.

I did go off on a couple of spotting trips, however, all by train. The first was to Leeds via Scarborough, returning straight to Bridlington by avoiding Hull. There were just four Standard Class 3 2-6-2Ts on the NE Region, two shedded at Scarborough and two at Malton. I copped the Scarborough engines at their home base, Nos 82026 and 82027. Neville Hill was the old NER shed at Leeds, and it possessed three of the impressive 'Q6' 0-8-0s produced by that company from 1913. I was lucky to see all three; Nos 63436 and 63449 were out on main-line duties, while No 63348 was on shed. Bunking the shed itself produced a miscellany of small fry. Of interest were two 'J94' 0-6-0STs from Ardsley, near Wakefield, Nos 68015 and 68049, and Stanier Class 3 2-6-2T No 40193 was there from Royston shed.

My second trip was also circular: Bridlington-York-Doncaster-

Hull-Bridlington. In the station at York was No 82028, the last of the
quartet of 2-6-2Ts on the NE Region that I needed. (I had seen No
82029 at Penrith during my return from Scotland in 1956). The station
inevitably produced some big stuff, including No 60013 *Dominion of
New Zealand*, the 'A4' with the deep-toned Canadian-style whistle,
'A1' No 60142 *Edward Fletcher*, and 'Deltic' No D9014, later to be
named *The Duke of Wellington's Regiment*. Class 'K1' 2-6-0 No 62005
was also there, destined eventually for preservation and further main-
line running. On shed I copped another 'A1', No 60124 *Kenilworth*,
two 'A2/3s', Nos 60515 *Sun Stream* and 60516 *Hycilla*, a couple of 'A3s',
Nos 60054 *Prince of Wales* and 60083 *Sir Hugo*, and a 'Brit', No 70030
William Wordsworth. Not a bad haul. By now all 45 of the unrebuilt
'B16/1' 4-6-0s had gone for scrap, but York possessed 18 of the 'B16/2'
and 'B16/3' rebuilds that were left. I copped three of the latter during the
holiday, Nos 61444, 61418 and 61463. As our Trans-Pennine trundled
briefly along the ECML on our approach to Selby, there occasioned
one of those strokes of luck that really made a spotter's day. I copped
'A4' 'Pacific' No 60021 *Wild Swan*, which passed us accelerating away
from the Selby speed restrictions with a northbound express.

Back home I took a two-week rest from gadding about on spotting
trips, but I did cop Class '4F' 0-6-0 No 44341 from Northwich and 'B1'
4-6-0 No 61381 from Leicester Central, both passing along the CLC.
My shed book told me the 'B1' was from Leicester, but I guess it had
been reallocated to Gorton as Leicester Central rid itself of all things
LNER.

Mike had made the acquaintance of a guy named Steve, and it
was he instead of Mike who joined me for another South Lancashire
invasion of London. On the way south our coach called at Watford for
a break – not the M1 services at the Gap, but the engine shed, where
I made just three cops. From there we made for Southall and Slough
sheds, before heading on into London. Nothing spectacular here, and
Slough was such a small shed, with two diesel shunters and two
0-6-0PTs on view. Inevitably our tour included the 'tried and tested'
Old Oak Common, but which on this occasion we left until later.[24]
This time, the former GER shed at Stratford came in for some scrutiny.
The Great Eastern section of the ER was in a period of transition from
steam to diesel, and we expected to collect a hoard of recently allocated
diesels together with some of the steam locos they were replacing. So
we next headed across London from Southall to do Stratford shed, by
which route I haven't a clue today.

Stratford supplied engines for services to East Anglia from London's

---

[24] Probably to maintain the visiting times stipulated on the shed permits.

Liverpool Street station. The engine sheds were positioned well to the west of the GER London-Cambridge line, and in between were situated the Great Eastern's carriage works, together with its attendant storage sidings. The locomotive workshops of the old GER, on the opposite side of this line, actually closed in 1962. However, locomotive repairs continued at Stratford in a machine shop situated between the two shed buildings, the Jubilee Shed and the smaller New Shed. Perhaps it goes without saying that Stratford MPD comprised the largest engine sheds in Britain, as we were about to discover. Access to the premises was gained through a tunnel under the Cambridge lines from the station.

While waiting by the tunnel entrance for the go-ahead to proceed, I had noticed a small advertisement pasted on one of the walls. It proclaimed that Georgie Fame would be appearing with his band, The Blue Flames, at the Flamingo Club. A couple of years later, when browsing through the wares of one of Liverpool's record stores, I came across an LP entitled 'Georgie Fame and The Blue Flames at The Flamingo'. I decided to buy it, and soon became hooked on his contagious style of blues. Appropriately, the opening number is entitled 'Night Train'!

Our party filed through the tunnel. What a great sprawl of railwayana lay before us at the far end! The distance from the entrance to the engine sheds themselves was about a quarter of a mile, following a route beside a loop line past the carriage repair shops; to us weary travellers the distance seemed many times greater. The shed was shortly to extinguish the last remnants of its steam allocation, but the 'Britannia' 'Pacifics', once the star turns on the principal expresses over the former GER system, were already long gone. We saw a couple of the initial batch of ten Class 40 diesels that replaced them, Nos D200 and D204. The first five were allocated to Stratford and the other five to Hornsey for working over the ECML. Of the steam engines that were left, many were in store. They were mainly of GER origin, comprising 'J15', 'J17' and 'J19' 0-6-0s, and 'J69' 0-6-0Ts. There was even a departmental locomotive (works shunter) on shed, a Class 'J66' 0-6-0T of 1886 vintage. Its departmental number was 32, formerly BR No 68370. Special mention must be made of No 61572. Classified as 'B12/3', this was the last surviving example of an inside-cylindered 4-6-0 in Britain, and was duly destined for preservation. Of the few remaining steam engines still in use at Stratford, there were 'B1' 4-6-0s, 'L1' 2-6-4Ts, GER 'N7' 0-6-2Ts, and Standard 2-6-4Ts. The Standard tanks were a surprise; according to our shed books, Stratford didn't have any. However, six of them were on view, Nos 80071, 80073, 80074, 80075, 80076 and 80077. All had 30A (Stratford) shedplates affixed, and had been transferred from Plaistow, which had served the London,

Tilbury & Southend line. Officially, the shed had closed following recent electrification of the line.

As for the main-line diesels, apart from the two Class 40s referred to above, the place was full of Brush Type 2s (Class 31), English Electric Type 3s (Class 37), BR-built Type 2s (Classes 24 and 25), British Thomson Houston (BTH) Type 1s, and North British Loco Type 1s. There were also numerous 350hp diesel-electric shunters, and a variety of smaller examples, including the unique Brush-built 0-4-0 diesel-electric No D2999.

None of us were looking forward to the long trek back to the coach after noting down about 130 numbers. As it was, both Steve and I were now becoming rather anxious about the whereabouts of some toilets, as there didn't seem to be any around. But there just happened to be some wartime air raid shelters near the carriage shops, so, after hanging back from the rest, we both dived into one of them. By the time we emerged the crowd was about to disappear from view beyond the carriage buildings. Rejuvenated, a quick sprint reunited us with the crowd, and we were now thankfully within sight of the exit tunnel.

Having done Stratford, we now followed the *Shed Directory*'s suggested itinerary by heading for Plaistow before going to Devons Road. As related above, Plaistow shed was now officially closed, but it was still being used as a storage point for locomotives. There were two Standard 2-6-4Ts there, Nos 80070 and 80103, both from Tilbury shed. It came as a big surprise to learn that the latter, barely five years old, was withdrawn from service for scrapping. At least, that was the official line – no doubt some parts of this engine were used as spares for others of its type. No 80070 was transferred to the WR. Not much older than the Standards were two of the LMS-designed tanks, Nos 42219 from Shoeburyness and 42254 from Tilbury, also marked as withdrawn. Although most of Stanier's three-cylinder 2-6-4Ts had now gone, No 42527 was still intact at Plaistow, as was another outposted LMS engine, 'Jinty' 0-6-0T No 47328, withdrawn from Shoeburyness, and five Class 'WD' 2-8-0s were in temporary storage from Tilbury. Devons Road was now totally dieselised, with seven Class 20 Type 1s and six diesel-hydraulic 0-4-0 shunters on shed for our visit.

Our party then headed for Old Oak Common by way of the sheds at Kentish Town (which supplied me with 'Jubilee' No 45620 *North Borneo*), Camden (only D372), King's Cross station (a meal break), and Willesden. At the latter was 2-6-4T No 42218, having been transferred from Shoeburyness. Old Oak supplied the expected bagful of cops, 39 in all for me, of which the most notable was pioneer 'King' Class 4-6-0 No 6000 *King George V*. The second surprise of the day materialised here in the form of seven Standard 2-6-4Ts, all of them in store. Why were these engines here? Following in the tradition of the old GWR, the WR didn't have any tanks of this wheel arrangement on its books, save for a few LMS Fowler examples at Swansea for working up that company's Central Wales line to Craven Arms and Shrewsbury. It transpired that the Standard tanks were in the process of transfer from the London, Tilbury & Southend line, and allocation was to be divided between Shrewsbury and Swansea sheds. Other examples followed later, finding their way to Croes Newydd (Wrexham) and Machynlleth on the old Cambrian section of the WR.

To conclude our London tour we called at Cricklewood shed, which was on our route home. Here we found two 'B1' 4-6-0s, Nos 61136 and 61192, both of Woodford Halse on the former GCR. They had come to Cricklewood for servicing, because the GCR shed at Neasden had closed.

Our next trip for another hoard of cops was North East England, but only after a three-week break. No Mike or Steve for this trip, though – I was on my own. Three classes of NER origin had evaded the scrapping inroads suffered by most of the pre-Grouping classes to this date. Though represented by just three classes, 'J27' 0-6-0s, 'Q6' two-cylinder 0-8-0s, and 'Q7' three-cylinder 0-8-0s, they survived in considerable numbers. These engines were still carrying on the good work for which they were intended, that of hauling freight trains around industrial North East England.

I'm not sure which route our driver took out of Manchester, but Northallerton was selected for the customary break. At 3.30am on a Sunday morning in mid-September, it was still pitch dark. There was just one locomotive on shed, Standard Class 2 2-6-0 No 78012. From there we called at West Auckland and Consett sheds. As well as an abundance of 'Q6s', there were also the occasional 2-6-0s of 'K1' and Standard classes. The latter included a couple of the rare Class 3s, Nos 77002 and 77003. On, then, to Blaydon shed, where we found 'A2' 4-6-2 No 60539 *Bronzino* and, among the 'B1' 4-6-0s, two namers, Nos 61025 *Pallah* and 61035 *Pronghorn*. Both of Blaydon's 'V3' 2-6-2Ts were on show, Nos 67636 and 67653, and an engine destined for eventual preservation was No 69023. This was one of 30 BR-built 'J72' 0-6-0Ts, identical to Wilson Worsdell's design of 1898. The remaining engines present were 'Q6s' and 'J39' 0-6-0s. Heaton shed produced a variety of 'Pacifics', 'A4' No 60002 *Sir Murrough Wilson*, 'A1' No 60137 *Redgauntlet*, 'A2' No 60538 *Velocity*, 'A2/3' No 60511 *Airborne*, 'A3s' Nos 60085 *Manna* and 60098 *Spion Kop*, a rare named 'V2' 2-6-2, No 60860 *Durham School*, and one more namer, 'B1' No 61241 *Viscount Ridley*.

Heaton shed also provided us with an interesting specimen, electric locomotive No 26500. It was one of two Bo-Bo locomotives (there was no sign of No 26501) built for shunting and running transfer freights over the steeply graded line, mostly at 1 in 30, from Manors down to Quay on the River Tyne. The Quayside branch was just over a mile in length, much of it passing through cutting and tunnel. After tolerating the noise and smoke from the struggling steam engines over previous years, many people must have given thanks when the branch was electrified in 1905. The two electric locomotives were withdrawn in 1964, being replaced by diesel shunters. However, the Quayside branch was closed in 1969.

Percy Main and the North and South sheds at Blyth contained mainly 'J27' 0-6-0s and diesel shunters. Travel between North and South Blyth entailed a frustrating 10-mile inland detour. Was it worth it? Well, yes. There were 19 'J27s' on North shed, helping to fill some 'gaps' in our *ABC* books.

Returning from the Blyth outposts, Tyne Dock shed was next. The class of 15 'Q7' 0-8-0s was still intact, and all were allocated to Tyne Dock. They were supplemented by a fair number of the 'Q6s', but there were also some 9F 2-10-0s and 'O1' 2-8-0s. All of these types were used for working heavy ore trains over the steeply graded route between Tyne Dock and Consett, and those engines allocated here were specially fitted with air pumps for operating the hopper doors of the bogie ore wagons. On a weekday, two locomotives, of any combination from the above, could be seen topping and tailing the heavy ore trains. Pity there was no such activity during our Sunday visit.

There was a bonus on shed by way of two named 'V2s', Nos 60964 *The Durham Light Infantry* and 60835 *The Green Howard, Alexandra, Princess of Wales's Own Yorkshire Regiment*. The massive curved nameplate of the latter was placed above the centre pair of driving wheels. Why these two 'V2s' were here was not clear; they were from Heaton and Gateshead respectively, and may well have been displaced from their home sheds as a result of dieselisation. (I wonder if the same applied to the 'A4' on Heaton shed.) Some of the 'O1s' were present, together with a selection of 'Q6' 0-8-0s. But what rotten luck! I copped 14 out of the total of 15 'Q7' 0-8-0s, and by the time we left I still needed two of the ten 9F 2-10-0s allocated here. 'Some people are never satisfied', as the saying goes, but who was to say that I would be visiting the area again?

Sunderland and West Hartlepool sheds provided more of the same mix as Blaydon (except for the 'A2'). So did Thornaby, but here there were numerous diesels of Classes 25, 27 and 37. Nos D248 and D279 of Class 40 were also present. When the BR Modernisation Plan emerged in the mid-1950s it was envisaged that steam would continue for some years later than was actually the case. It is therefore ironic that this depot was constructed specifically as a 'modern' steam shed after the Plan was announced, yet here were several diesel types, with hardly a steam loco in sight. However, constructed on the roundhouse principle, which afforded ample space between shed roads radiating from the central turntable, Thornaby perhaps served the diesel better than any straight-road steam shed could have done.

Before heading for home, we called at Darlington shed. I copped its two 'A3s', Nos 60040 *Cameronian* and 60075 *St Frusquin*. Darlington kept at least one 'A3' in steam to cover for diesel failures on the principal main-line services. I copped 11 of Darlington's 13 'J94' 0-6-0STs, together with one from West Hartlepool. There was also an oddity allocated to Darlington in the shape of LMS 2-6-4T No 42477. There were also some cops for the taking of locomotives on shed awaiting their turn for overhaul at the works. Before we departed on our journey home I copped 'Deltic' No D9012 *Crepello* heading an express along the main line.

At home the grapevine informed us that the Central Wagon Works at Ince, near Wigan, was scrapping BR steam locomotives. Mike and I paid a visit and found six GWR 0-6-0PTs there, Nos 5761, 5789, 6760, 8727, 8750 and 8793. Two LMS engines were also present, Class 3 2-6-2T No 40174 from Blackpool and 'Jinty' 0-6-0T No 47470 from Lancaster. On a subsequent visit, 'Duchess' No 46243 *City of Lancaster* and some 'B1' 4-6-0s were among the unfortunates awaiting the cutter's torch.

A visit to Shrewsbury in October 1962 revealed more of the Standard 2-6-4Ts that had been transferred to the WR, Nos 80069, 80078, 80079, 80097, 80134 and 80135. They were eventually shared out between Croes Newydd, Swansea and Shrewsbury itself. Two 'Castles' were on shed, Nos 4080 *Powderham Castle* and 7016 *Chester Castle*, and at the station I copped diesels Nos D1004 *Western Crusader* and D814 *Dragon*.

Two day trips with the South Lancs Club followed, the first to Doncaster and sheds in the Leeds and Wakefield areas, the second to sheds around Stockport and Manchester. The latter included another visit to Gorton Works, but the only engine worthy of note was the solitary named 'WD' 2-8-0, No 90732 *Vulcan*. Then, peering over the wall into Beyer Peacock's yard, we saw newly built D7069, a Type 3 diesel-hydraulic. Although in pink works primer, it already had stainless steel figures affixed indicating its fleet number.

The Yorkshire run was more fruitful, even at this late hour. The unique 'A1/1' No 60113 *Great Northern* was on Doncaster shed. It is well known among railway circles that this loco was the infamous rebuild by Thompson of Gresley's pioneer 'Pacific'. 'Ugly' is an adjective commonly applied to No 60113; I think the outline shape of the engine's smoke deflectors influenced the rather ungainly appearance of its front end. Much to my disgust later on, I failed to record the locomotive on film. A surprise on Doncaster shed this day was LMS three-cylinder 2-6-4T No 42502, together with one of its Fairburn cousins, No 42687. Both locos were from Shoeburyness, and were no doubt awaiting their turn for the cutter's torch in the works, where we found another three-cylinder tank, No 42529, and another Fairburn, No 42219. Of note in the works were 'A4' No 60007 *Sir Nigel Gresley* and 'V2' No 60800 *Green Arrow*. Having been withdrawn from service, the 'V2' was in the process of being restored for preservation under the auspices of the BTC. *Sir Nigel*, however, had a few more years' work to do for BR before being purchased by the 'A4' Locomotive Preservation Society in 1966. We saw a veteran GER 0-6-0 at the works, 'J17' 0-6-0 No 65567, for scrapping. Its appearance at Doncaster was perhaps significant because, as noted earlier, the GER Stratford Works in London was to close.

The number of cops achievable at Doncaster was now diminishing, although a total of 65 for both shed and works made the trip worthwhile, particularly as I had copped *Great Northern*. And at the sheds of Normanton, Wakefield, Ardsley and Stourton there were plenty of mixed-traffic and freight locos on view, of both LMS and LNER types. South Yorkshire was also noted for its plentiful supply of 'WD' 2-8-0s, and these four sheds yielded 26 examples for me. It wasn't just Doncaster that provided celebrity engines either, for I copped two of Ardsley's 'A3s' on their home shed, Nos 60092 *Fairway* and 60077 *The White Knight*. Then on Leeds Neville Hill shed three more 'A3s' entered my book, Nos 60038 *Firdaussi*, 60081 *Shotover* and 60084 *Trigo*. *Firdaussi* had not long been allocated to the former LMS shed at Leeds Holbeck to work over the Midland main line to Carlisle (thence to Glasgow St Enoch via the GSWR route). On busy summer Saturdays these rosters were supplemented by 'Pacifics' from Neville Hill of both 'A3' and 'A1' classes.

So concluded the activities of 1962. The 'winds of change' were freshening up as Cliff Richard was proclaiming he was a 'Bachelor Boy' and Elvis Presley was at No 1 with 'Return to Sender' – maybe an appropriate request to aim at Dr Richard Beeching's Report, which was expected in a few months' time? Dr Beeching had been appointed as the BTC's new Chairman in 1961, and was in the process of preparing his far-reaching report for the reshaping of our railways. What would 1963 have in store (if that is the right word!) for the railway, and in turn for the enthusiast?

The year 1963 dawned with the installation of the new British Railways Board, which replaced the British Transport Commission. Having been a member of the BTC, Dr Beeching was appointed as its Chairman. The Government had charged him with formulating a plan to turn our railways from a loss-making enterprise into one that 'paid its way'. Extracts from Dr Beeching's report, *The Reshaping of British Railways*, were published in the railway press in May 1963. It would be fair to say that almost everyone found it shocking, not least the railway enthusiast, and the report was often referred to as 'Beeching's Bombshell'. It is not the purpose to discuss the report here in detail, but a few brief comments will be appropriate.

It seems that the Doctor based his recommendations purely on economic grounds, with not much thought to social needs, particularly on the side of passenger traffic. He proposed that 270 passenger services should be withdrawn, which would result in the closure of 2,363 stations and halts. Of local significance, the closures would have included the Liverpool to Southport electric services and my beloved trains to Wigan North Western. (Happily, both services are thriving today.) Most of these closure recommendations were socially unacceptable and, because of the furore they generated, tended to overshadow the good points of the report. Principal among these was the elimination of non-vacuum-braked goods wagons, and the introduction of bulk-carrying freight trains, fully braked. We can see the results of the latter point today but, thankfully, many of the passenger services proposed for withdrawal have survived.

On the motive power front, remarks appeared in the railway press that the then BTC seemingly wanted to rid BR of as many steam engines as was practically possible before the new Board took over. Certainly, the last three months of 1962 saw greater numbers withdrawn from capital stock than during previous months. This proved to be a portent of things to come, for the new deadline for the elimination of steam was now to be 1968 instead of 1975 or thereabouts as originally envisaged. The previous year had witnessed the extinction of several classes of steam locomotive. The most noteworthy of these were the unique Standard 'Pacific' No 71000 *Duke of Gloucester*, the LMS 'Princess Royal' 4-6-2s and 6P unrebuilt 'Patriot' 4-6-0s, and the 'WD' 2-10-0s. It is also remarkable that the entire GWR 'King' Class 4-6-0s were withdrawn within the 12 months[25], as were the LNER 'Q7' 0-8-0s of which we had seen all but one at Tyne Dock shed earlier in the year. Other exterminations were 'old favourites' of this particular spotter, the LMS Fowler and Stanier Class 3 2-6-2Ts and Class 2P 4-4-0s, together with the LNER 'K2' and 'K3' 2-6-0s and the post-war 'L1' 2-6-4Ts. The first withdrawals had also taken place of what young spotters of earlier years had considered to be sacrosanct, namely the LMS 'Duchess' 'Pacifics' and 'Royal Scot' 4-6-0s, and the LNER 'A4', 'A2' and 'A2/3' 'Pacifics' and 'V2' 2-6-2s; inroads were also being made into the post-war classes of LNER 'K1' 2-6-0s, the GWR 'County' 4-6-0s, the first five 'Clan' 4-6-2s (those based on the ScR at Polmadie), and some Ivatt LMS Class 2 2-6-2Ts. And of course there was the Standard Class 4 2-6-4T, No 80103, which we saw at Plaistow. Thus it was felt that our rate of shed-bashing should be stepped up in order to see as many engines as possible before they disappeared. As we shall see shortly, the situation was seriously attended to!

Meanwhile, Arctic-like weather conditions had set in after heavy snow around the turn of the year. Fine but cold weather followed, interspersed with more snowfalls that settled on top of the already frozen stuff on the ground, conditions that persisted for a couple of months into 1963. The resultant effect on our railway system provided not a few headaches for the operating authorities. Thousands of trains, both passenger and freight, were cancelled in January alone due to the 'Big Freeze'. In the railway journals, we read of mothballed steam locomotives, even some that had already been withdrawn, being restored to traffic to replace failed diesels. Many of the diesels' train heating boilers froze (our carriage stock was still steam-heated), and oil in the locos' engines became a little too viscous. Apart from all that, our railway was not geared up for the maintenance on a large scale of the 'modern' form of traction. With a few exceptions, diesel locomotives were stabled at steam locomotive depots, with their associated dust and grime. These were totally unsuitable conditions for precision-conscious diesels.

On the lighter side, unusual locomotive workings on special trains were now materialising in increasing numbers. Advertisements of such

[25] No 6018 *King Henry VI* was given a temporary reprieve to run a special train in April 1963 between Birmingham Snow Hill and Swindon Works. This train was sponsored by the SLS to commemorate the passing of the 'King' Class 4-6-0s.

appeared in the 'forthcoming events' columns in the railway press, and one of these proclaimed that an unrebuilt SR 'West Country' 'Pacific' was to run from London Marylebone to Crewe in February. Organised by the Home Counties Railway Society, the train was routed from London via Birmingham New Street and Wolverhampton High Level. At Crewe, society members were to receive the privilege of having their train hauled onto the works sidings in order to tour around the site. Visits to North and South sheds were to follow.

It was another of those bitterly cold February Sundays as Mike and I stood with some like-minded individuals at the south end of Crewe station awaiting sight of the celebrity. The expected arrival time came and went, and still we waited. Just as at Chesterfield the previous February, the cold wind penetrated our clothing. The station cafeteria was situated close by, beckoning for custom with hot drinks, etc. I anticipated taking a photograph of the engine. Sure as eggs are eggs, if I moved away the train would be sure to come. So we waited some more. In the end the cafeteria won; Mike and myself were not the only ones to succumb, as we trooped off for some sustenance.

Sod's law ruled again!

'It's here! It's here!' voices called out.

By now it was too late for a photo. As we all bailed out of the cafeteria onto the platform, No 34094 *Morthoe* glided past us, drawing its train to a halt about an hour and a half late. A mêlée resulted as passengers also bailed out onto the platform, and the story unfolded about their experiences en route north. Apparently the 'Pacific' had got into difficulty at Wolverhampton, stalling on a crossover outside the Low Level station. Because of the position of the train, it was some time before a diesel shunter could be positioned at the rear to give some assistance.

Threading our way towards the engine through the disgorging passengers, we observed that *Morthoe*'s crew looked utterly 'cheesed off'. The fireman uncoupled their steed, as the train was now to be hauled into the works by a 'Black 5'. *Morthoe* retired to North shed for servicing and, with the '5' in place, the call rang out for passengers to reboard the train.

'Come on,' said Mike, 'let's go with them!'

With apologies to the Home Counties Railway Society, we did and, to keep out of view of any stewards until the train moved off, the pair of us crammed into one of the toilet cubicles. (It is uncanny how air raid shelters and toilets came in handy for the wrong reasons!) We managed to stay with the crowd throughout the complete tour, which took in the North and South engine sheds in addition to the works. Between the three establishments a fleet of five Crosville buses had been laid on, and the whole 'operation' went like clockwork.

In the works we copped 21 'Western' (Class 52) diesels under construction, Nos D1053 to D1073. I also copped the last BR steam engine to be built, 9F 2-10-0 No 92220 *Evening Star*. There were nine more 9Fs in the works for overhaul, but otherwise not much steam was in evidence compared with past years. Dusk was falling as we toured Crewe South shed, where I copped rebuilt Crosti 2-10-0 No 92020 and four other locos. Rather exhaustedly, we tramped around North shed in the dark. *Morthoe* was there, breathing smoke and steam, having been stoked up in readiness for its return south. There was also a 'B1' 4-6-0 on shed, No 61409, the last numerically of its class. It was in an appalling state externally, its boiler barrel ringed with limescale. Seemingly this engine had worked into Crewe on a freight midweek, and the story was that North shed had 'bagged' it in order to pilot the 'West Country' on the returning special. In view of the experience of the 'Pacific' on the northbound leg, perhaps someone at Crewe had second sight?

Mike and I returned to the station with the Home Counties party, and casually went our own way once we had passed the ticket barriers. Back at the south end we witnessed the departure of Nos 61409 and 34094 from the station. The steady decisive exhaust beat of the 'B1' contrasted starkly with sound of the three-cylinder chattering of the 'Pacific', which was punctuated by bouts of wheel-slipping. For the record, Crewe North shed supplied me with GWR 4-6-0 No 4907 *Broughton Hall* from Cardiff Canton and 'Brit' No 70018 *Flying Dutchman*, by then based at Longsight, Manchester. The day had turned out well, except for the fact that I didn't manage to photograph *Morthoe*.[26]

The next South Lancs tour took us to Bristol, Swindon and Gloucester, which naturally yielded another plethora of GWR locos, named and unnamed. We made our first and only venture onto Somerset & Dorset territory by visiting Bath (Green Park) shed. The S&DJR remained an independent railway until 1930, after which the line and infrastructure passed into Southern Railway ownership, while the locomotives and rolling stock remained the responsibility of the LMS. Thus, following nationalisation, the Southern Region administered the line until regional reorganisation in the 1960s transferred it to the WR

Two of the five remaining S&DJR 2-8-0s were on view there, Nos 53808 and 53810. All 11 of the class were allocated to Green Park throughout their lives but, as related earlier, the first six had already been withdrawn. It being a Sunday, we expected to see more than two on shed, but later in the day we found No 53806 on Swindon shed and

[26] The next Southern 'Pacific' I saw on the WCML was No 34079 *141 Squadron*, which I managed to photograph at Stafford during another South Lancs Club tour.

No 53807 on Barnwood, the old Midland shed at Gloucester. Both were withdrawn, and it wouldn't be long before these two locos suffered under the cutter's torch.

On Swindon shed was No 4079 *Pendennis Castle*, one of a few to eventually pass into preservation, albeit this one in due course being exported to Australia. In contrast was the sad sight of a another 'Castle' 4-6-0, No 5017 *The Gloucestershire Regiment 28th 61st*, on the scrap line together with some small fry. Even worse, two withdrawn 'King' 4-6-0s were in a rather decrepit state at Swindon Works, Nos 6018 *King Henry VI* and 6025 *King Henry III*. In contrast to these was an ex-works 'Grange' 4-6-0, No 6824 *Ashley Grange*. While in town, our party paid a visit to the then recently opened Swindon Railway Museum, containing GWR artefacts. Everybody proudly claimed all four standard gauge exhibits as cops, ie 'Dean Goods' 0-6-0 No 2516, 4-4-0 No 3440 *City of Truro*, 4-6-0 No 4003 *Lode Star*, and 'modern' 0-6-0PT No 9400. Perhaps cruelly, no one was interested in the broad gauge replica of *North Star*, one of the early engines that helped to pioneer railway travel.

Leaving Swindon, both Gloucester sheds were sampled on our way home. In addition to No 53807, we copped two more Midland 0-4-0Ts, Nos 41535 and 41537, sisters to those seen at the Chesterfield steelworks on that cold February Sunday in 1962. Horton Road was the former GWR shed, but we found a handful of GWR locos on the ex-Midland establishment of Barnwood, including 'Castle' 4-6-0 No 5049 *Earl of Plymouth*.

There was a month's rest now, before I was off again on my next South Lancs tour towards the end of March. This took me to South Wales, and introduced me to a private scrapyard at Barry. This belonged to Dai Woodham, and was one of many private scrapyards to which BR was now selling its steam engines instead of scrapping them at its own works sites. However, instead of cutting up locomotives on an ad hoc basis, Mr Woodham decided that while there was a plentiful supply of freight wagons (particularly the short-wheelbase four-wheelers), he would concentrate on cutting up these, leaving the steam engines as a last resort. No wonder the yard at Barry was destined to become a place of pilgrimage for a great many enthusiasts, wanting to cop or just photograph the engines gathered there.[27]

Woodham's yard was our first port of call after travelling down

[27] In time, more than 200 steam locomotives were assembled at Woodham's for scrap, but in fact just two were cut up. The remainder were resold for private preservation, the last loco moving out in 1989. Dai Woodham received an MBE for his services to railway preservation but sadly died in 1995, a year after closure of his yard.

overnight from Manchester. It was still dark when we arrived, and quite foggy. There was no lighting of any sort to guide us through the lines of locomotives gathered there and, to add to the eeriness of the place, fog horns were sounding at regular intervals to warn shipping of the proximity of the coastline. For most of the party, myself included, this was our first visit to the scrapyard, and once again the question was mooted, 'What are we doing at such an unearthly place at this hour on a Sunday morning?'

Cyril, the organiser of all these tours, was obviously used to this situation, and had ensured that a few torches were available, not only to find our way around, but to identify the incumbents. Progress through the lines of locomotives was slow, as it proved difficult to identify some of them, mainly the GWR types that at this time predominated in the yard. Many front numberplates had been removed, as had most of the cast cabside numberplates carried by GWR locos, probably by souvenir-hunters.[28] Torches were thus directed to the coupling rods on the wheels, onto which the engine's number was stamped during works visits. We had to search diligently for these stampings, for when spare rods were affixed from other locomotives the numbers of both engines were stamped on them, one of them purporting to be crossed out! Imagine the length of time we spent doing this, so that by the time we had finished daylight was breaking. And what were those big engines at the end of one of the tracks? Two 'Kings' – Nos 6023 *King Edward II* (which I copped) and 6024 *King Edward I*.

There were gasps, then an air of sadness prevailed as we all gazed disbelievingly at these 'Kings of the steam era', lying forlornly, shrouded in the drifting mists of a cold, damp early morning. But we couldn't linger here, and headed for the shed at Barry. Then it was onward to Radyr, Llantrisant, Caerphilly Works, Abercynon, Merthyr and Aberbeeg. We even took in the sub-sheds at Dowlais Cae Harris and Rhymney. What outposts these were, up amongst the Valleys!

Many of the sheds contained small freight and mixed-traffic engines, such as 0-6-2Ts and the inevitable 0-6-0PTs. It wasn't until we arrived at the larger sheds of Pontypool Road and Newport Ebbw Junction that we saw any named GWR engines. There were also some Standard 9F 2-10-0s on Ebbw Junction, including No 92250. This engine, numerically the last in the class, was fitted in 1960 with an exhaust system incorporating what rejoiced under the title of a Giesl Oblong Ejector (named after its inventor), and once again contradicting BR's dictat of 1955; the fitment was a rather belated attempt at fuel economy. The

---

[28] In time, the collection of numberplates, and particularly nameplates, proved to be a good investment. Many have fetched high prices at auctions.

first of the 'Grange' Class was also there, No 6800 *Arlington Grange*.

As a sign of the times, it was noticed that an increasing number of sheds now sported a scrap line of condemned locomotives; that at Ebbw Junction comprised 19 engines, and 11 occupied another at Severn Tunnel Junction. At the latter was 'WD' 2-8-0 No 90565, all the way from Southall. In view of BR's revised scrapping policy, this engine was obviously on its way to one of the private scrapyards in South Wales. Among the larger engines present on these scraplines were GWR 2-8-0Ts Nos 5214 and 5227, and one of the impressive 2-8-2Ts, No 7224. To round off our tour, we called at the sub-shed of Lydney, where I copped five of the lightweight Class '1600' 0-6-0PTs of F. W. Hawksworth's post-war design, together with a couple of Collett's '5700' Class.

Now for the 'big one'! I decided to embark on the South Lancs Club's four-day tour of Scotland. This apparently was an annual event, and in 1963 took place over the Easter weekend of 12-15 April. Being a family man, Mike had commitments over Easter, and understandably couldn't make the trip with me.

The tour was to start from the usual place outside Victoria station in Manchester, but at 8.30 on the Good Friday morning. Most public transport systems in those days operated a Sunday service on Good Fridays, including the railways. Thus to arrive at the departure point on time entailed catching the first train of the day from Liverpool Central, the 7.15am, but there was no No 79 bus to get me into the city sufficiently early. I therefore had to scurry along to Broad Green to catch the first No 6 of the day, scheduled to pass at 6.15am. Waiting in the cold morning opposite Thomas Lane, I was 'on pins' as the time elapsed. Then, sure enough, I sighted the bus approaching from Bowring Park, along the dual carriageway that straddled the tram tracks.[29] I made the train all right, and thankfully there were no hitches on the way to Manchester Central. From there, I commandeered a taxi and arrived outside Victoria station at about 8.10am. Thankfully I settled into a seat next to the aisle. A lad from the Manchester area, whose name has escaped me over the years, was already sitting by the window. We became mates for the tour, swapping seats throughout.

On our journey to the Border we called at Lancaster and Carnforth sheds, both 'done' in brilliant sunshine. I didn't cop many engines at these places, though: five local steamers at Lancaster and a couple of diesel-electric shunters at Carnforth. Heading off into the then Westmorland hills, the weather turned dramatically to snow, and it was

[29] The carriageway was singled in 1973 when the M62 motorway was constructed and now dominates the scene.

a very wet Oxenholme shed that was our next port of call. No cops here for me, though I did try taking a photo of rebuilt 'Patriot' No 45545 *Planet* on a northbound train. However, the light was so dull that it hardly turned out at all. 'Jubilee' No 45652 *Hawke* also passed on the main line, while on shed were Fowler 2-6-4Ts Nos 42319 and 42359, used for banking trains up to Grayrigg summit.

The next shed stop was Dumfries on the old GSWR route from Carlisle to Glasgow St Enoch. At this shed was the inevitable scrapline, a common feature at many sheds now. On this particular one was an oddity in the shape of a 'J72' 0-6-0T. No 68750 was an NER design, and was en route to a scrap dealer somewhere in SW Scotland. Similarly, we later found LYR 0-6-0 No 52275 on Hurlford shed. It was in this corner of Scotland that the last of the LMS Class 2P 4-4-0s had eked out their lives. As related earlier in this chapter, this type was now extinct in BR service, but there were many still intact, languishing on scraplines at the sheds we visited in this area. Keeping them company were hosts of withdrawn CR veterans of 0-6-0 tender and tank types, together with some Stanier Class 3 2-6-2Ts. Before reaching Hurlford, we looked in at the sheds at Ayr and Ardrossan. More of the same was in evidence here, but there were also various 'Black 5' and 'B1' 4-6-0s, and both LMS and Standard 2-6-4Ts still in normal use.

'There's a scrapline at a place called Lugton,' someone remarked during the course of our wanderings. Apparently, rumour had it that some of Corkerhill's 'Jubilee' 4-6-0s were stored there, which most of the crowd wanted, including myself. So although it was now quite dark, we just had to find the place. Reference to a map revealed that Lugton is approximately halfway between Hurlford and Glasgow, the latter our destination for the night's stopover. But just where was this scrapline? Driver Fred scoured the network of roads while, with the interior lights extinguished, a few of us kept a lookout for anything silhouetted that bore the slightest resemblance to a steam locomotive. The impression was that we were going around in circles, to the accompaniment of 'It must be here somewhere', as though someone was continually playing a loop tape on a tape recorder. As tiredness began to overtake us, there it was, a group of dark familiar-looking shapes. We all bailed out of our coach in a state of relief. With torches up front, our party headed towards the ghostly objects to which we had come to pay homage. Emphasising the eeriness, the wind howled around the place. There was a barn or whatever close by, with a loose door continually swinging open and slamming shut.

Yes! Yes! Yes! Yes! I got four of the Corkerhill 'Jubilees' I needed, Nos 45621 *Northern Rhodesia*, 45665 *Lord Rutherford of Nelson*, 45707 *Valiant* and 45711 *Courageous*. There were five other locos there: 2P 4-

4-0s Nos 40620 and 40621, CR 0-4-4Ts Nos 55206 and 55225, and CR 0-6-0T No 56266. Despite the frustration in the fact that No 45727 *Inflexible* was missing, we'd had a very satisfactory finish to the day, and all wearily headed back to the coach and on to Glasgow for the night.

Cyril had got his organisation to a fine art, our party being divided between three bed-and-breakfast establishments. At one of these, I and my Manchester friend were billeted to share a room with The Poet. Dog tired, we settled down for a good night's sleep, not bothering to ask The Poet for a lullaby. But then when morning arrived:

'Bzzzzzzzz! Bzzzzzzzz!'

'What the dickens was that?'

The Poet was using an electric shaver. It was the first time I'd encountered one; they weren't yet a common animal, not in our age group anyway. Well, it was certainly a novel form of alarm clock, which effectively, if startlingly, aroused us from our slumbers.

The morning commenced with a blitz on Glasgow's sheds. Parkhead depot contained nine Clayton Type 1 Bo-Bos, including the first of the class, No D8500. This loco had taken to the rails towards the end of 1962 but, after the delivery of further examples, faults were discovered within the diesel engines themselves, namely crankshaft failures. Thus the entire class so far built was temporarily withdrawn and returned in stages to the manufacturer at Derby for engine modification. They eventually reappeared in service during May. Ironically, BR had decided to adopt the Claytons as the standard design in the Type 1 power range (up to 1,000bhp). Despite the modifications, the Claytons did not prove as reliable in service as the English Electric Type 1s, so that by 1971 BR had dispensed with a class that totalled 117 locomotives. However, a handful were sold to private industrial operators and preservationists. To cover for the temporary withdrawal of the Claytons in 1963, the ScR reinstated some recently withdrawn steam locomotives, including the three Stanier 8F 2-8-0s at Polmadie, and was loaned other engines from the NE Region.

Among the many cops at St Rollox were 'A4' No 60004 *William Whitelaw*, and at Eastfield was 'J36' 0-6-0 No 65222 *Somme*. On Corkerhill was the 'missing' withdrawn 'Jubilee', No 45727 *Inflexible*. Celebration time again! And the joy was repeated at Polmadie, for at last I completed the 'Clan' Class 'Pacifics' with No 72003 *Clan Fraser*. Alas, the joy was tinged with sadness for, as related above, it was already withdrawn, sharing siding space together with its other four Polmadie classmates.

On the way to Edinburgh we called at Bathgate shed, and another scrapline, this one containing eight 'V2' 2-6-2s. Keeping company with them were a couple of 'N15' 0-6-2Ts, 'B1' 4-6-0 No 61244 *Strang Steel*, and a couple of interesting 4-4-0s. One of these was No 62484 *Glen Lyon*, one of the celebrated 'D34' Class that worked the West Highland line between Glasgow and Fort William; the other was No 62685 *Malcolm Graeme* of Class 'D11/2'. This engine was one of several post-Grouping engines built for the Scottish area of the LNER, developed under Gresley's direction from Robinson's GCR design which were classified 'D11/1'.

Continuing onward to Scotland's capital, Haymarket, Dalry Road and St Margaret's sheds were next on our itinerary. There weren't many engines on Haymarket all told. Nevertheless, I copped 'Deltic' No D9019 (then unnamed), 'A4' No 60024 *Kingfisher*, 'A1s' Nos 60132 *Marmion* and 60159 *Bonnie Dundee*, and five EE Type 4s (Class 40). Dalry Road was the old CR shed, which served Edinburgh's Princes Street station. As would be expected, it contained some stored engines, including three CR examples, but more surprisingly LNER 'D49/1' 4-4-0 No 62712 *Morayshire*, another engine that eventually found its way into preservation. St Margaret's produced a host of mixed-traffic and freight engines, particularly 0-6-0s of NBR vintage. 'A4' No 60019 *Bittern* was, however, a surprise cop.

Perth was our next 'stabling point' for bed and breakfast. The Forth Road Bridge was still under construction, being completed in 1964. Our route therefore took us around the Firth of Forth almost as far as Stirling, our port of call on the following night, and our last for bedding down in Scotland. Thus we left the engine shed to be 'done' on the way back.

Travelling westward from Edinburgh along the shores of the Firth of Forth, we came across an isolated scrapline at Bo'ness. This one contained 15 engines, three of which were LMS Class 3 2-6-2Ts from Dawsholm shed, Nos 40159, 40177 and 40200. Also on the south bank of the Forth was Grangemouth, whose shed provided six Class 'WD' 2-10-0s, Nos 90755, 90757, 90765, 90766, 90769 and 90774, all of them withdrawn (and class extinct).

At Perth the engine shed beckoned prior to booking in at our 'barracks'. Some 'Duchess' 'Pacifics' were there, including Nos 46244 *King George VI* and 46256 *Sir William A. Stanier, F.R.S.* Ahh! Memories of my journey to Scotland in 1956, when I spotted the latter at Carlisle. And yet another scrapline materialised, containing two engines we didn't expect to see. These were of GWR design, Class '1600' 0-6-0PTs Nos 1646 and 1649.

These two locomotives were sent north of the Border in the late 1950s, as replacements for a couple of ageing Highland Railway engines. The former HR main line between Dingwall and Wick possessed a branch line to Dornoch, and this branch was worked by the last two surviving

HR 0-4-4Ts, Nos 55051 and 55053, one being kept as spare engine. These two veterans had continued in use for as long as possible because of their light axle-loading, but were becoming life-expired by the late 1950s. The Class '1600' pannier tanks seemed to be the only suitable alternative with a similar axle-loading. So No 1646 was sent north from Wrexham's Croes Newydd shed in 1956 to replace No 55051, and No 1649, from St Philip's Marsh, Bristol, followed in 1959, replacing No 55053. Now the panniers were themselves withdrawn, aliens among some Caley 4-4-0s and 0-4-4Ts, and other LMS examples in the form of Class 4F 0-6-0s and Class 3 2-6-2T No 40150.

Three Clayton Type 1 diesels were on Perth shed, Nos D8503, D8504 and D8511. Presumably these had been returned from their manufacturers suitably modified.

After our night in Perth we were off to Dundee, Forfar and Aberdeen. What a beautiful view of the green North Sea as our coach approached the Granite City from the south! Aberdeen had a clinically clean appearance, which is really all that sticks in the memory from all those years ago. Cops in the form of 'A3' No 60089 *Felstead* and 'A4' No 60009 *Union of South Africa* were on shed here. Otherwise, nothing remarkable was copped at any of the aforementioned sheds, nor at Kittybrewster (all diesel), Montrose, Thornton Junction, Dunfermline or Alloa. Once again hoards of stored locomotives and mixed-traffic engines diminished the gaps in our *ABC* books. We all returned to Stirling well satisfied, and looking forward now to returning home. Stirling shed was left until the following morning, as the party split up for the last time into groups for our B&B lodgings. My group was in for an unexpected surprise, as our landlady very kindly laid on a late evening meal for us, a tasty mixed grill. That's real Scottish hospitality for you!

There wasn't a great deal on Stirling shed the following morning. The day had dawned with brilliant sunshine, though, which afforded a very pleasing photograph. Taken from inside the shed looking towards the eastern end, the sun was reflected from some of the occupants, with one of our party members silhouetted while taking notes. Departing Stirling, we took in the sheds at Polmont, Kipps, Hamilton and Motherwell, en route to Carstairs. There, to everyone's dismay, we found a couple of withdrawn 'Duchess' 'Pacifics', Nos 46231 *Duchess of Atholl* and 46232 *Duchess of Montrose*, both ex-Polmadie. There was also another withdrawn 'WD' 2-10-0, No 90768. However, the biggest surprise of all passed by on the main line. This was 'Brit' No 70037 *Hereward the Wake* heading a Liverpool to Glasgow train. Amazingly, this engine was still allocated to Immingham on the ER, as proclaimed by the 40B shedplate that the engine was sporting on its smokebox door.

Leaving Carstairs behind, it was 'Destination Manchester'. However, owing to the amount of time spent at the sheds this day, we didn't arrive back at Victoria station until 10.40pm. This was too late for my last train to Liverpool, which left Central at 10.30pm. What to do now? To phone home was the first priority.

'If I get a taxi, could you pay for it, Dad?' asked a tired and skint young man.

What the cost would have been doesn't bear thinking about, as the taxi driver would need to get back to base, probably without a fare, in the early hours of the next morning. So, a taxi being out of the question, Dad phoned some friends who lived at Heaton Norris near Stockport, and asked if they could fetch me and put me up for the night. As a sales representative, this friend apparently visited Liverpool every Tuesday, so it would not be a problem to drop me off at home that day. So after a night spent on a pile of blankets spread out on their kitchen floor, I at last found myself being whisked back home, still in a half dazed state after my uncomfortable night. Many thanks to those friends though, for without their assistance I don't know what I would have done. Despite all that and losing a day's pay at work, the tour around Scotland had been wholly worthwhile and I thoroughly enjoyed the adventure. The whole trip had cost just £6 10s.

Another complete break from railways followed, during which the 'Beeching Bombshell' was dropped. I was a little overwhelmed by it, but I just refused to believe that all the proposals would be implemented. They weren't, thankfully. Nevertheless, the writing was on the wall for steam power, and I therefore decided to continue hunting down the surviving steam stock, including any withdrawn engines that still remained intact, just to enable me to underline their numbers in my books.

So, one month later, I took off on another South Lancs Club tour, this time to East Anglia. It was a heck of a run just to collect numbers mainly of mixed-traffic and freight engines, and diesel locos of Types 2 and 3. Into the bargain I did experience yet another part of the country I hadn't previously visited. I already knew that East Anglia was renowned for its flatness, but such an impression did this feature make that images of vast skies and distant horizons readily stick in the mind.

Of interest among the diesel shunters were some examples built by the LNER, numbered in the 15000 series, while noteworthy steam cops among the mundane were 'Brit' No 70006 *Robert Burns* on March shed and 'A3' No 60047 *Donovan* on New England. There was a scrapline at the latter, containing 'V2' No 60832 and five 'WD' 2-8-0s. Returning through the Midlands, we called at Derby to find 15 Clayton Type 1s, returned from Scotland for engine modifications.

At about this time there were two significant developments in my life. First, I was encouraged by colleagues at work to join the Sports & Social Photography Club. It was pointed out how much cheaper it would be if I were to process my own films and make prints from them myself. So I purchased a developing tank together with an enlarger and associated equipment, and spent many nights in an adapted darkroom printing photos from my Scotland tour. Comments from the club members (like 'Your photos are not sharp enough') rather dampened my self-congratulation. The criticism was constructive, though. What I needed was 'a decent camera', and a need to be selective in the type of film developer I bought. Matters were put to rights, and I bought a new camera when my next birthday came round the following January.

Meanwhile, Dad had been introduced to Chris, who had joined the staff at the Co-operative store in Liverpool where my father had been employed for most of his working life. Discovering that Chris had an interest in railways, Dad arranged for us to meet shortly after my return from Scotland, and thus began a friendship that continues to this day.

Chris's first outing with me (and Mike) was another SLS visit to Doncaster Works and shed. In the works on this occasion were 15 Brush Type 2s (Class 31) whose Mirrlees engines had suffered major defects in the crankcase structure, resulting in fracture. Not all the Mirrlees engines failed, but it was decided to re-equip the whole class with English Electric engines of 1,470bhp as works visits became due for each locomotive. With this engine the locomotives remained within the Type 2 power range, and by 1969 all 263 examples of Class 31 had been modified. Overhauls of express steam passenger locos were now becoming rare, but in the works on this occasion I copped 'A4' No 60006 *Sir Ralph Wedgwood* and 'A3' No 60053 *Sansovino*. 'A4' *Mallard*, holder of the world speed record for steam, was in the process of being restored cosmetically for static display at the then British Transport Museum at Clapham, London. Sister loco No 60010 *Dominion of Canada* was also in for overhaul, and would be sent to Scotland to work the Glasgow-Aberdeen expresses over the former LMS route. (We shall encounter No 60010 again a little later on.) Class 'N2' 0-6-2T No 69523 was withdrawn from service, but was destined for preservation by the Gresley Society. There was nothing startling on Doncaster shed this time around, but I did cop 'Brit' No 70035 *Rudyard Kipling*, visiting from Immingham.

Because of working commitments, it was not always possible for Chris to join every railway jaunt. Nevertheless, we visited each other regularly, discussing times past and showing our photographs. So, sometimes with Mike, I continued going to the likes of York, Crewe and Shrewsbury, although these places were not now providing cops in large quantities. Let's face it, the supply had to dry up sometime. Anyway, that didn't bother me as much now, as I was becoming more interested in railway photography. More artistically than before, I was beginning to photograph trains rather than locomotive 'portraits'.

So one fine Saturday I ventured to Shrewsbury with Mike, where I copped No 1027 *County of Stafford*. It was awaiting its next turn of duty, parked in a siding near the signal box at the south end of the station. The 'County' 4-6-0s were now becoming rare birds. A total of 30 were built of this post-war design, and 19 started 1963 still on BR's books, but No 1027 had been withdrawn by November, together with eight others. As luck had it, I managed to include No 1027 in a photograph taken of a departing train. Bound for the West of England, it was unusually double-headed by two diesels, 'Warship' No D817 *Foxhound* and 'Western' No D1066 *Western Prefect*.

I hadn't yet visited the former LYR Horwich loco works, but the matter was rectified at the end of June, courtesy of the SLS once again. The 22 cops I made included some interesting ones. LYR 2-4-2T No 1008 (ex-BR No 50621) was being restored for preservation, and I also copped the works narrow-gauge shunter *Wren*, which bore no number. Other LYR veterans on show were three standard-gauge works shunters, still bearing their LMS numbers, 11305, 11324 and 11368, while another old 'un, 'Pug' 0-4-0ST No 51218, was found on Bolton shed to complete the LYR contingent. I called at the wagon works at Ince on my way home, and copped 'B1' No 61206, late of Woodford Halse on the former Great Central main line. A big surprise, alas a sad one, was the sight of 'Duchess' No 46238 *City of Carlisle*. Indeed, on yet another visit later in the year I found No 46243 *City of Lancaster* in company with two more 'B1s', and 'Jubilees' Nos 45623 *Palestine* and 45681 *Aboukir*. Oh, how we cursed at the repeated sightings of such locos in our younger years. These visits to scrapyards were proving to be so remorseful!

In July I and my parents spent a few days staying with my aunt, late of the farm near Stafford. My uncle had passed away in the intervening years and, after running the farm for a while afterwards, my aunt retired to a bungalow in the village of Eccleshall. I spent some time at the station taking photographs while the family went on a shopping spree in the town. Best shot of the day was of a 'Black 5' 4-6-0 entering the station with a train from the north; I also caught two 'Duchess' 'Pacifics' on film, Nos 46240 *City of Coventry* and 46229 *Duchess of Hamilton*. Disappointingly, my shot of the latter turned out very slightly blurred. It transpired that the shutter in my Ilford Sportsman had become defective, and it packed in completely during a visit to London with

Dad on the Wednesday! (I really did need a new camera.) Our trip to London, costing £1 13s 6d from Stafford, was more of a sight-seeing visit, although we did briefly pop into Paddington station, where some 'Warship' and 'Hymek' diesels were humming around. 'Brit' No 70054 *Dornoch Firth* hauled us up to the capital, but we had a measly Class 40 diesel for our return run.

There was better luck for me later for, instead of returning home from Stafford, we headed north to stay with my aunt and uncle at Dalton. Travelling up on the Thursday, we were able to catch the down 'Lakes Express' (which didn't stop at Stafford on Saturdays). The train, comprising 15 coaches, rolled into the station behind a Class 40 diesel, which then laboured up the 3 miles from Stafford at a gradient that averaged at 1 in 500 to Whitmore Summit. At Crewe 'Royal Scot' No 46165 *The Ranger (12th London Regt.)* substituted our diesel. This was a privilege! Not only that, but the load was increased after a 'Jinty' 0-6-0T attached a van to the rear of the train. *The Ranger* made good pace up to Weaver Junction, where the Liverpool line bears left and the main line to the north starts to climb. Speed noticeably dropped up the 1 in 135 climb to the bridge across the Manchester Ship Canal, but was followed by a brisk pace down the other side, also at 1 in 135. Beyond Warrington is Winwick Junction. A speed restriction here for the right-hand bend was followed by upward gradients varying from 1 in 132 to 1 in 470, ensured a crawl as far as Golborne. The story was the same for Wigan. Then, once past Standish, speed picked up again as the line is mostly downhill to Preston, where a stop was made. Leaving Preston behind, *The Ranger* managed some decent speed along the relatively level stretch of line that now parallels the M6 motorway. Indeed, construction of the motorway was taking place, and was probably viewed with apprehension by many railwaymen, as the motorcar and lorry were already steadily 'overhauling' the trains as a means of transport. 'What could Dr Beeching do?' or, more to the point, 'What would he do?', were questions in the minds of both railway employees and spotters alike.

During July and August the 'Lakes Express' was made up of three portions, to Workington, Windermere and Whitehaven. The Whitehaven portion, in which we were travelling at the rear of the train, was detached at Lancaster (the other two would be split at Oxenholme). Forward from Lancaster, one of the recently transferred Co-Bo Type 2s took our train around the coast of Morecambe Bay to Dalton, and so to our 'digs'. Some digs! It was a beautiful semi-detached, situated on high ground above the town. The view from the rear looked out eastward across rolling countryside, and the line from Carnforth could just be discerned in the distance as it emerged from Lindal Tunnel. While there I couldn't resist yet another trip to Carlisle. There were only ten cops for me this time, but I couldn't take any photographs. I guess I just enjoyed being there!

By now Liverpool's Beatles had firmly established themselves on the music front. Their master stroke was a song entitled 'She Loves You', which spent 31 weeks in the charts. I think this endeared earlier generations into recognising the band's talents. A glut of new bands followed in their wake into the big time, competing with the longer-established artists. Other Liverpool bands, Gerry and the Pacemakers, The Searchers and Billy J. Kramer and the Dakotas all had hits, as did Brian Poole and the Tremeloes, and one Frank Ifield, who sang 'Confessin''.

I managed to have my Ilford Sportsman repaired in time for two more South Lancs trips, the first taking me to the East Midlands on 1 September. This tour included Annesley shed, where we saw five more withdrawn Class 'O1' 2-8-0s. Their replacements were some 9F 2-10-0s, of which I copped eight at the shed. On Colwick shed I copped 13 of the 15 Ivatt Class 4 2-6-0s amongst the LNER stuff. Many of the Ivatts had probably been allocated new to the ER, most of the class having been built following nationalisation and adopted as the basis for the Standard design. The two I didn't cop had likely passed my Childwall home. The same goes for Colwick's 'WD' 2-8-0s, of which I copped nine out of the 19 present. I was a few years too late to see any of the Beyer-Garratt articulated locomotives at Toton, these having been replaced by 9F 2-10-0s in the late 1950s. Latterly the ten prototype 'Peak' Class diesels had been transferred here, seven of which, Nos D1, D4, D5, D6, D7, D8 and D10, were on shed during our visit.

Back on the North Eastern beat a fortnight later, there was a most interesting visit to Darlington. Outside the works was Class 'J21' 0-6-0 No 65099, a design of 1886 vintage. Having been withdrawn a while earlier, it was to be retained to provide spares for another example of the class, No 65033, which was to be preserved. The latter engine eventually found a home at the Beamish Open Air Museum. There was a separate breaker's yard close to the works; some locomotives were still intact, awaiting the cutter's torch, while others were in various stages of being cut up. The latter were still identifiable, as the engine numbers were still legible on cab or bunker sides. We found the remains of Class 'T1' 4-8-0T No 69921, an NER design of 1909 used for heavy shunting operations. In contrast, there were two of the diminutive Class 'Y1' 0-4-0T Sentinel-type shunters, Nos 68149 and 68150. These were geared steam locomotives, and were built for light shunting work. Although they were 'in pieces', they could arbitrarily count as cops. All were of types I hadn't seen before.

Darlington shed provided the biggest surprise of the day. Three 'Clan' 'Pacifics', Nos 72000, 72001 and 72003, were parked close to each other amongst some LNER and 'WD' types. All were awaiting the cutter's torch, be it at Darlington Works or at a private breaker's yard, I'm not certain. On shed I copped 'A3' 'Pacific' No 60051 *Blink Bonny* and 'V2' 2-6-2 No 60809, which possessed two massive plates to accommodate the name *The Snapper, The East Yorkshire Regiment, The Duke of York's Own*.

There was a lull in the proceedings from now until mid-December, when I couldn't resist a trip to London with the South Lancs. It was a bitterly cold day, the likes of which I had become used to by now. Once again Old Oak Common shed unbelievably yielded a hoard of cops, although half of these were diesel-hydraulics. Stratford was now completely given over to diesel traction, save for providing sanctuary for Class 'N7' 0-6-2T No 69621, which was destined for preservation. As on the Great Eastern, the Great Northern section was also completely dieselised by now. Finsbury Park shed had on view the white-painted *Lion*, the prototype Co-Co diesel from BRC&W referred to earlier. However, steam still showed itself at Hornsey depot in the form of 'B1' 4-6-0 No 61194, which had been commandeered for use as a stationary boiler. It wouldn't be going anywhere, except to the carriage sidings to provide steam heating for coaching stock (and eventually to the breaker's yard).

Following my birthday in January 1964 I finally had enough money to buy another camera, and chose a 35mm Yashica J. It possessed a 45mm fixed lens, and cost about £25, equivalent to about three weeks' take-home wages for me. (I would have preferred an SLR [single lens reflex] model, but needed to save for a lot longer to be able to afford one of those.) Anyway, the Yashica gave me a whole new meaning to the word 'sharpness'! I still have the camera, which I keep in case it is needed in an emergency.

I tried colour film for the first time using the new camera. Inevitably, some shots had to be of trains, and my first attempts were taken at Wrexham, courtesy of Chris and his car. The old GCR shed at Rhosddu was closed, but we found three GWR locos stored inside: 2-6-0 No 6301, and 2-8-0s Nos 3831 and 3846. The GWR shed at Croes Newydd had been transferred to the LMR in 1963, together with those at Shrewsbury, Oswestry and Machynlleth. Despite this, there were 18 GWR locos on view at Croes Newydd, but an influx of Standard types was evident. Six of these were Class 4 4-6-0s, and included a double-chimneyed example, No 75026.

The light at Wrexham was not particularly good for a colour film rated at 64ASA, but I did achieve some sharp if dull images, which at least gave me some satisfaction. The same applied at Aintree where, on Grand National Day once again, two ECML Pullman cars made an appearance. Together with a former 'Devon Belle' observation car, they brought up the rear of a train from Cleethorpes, hauled by a contrastingly grubby 'Patriot' 4-6-0, No 45522 *Prestatyn*. One of the WR diesel Pullman sets formed a race special from Swansea, apparently for the second year running. The trend continued for a few years more.

Towards the end of March I decided to do something a little different, a go-it-alone trip to London to see what I could achieve with my new camera. I therefore planned a sight-seeing tour combined with a visit to Clapham Junction to photograph some Southern steam in action. This was a tall order so, to make the most of a whole day, travelling overnight seemed a good idea. On Fridays there was a choice of two trains to London on either side of midnight. I decided to catch the first, which was the Fridays-only train. It departed from Lime Street electric-hauled and good progress was made to Crewe, but I was about to discover how painfully slow overnight trains could be. Having arrived at the 'Big Junction', I stared bleary-eyed out of the carriage window as station hands set to work unloading and loading baggage. There were seemingly long silences interspersed by calls between station staff and by the rumble of luggage trucks being dragged, either electrically or by manpower, along the platforms, transferring sacks from one train to another. More sacks arrived for loading onto my train and the sounds of train movements followed from elsewhere in the station, but frustratingly out of sight.

Electrification of the WCML between Crewe and London had advanced as far as Nuneaton by now, some trains having electric haulage to and from this point from 2 March. Thus when my train eventually departed from Crewe, I was puzzled as to why I could hear a steam engine at the front, a 'Jubilee' 4-6-0 by the sound of it. Anyway, I wasn't going to complain. On the contrary, it was such a rare privilege.

Progress up the WCML continued as far as Bletchley, where, in common with other overnight trains to London from the north, my train was diverted away from the WCML to enable the rebuilding of Euston station to progress by night, unhindered by train movements. With the 'Jubilee' 4-6-0 still on the front, the train now continued westward along the LNWR Cambridge to Oxford line. Near Calvert, by means of a connecting spur inserted during the last war, it gained the GCR route into London, the last main line constructed into the capital. From Ashendon, the GCR shared tracks with the GWR as far as South Ruislip. By the time my train had reached here, dawn was just about breaking, and I kept a lookout for things GWR or LNER. I did catch a glimpse of a GWR Prairie tank, No 6112, but at 6.00am there was not yet much traffic about. Beyond South Ruislip the GWR and GCR routes divided, the former to London Paddington, while my train followed the latter via Wembley into Marylebone. The time was somewhere between 6.15 and 6.30am.

Having been awake throughout the 6-hour journey, I thought I was in an imaginary world as I wearily set foot onto the platform. There were just four of them.

'Not a very big station for a London terminus,' I thought.

However, the place was graced with the presence of two steam locomotives at the buffers. One of them was an LNER 'V2' 2-6-2, whose number I didn't record. Standing alongside it was the engine that had just brought me from Crewe, none other than No 45552 *Silver Jubilee*, numerically the first of the class. It was in a rather shabby condition, as were many steam engines at this time. The engine still retained its 'raised' numerals on the cabsides, which were a legacy of this locomotive's history.

No 45552 had started life at the end of 1934 as LMS No 5642, sporting LMS red livery like its 113 classmates already in service. All were then unnamed, but the following April it was announced that No 5642 would be named *Silver Jubilee* in recognition of the 25-year reign of King George V. It was also decided to repaint it into high-gloss black, the engine also receiving many chrome-plated embellishments in the process, intended to portray a silver effect. Refurbishment was well advanced when the decision was made for these 4-6-0s to be known as the 'Jubilee' Class. The name *Silver Jubilee* was selected for the leading engine numerically, and thus the identity of No 5642 was swapped with that of the original No 5552. Included in the 'silver' embellishments were chrome-plated numerals affixed to the cabsides. At nationalisation the addition of a figure '4' became necessary, and the engine became No 45552[30].

Before making for Clapham Junction, I first headed for Paddington station, believing that there would be some activity there, but this too was quiet. Well, what did I really expect? The WR was scheduled to rid itself of steam during 1964, and all of the local suburban traffic was now operated by DMUs. There was one gem, though, as far as I was concerned, in the form of 'Castle' Class 4-6-0 No 7005 *Sir Edward Elgar*, which I duly photographed in colour. Alas, this express passenger locomotive was being used as Paddington's station pilot, moving around

[30] There is a twist to this tale. Some of the chrome-plated figures were stolen during temporary storage of the engine in the early 1960s. On the night it hauled my overnight train to London, these had been replaced by wooden replicas, painted over. *Silver Jubilee* was finally withdrawn the following September.

parcels stock that had arrived overnight. Maybe the engine itself had brought in a parcels train and, if so, it was a pity I hadn't been there earlier to witness its arrival. I was pleased with the photograph, though, which was taken when the morning light was still at 'half strength' and the station lights were still burning.

Clapham Junction seemed very complicated. Basically, it accommodated the former London & South Western Railway (LSWR) main lines from Waterloo, which divided here for Southampton and Bournemouth, and for the South West of England. The London, Brighton & South Coast Railway (LBSCR) lines from Victoria, having run parallel with the LSWR tracks for some miles, also diverged at Clapham to Brighton and other nearby resorts. This may seem an oversimplification, as Clapham also had to contend with trains using the cross-London link to the former LMS and GWR systems, and empty stock workings at the nearby carriage depot. From the east end of the station I could see the principal signal box for the junction, which was supported on girders spanning the LSWR tracks. It gained notoriety in 1957 when a partial collapse of some of the girders occurred; corrosion of some steel plates was discovered during the ensuing investigation and was confirmed as the cause of the disaster.

I caught my first real glimpse of Southern 'Pacifics' at speed. Eight of these machines passed through the station, four 'Merchant Navy' Class and four 'light Pacifics', the latter all in rebuilt form. The remaining types I saw during my couple of hours' stay comprised four Standard Class 3 2-6-2Ts, a Standard Class 5 4-6-0, and one 'S15' 4-6-0, the only other Southern type I saw. The Standard 2-6-2Ts seemed exclusively in use on empty stock workings between the carriage sidings at Clapham and the SR's two principal main-line termini, Waterloo or Victoria.

The next part of the day was spent photographing many of the stereotyped views of London, including the well-known aspect of the Houses of Parliament from across the Thames. Who remembers this view, used by BBC Television as a caption to precede each evening's viewing? (Those were the days when there was a break in transmission between 6.00 and 7.30pm.) The annual University Boat Race was being enacted this day. At the time it always took place in the afternoon, and I decided to take a tube train to Gunnersbury to see the latter stage of the race. Alas, I arrived just as everyone was heading away from the river, the participants and following convoy having already passed! Well, at least I saw a little of West London from a tube train, which travelled at ground level for a considerable part of the way. Back at Euston for my train home, I had more bad luck. 'Duchess' 'Pacific' No 46245 *City of London* was at the top end of the station.

'Good,' I thought, 'a colour picture. Oh, drat!'

I had just used my last frame of film to photograph the Big Ben clock tower – again. Tough!

I made two more trips to London that summer, again using the night Fridays-only train. Trouble was, I had to miss most of ITV's *Ready, Steady, Go!* pop music show, which was on air live usually between 10.00 and 11.30pm. Mention of this particular programme nearly always brings to mind the Rolling Stones. They seemed to appear more than anyone else and, about this time, they could often be heard belting out their hit 'It's All Over Now'. By coincidence, but in complete contrast, Roy Orbison was also in the reckoning with 'It's Over', which he quickly followed up with 'Oh, Pretty Woman'. These were the heady days of popular music, running in the wake of Beatlemania. There is too much to mention here, except perhaps my favourite turns like the Stones, Roy Orbison, The Animals and Chris Farlowe – also Sounds Incorporated, the 'instrumental' group that backed many of the stars, including Little Richard for some of his live TV performances.

Sight-seeing would be barred from my two further trips; I would be concentrating solely on visiting railway establishments. My first visit to London had already proved that trying to combine the two instils a tendency to rush around. Apart from Clapham Junction, I had a look at the Transport Museum on the Common, and at Westbourne Park station, on the GWR main line out of Paddington. Here I caught another 'Castle' 4-6-0 on film, though not in the way I would have preferred – No 5055 *Earl of Eldon* was hauling empty stock between Paddington and Old Oak. I photographed some diesel-hydraulics and a few remnants of steam that passed through the station. At Clapham the mixture was as before, together with the bonus of seeing one of Bulleid's prototype electric Co-Co locomotives, No 20003. It passed through on the LBSCR lines, hauling a boat train from London Victoria to Paris (via Newhaven). Of interest at the Railway Museum I found world speed record holder No 4468 *Mallard* (encountered under restoration at Doncaster the previous year), Midland Compound 4-4-0 No 1000, and GCR 'Director' 4-4-0 No 563 *Butler-Henderson*. I had seen *Butler-Henderson* several times during the mid-1950s, passing my home in Childwall as BR No 62660.

To conclude the 'Southern' theme, there was a South Lancs tour to this part of England in April 1964. This would be my only visit deep into Southern Region territory while steam persisted, and obviously I was going to cop just about everything I clapped eyes on. The only locomotives worthy of special mention were another of Bulleid's electric Co-Cos, No 20001, which passed on the main line at Three Bridges, and 'USA' Class 0-6-0T No 30072 on Guildford shed. The 'USA' was destined for preservation on the Keighley & Worth Valley Railway, due to reopen in 1968. We did Nine Elms shed at something like 7.00am. At this massive shed, some Bulleid 'Pacifics' were getting up steam out in the yard. But it was obvious that the heydays of this place were now in the past. With the few steam engines on view, these big engines seemed comparatively insignificant in the otherwise vast emptiness of the shed yard. Nevertheless, having said that, I made 42 cops at Nine Elms, which perhaps gives some idea of its size. For the record, the remaining sheds visited were Hither Green, Norwood Junction, Redhill, Brighton and Feltham. Paradoxically, having visited Brighton, I hadn't seen the sea!

While I still kept in touch with Mike, Chris now became my main companion in the quest for hunting the dwindling number of engines that remained. I was still 12 months away from buying a car and learning to drive, although Chris had been driving for about two years. So his Standard 10 was pressed into service early in April for a trip to Carlisle. The journey took about 3½ hours, most of it using the A6. This entailed negotiating Kendal and Penrith, with the climb over Shap in between, with its twists and turns. In addition, we encountered the extensive road works at the end of the 'Preston By-pass', involving construction of the flyover junction connecting with the A6 (and later the M55 motorway to Blackpool). Following the A6 as far as Galgate, near Lancaster, we joined another stretch of the M6 to its northern limit just beyond Carnforth. Its extension to Carlisle was yet a decade away.

Before venturing to Kingmoor shed we decided to visit Newcastle via the DMU service. We couldn't gain admittance to the MPD at Gateshead (who could?), but both of us copped 'A4' No 60020 *Guillemot*, which was standing forlornly in a siding, withdrawn from service. There were just six other cops for me at Newcastle, although I did manage some more colour pictures, despite yet another dull day. I captured some 'Deltics', one of which I photographed traversing the King Edward Bridge at the head of the up 'Queen of Scots Pullman' train.

Back at Carlisle, we 'did' Kingmoor shed, and I couldn't believe my luck. I needed two of the surviving 'A3' 'Pacifics' and both were on shed that day, Nos 60041 *Salmon Trout* and 60052 *Prince Palatine*. What a place to cop them, having just returned from 'Eastern' territory! Not only that, but I also copped 'Jubilee' 4-6-0 No 45697 *Achilles*, one of the four[31] I required to complete the class. To conclude the trilogy, 'Brit' No 70003

---

[31] Two of the other three were Nos 45682 *Trafalgar* and 45685 *Barfleur*, both of which I saw on Bristol Barrow Road shed during another South Lancs tour at the end of April. I didn't manage to see No 45605 *Cyprus* of Leeds Holbeck, still extant at the time, nor No 45702 *Colossus*, by now scrapped. Ironically, the latter had been allocated closer to home at Newton Heath.

John Bunyan was also on shed; having copped No 70039 at the station earlier in the day, copping *John Bunyan* completed the 'Britannia' Class 'Pacifics' for me! Some day.

'Jammy ******!' remarked Chris.

Another trip to Carlisle followed during the summer, by which time Chris had swapped his Standard 10 for a Hillman Minx. (I liked the car so much I bought one myself the following year!) The day was quite remarkable for more of the wrong reasons. It was our intention this time to obtain some photographs; however, rain fell incessantly for most of the day, spoiling our chances. After looking at various locations in the area along the WCML, we decided that there was nothing else for it but to return to the access road to Kingmoor shed, sit in the car, and watch the trains go by. An up fitted van train passed by on the main line, headed by no less than 'Duchess' 'Pacific' No 46254 *City of Stoke-on-Trent*. Oh, how we still rue the moment we failed, on what was to be our last opportunity, to photograph a 'Duchess', rain or no rain. Never again were either of us to see one of these fine machines in action, working for BR. All but one of them were withdrawn that August, followed by the last, No 46256 *Sir William A. Stanier, F.R.S.*, no less, in September.

Darkness fell a little early, owing to the overcast weather, and the rain was the cause of a nasty experience or two on the journey home. Beyond Penrith we continued along the A6, and it was pitch black as we reached Shap. Once over the summit, Chris bravely followed the road as it snaked down towards Kendal. Suddenly, as we swung round a bend, some rocks came into view in the car's headlights. Chris dared not brake too sharply in the wet conditions, and couldn't avoid crunching his Minx over the rocks. He kept going, as the car seemed none the worse. At the first opportunity, though, he pulled into a lay-by for a break, and probably to relieve his anxiety a little. We had now run out of the rain, at least for a little while. So, having dispensed some coffee from our flasks, we wound down our windows to let it cool. Next, the sound of a heavy lorry came drumming up from behind and, as it passed us, a deluge of water came spewing through Chris's open window.

'Looks as though I've stopped in a pool of water,' he murmured, among other things. I couldn't resist remarking about his coffee now tasting like mud!

The incident involving *City of Stoke-on-Trent* sparked off what Chris and I still commonly refer to as the 'five-year syndrome'.

'Think of all the things we could have done, had we been born five years earlier,' we began saying. Yes. Taking more photographs of 'Duchesses' than we actually did would have been one thing. Photographing the railway from the lineside would have been another, instead of continually hurtling around the country in search of engine numbers. The Waverley Route from Carlisle to Edinburgh, the GWR routes through Llangollen and Talerddig, and the Cambrian coast line all spring to mind, not forgetting the Settle-Carlisle line. However, we continued to 'hurtle' around the country for a while yet, into 1965 in fact, but we now combined our activities with at least some effort at photography.

The end of our association with the South Lancashire Locomotive Club was approaching. Our final trips, to Crewe, Derby and Darlington, actually took place in 1965. However, I would prefer to conclude the 'South Lancashire Years' with two escapades that took place in October and November 1964.

Edinburgh and Glasgow were once again our destinations for the overnight October tour. Heading initially for Edinburgh this time, the first port of call was Hawick on the much-lamented Waverley Route, which provided the usual break for driver and passengers. The time was around 3.30am as the crowd of 50 trooped out of the coach, through a gate and along a path that led past the goods yard to the shed. En route we were disturbed by shouts from above. Hawick's tall signal box was close by, and a couple of Scotsmen therein began bawling at us. I think they wanted us to 'clear off'. In the ensuing raucous exchange, our leaders tried to explain that we were in possession of a permit, but it was no good. I guess they were not too familiar with our dialect, nor we with theirs for that matter. So, ignoring their shouting, we carried on to the shed. For the record, there were just six locos there: Type 2 diesel (Class 26) No D5316, 'Standard 4' 2-6-4T No 80113, 'Standard 4' 2-6-0 No 76049, and 'Standard 2' 2-6-0s Nos 78048, 78047 and 78049. I was now suffering from previous visits to Scotland, and copped only the last two of this little lot! On returning to our coach we found the police waiting for us at the gate. They just ushered us out and no charges were pressed. I suppose that, if we were in possession of a permit, there was nothing they could do. I dare say half of Hawick had been disturbed by the racket earlier, and maybe by midday the whole town had heard about the crowd of nuts who invaded their engine shed in the middle of the night!

Not surprisingly, Chris gained a far greater quantity of cops than I was able to muster. However, I did manage some new steam numbers, together with a load of diesel shunters and Type 2s, now commonplace at most of the sheds in Scotland. Highlight of the day for both of us proved to be the copping of 'A4' 'Pacific' No 60016 *Silver King* on Edinburgh's St Margaret's shed. At Glasgow Polmadie we found nine Clayton Type 1s on static test in the diesel maintenance depot, following their return north after engine modifications at Derby. The din from all these engines under throttle remains clearly in the memory.

The remaining South Lancs trip was another rail/road affair, by train to Wolverhampton followed by a coach tour around West Midlands sheds. Chris and myself opted to travel to Wolverhampton directly from Liverpool, and we duly met the South Lancs party there. 'The Ark on Wheels' would have been a fitting description for the sight that greeted us outside High Level station! Our 'coach' must have been a pre-war creation, for it had a wooden body and possessed an all-crash gearbox. On moving off, the vehicle had almost stopped again by the time our driver managed to engage second gear!

In this crate we plodded around, visiting Oxley, Bescot, Bushbury, Aston, Saltley and Tyseley. At this late stage the former GWR sheds of Oxley and Tyseley were now administered by the LMR. However, the LMR retained some GWR locos at these establishments for some time, and there were even two 'Castle' 4-6-0s on Oxley shed, Nos 7023 *Penrice Castle* and 5063 *Earl Baldwin*. I photographed the latter engine, despite the fact that the weather was turning quite misty. The resultant photo seems rather appropriate, as the engine was standing forlornly, almost despairingly, awaiting its fate as the mists closed in. There was a similar situation at Bescot shed, where I photographed one of the surviving 'Super D' 0-8-0s, No 48895. At Tyseley shed we saw Prairie tank No 4555. This engine was to become something of a star. Withdrawn from BR stock, it was sold to a consortium that included the late Patrick Whitehouse, of the one-time BBC's *Railway Roundabout* fame. By agreement, it was maintained at Tyseley, and even found itself in use heading local freight trains for BR.

By the time we had 'done' Tyseley shed, visibility had deteriorated somewhat. Stourbridge shed was on our itinerary but, as time was running out, we wisely decided to head straight back to Wolverhampton to catch our respective trains home. Straight back? The trek to the station took an absolute age, as we crawled through the now quite thick fog. I don't know if our driver even bothered to get the old bus into second gear. Eventually we were very grateful to find ourselves plodding through the streets of Wolverhampton. By this time most of us were feeling decidedly uncomfortable, and upon reaching the station there was a stampede for the toilets.

14
Number-spotting – an old
habit dies hard

The year 1965 started with promotion at work from being an engineering apprentice to becoming a staff member. Promotion? I could have earned more money had I remained on the production side! However, my salary would increase over the years. Despite the drawback, I was able to purchase a car with a little assistance from Dad. Influenced by the fact that Chris owned a Hillman Minx, I bought a 1600 model, three years old and costing £430. To assist with my driving practice, Chris accompanied me to places like Winwick Junction, near Warrington, and to Springs Branch at Wigan, to photograph some trains. Photography was the main inspiration now that we had quit the South Lancs Club. But what was there left to photograph? The 'Duchesses' had gone, and there were just two 'Royal Scot' 4-6-0s left. We managed to snap one at Wigan, No 46140 *The King's Royal Rifle Corps*. After that the only LMS express passenger types left were a handful of 'Jubilee' 4-6-0s, and most of these were allocated to the NE Region. What remained to be seen around our neck of the woods were purely mixed-traffic and freight types of LMS and Standard designs. The Standards by now included the whole 'Britannia' 'Pacific' class, no doubt to offset the withdrawal of the LMS 'Duchesses'. The issue smacked of the work of accountants. The outcome was that the 'Brits' were occasionally hard-pressed to maintain some of the schedules given to them, and arguments have persisted that some of the 'Duchesses' should have been retained.

I passed my driving test at the second attempt in July 1965, and the following September Chris and I embarked on what transpired to be our final spotting fling. We chose such extreme destinations as Woodham's scrapyard at Barry, followed by a run up to southern Scotland. We took my recently acquired Minx so that I could experience some long-distance driving, although I recall that Chris did more than his fair share.

There were more than 100 steam engines at Barry by 1965. With Southern types now supplementing LMS and GWR examples, not to mention three Standards, the result was that we both obtained another host of cops. I came away from the place with little else, for while changing films in my camera later at Bristol's Temple Meads station, I left my exposed film, full of images of Barry incumbents, on a platform truck! The Standard examples we saw at Barry were 2-6-4T No 80067 and 9F 2-10-0s Nos 92207 and 92245. Among the Southern contingents were 14 Bulleid 'Pacifics', some of which I'd seen on my excursions to London only the year before. LMS 'Jubilee' 4-6-0 No 45699 *Galatea* was there at this time, as was S&DJR 2-8-0 No 53809. (The latter has been restored, while *Galatea* is still in ex-Barry condition at the time of writing.)

Severn Tunnel Junction and the Cardiff area provided scores of diesel cops. Finding a steam locomotive actually in steam was like spotting an oasis in the desert. Anything we found in steam was photographed, even if it was some distance away. While at Bristol Temple Meads we saw the Brush prototype diesel *Falcon*, at that time still numbered as D0280. With my new film loaded, I photographed it just before it departed, and it was probably my anxiety to capture it that led to my absent-mindedness in forgetting to pick up my exposed film. Following the departure of *Falcon*, we were treated, if that's the correct term, to the appearance of a couple of Bulleid 'light Pacifics', Nos 34039 *Boscastle* and 34010 *Sidmouth*. They weren't in steam, though, but en route to Woodham's scrapyard at Barry. 8F 2-8-0 No 48117 was towing them, and ran round its 'train' before setting off in the direction of South Wales.

The weather was dry but rather overcast for our stay in South Wales, but the sun was 'cracking the flags' as we departed for the north. Instead of going home for a break of journey, I had arranged for us to stay the night at my aunt and uncle's home in Dalton. We duly arrived about 10pm, and my good aunt made us a cooked meal before we settled down for the night.

The following morning was overcast once more, as Chris and I headed up through the Lake District. Beyond Windermere we climbed over the Kirkstone Pass; patches of mist drifted through the mountains, the tops of which were themselves enveloped by cloud. After a pleasant drive alongside Ullswater, we continued northward to join the A6 near Penrith.

We called in at Carlisle's Citadel station, where we found 'Brit' No 70001 *Lord Hurcomb* and a miscellany of steam and diesel types; then, after the break, we finished up journeying all the way to Edinburgh to find some 'digs' for the night. The rain poured down upon our arrival, and we particularly noticed the drop in temperature, as my car had no heater (the fitting of such contraptions was not a standard feature of British cars, even by the 1960s – you had to buy a 'de-luxe' model to find one already fitted). The day had been long beyond our expectations, and we were mighty glad to find somewhere to get our heads down for the night.

The following morning the sun shone, but all too briefly. Taking advantage, we took a few quick photographs in the Scottish capital, and walked up the famous Princes Street to shop for a few souvenirs. After visiting St Margaret's shed we headed for Dalton via a very circuitous route, calling in at Hurlford, Ayr and Dumfries sheds! There were plenty of local workhorses still resident at these places, but it is worth noting that quite a few of them had been transferred to Scotland from LMR or NER sheds. One wonders if they had migrated during the mid-1960s when the ScR was experiencing problems with the diesel engines in its NBL Type 2s.[32] It looks as though the ScR decided to hang on to what steam locos it acquired until the demise of steam from the region in 1966.

We'd had a bellyful of chasing after loco numbers for the moment, and headed away towards England again. There was yet more rain, and the nearer we got to the Lake District the heavier it became. Needless to say, both of us felt the need for a heater in this car, and had to wrap up to counteract the cold. It was a black night as Chris took over driving once more as we headed towards the Lake District. Having passed Ullswater, we started to climb through the Kirkstone Pass. I glanced at the petrol gauge and couldn't believe my eyes. The needle had settled on 'empty', and I drew Chris's attention to this. There was a petrol station at the top but, tough luck, the place was in darkness, obviously closed. That was all we needed, no petrol in a cold car!

'Right,' Chris continued, 'you're not supposed to do this, but...'

He switched off the engine and let the car coast down most of the way to Bowness, where we prayed we would find a petrol station that was open. We did, and it was. But there was surprised relief when, despite having taken on board a couple of gallons, the petrol gauge remained on 'empty'.

'After all the rain, the dampness must have short-circuited the gauge,' explained Chris.

We made it to Dalton OK, and the following morning the petrol gauge was working. So all was well as we departed for home.

One of the first things I did after my return home was to have a heater fitted to my car. As no carpets were fitted either, Dad fixed me up by shaping four pieces of remnant to fit front and back. A fog lamp, which I fitted myself, completed my requirements.

Now complete with heater, I drove to Crewe with Dad and Chris in March 1966 to view 'A4' No 60019 *Bittern*. The 'Pacific' was working a Williams Deacon's Bank Club tour from Manchester to Derby, and stopped off at Crewe en route. We saw the train a second time at Longton on the line to Stoke.

[32] By this time BR had replaced the NBL engines in 20 of these Type 2s with Paxman engines of 1,350bhp. Nevertheless, the whole class of 58 locos became extinct in 1972.

The WCML was within about 15 miles of home so, now I had a 'set of wheels', I was able to make frequent trips to photograph the trains. An aunt of Mum's lived close to Dallam at Warrington; so after dropping her off there Dad and I proceeded to either Dallam shed or Winwick Junction a few miles north for a couple of hours' photography. The WCML had been quadrupled in 1881 over the 4½ miles between Warrington and Winwick. North of the junction, one pair of tracks follow the original route to Earlestown, formerly Newton Junction, on the L&M line. The cut-off main line, opened in 1864, curves sharply away from the 'Newton' tracks, and climbs at gradients of 1 in 132/156 as far as Golborne, passing under the L&M line in the process. The four tracks up to Winwick Junction were reasonably busy. A fine evening was good for photography, as the sun was at a low angle to produce some good lighting effects.

Vulcan Works is situated in the vee formed by the Earlestown and cut-off lines. It once possessed its own rail connection to the Earlestown line, over which passed many diesel locomotives destined for service with BR. The most revered among the latter must be the 22 Class 55 'Deltics'. The establishment was renowned for the production of many steam and diesel locomotives for export, too. As most of these were out-of-gauge for passing over BR metals, they were transferred by road transport to Liverpool Docks for shipment.

Acton Grange Junction, on the south bank of the Manchester Ship Canal, became another favourite photographic location. Here the line to North Wales diverges left from the southbound WCML, crossing it on a flyover further south to continue through Frodsham and Helsby to Chester. There is still plenty to interest the observer at Acton Grange. It was the Ship Canal that necessitated the deviation of the main lines via the high-level girder bridge seen today, to leave sufficient clearance for the large ships that once frequently passed along the canal. The deviations opened in 1893. Between Acton Grange Junction itself and the village of Moore, a lane off the A558 Runcorn road crosses the forked Crewe and Chester lines before continuing down to the canalside. The lane provided good photographic vantage points for both lines, but shrubbery and trees restrict the options somewhat today. From the lane can be seen the original track formations of the Grand Junction Railway and the Birkenhead Railway[33] prior to the construction of the deviations. The two routes joined at Walton Old Junction, now on the

[33] Formerly known as the Birkenhead, Lancashire & Cheshire Junction Railway, its original plan was for a line between Hooton on the Chester to Birkenhead line and Heaton Norris, Manchester. It stopped short at Warrington, the result of railway politics, which also saw the company construct a 'branch' from Helsby to Chester. The latter ultimately formed a trunk route from the North of England to North Wales.

north bank of the canal not far from Bank Quay station. Up to about 1970 tracks were still in situ at Acton Grange for some distance along the course of the old Chester line, being used as long sidings for the storage of condemned rolling stock. Slow freights also used them as a refuge to allow trains with greater priority to overtake.

I preferred to photograph around Acton Grange and Moore than at Winwick. There was better scope for picture composition, and there was also a greater variety of trains to photograph. The most notable of the freights were trains of oil tankers to and from the Stanlow refinery, which used the Chester line as far as Helsby Junction. Steam power in 1965 and 1966 could still be seen on passenger work, with 'Britannia' 'Pacifics' and 4-6-0s of both 'Black 5' and 'Standard 5' variants in evidence. Freight trains produced 'Jubilee' and 'Black 5' 4-6-0s, and Stanier 2-6-0s and 2-8-0s, with the rare appearance of a 'WD' example. Class 9F 2-10-0s predominated on the Stanlow oil trains; sometimes they worked in tandem with another member of the class or perhaps with a 'Black 5'.

Two unfortunate episodes in the vicinity of Moore mar the memory of my visits. A fatal crash occurred in May 1966 on the Crewe line. Some wagons loaded with soda ash broke away from a Northwich-St Helens train while it was climbing to the Ship Canal bridge. Rolling back, they collided with a northbound Euston-Stranraer train headed by Class 40 No D322, killing the crew. The second accident took place in September of the following year, again on the Crewe line. On this occasion, some of the stock of an overnight Euston-Barrow train became derailed just to the south of Acton Grange Junction. Fortunately, there were no fatalities this time.

Earlier in 1966 I acquired a Nikkorex camera from a family friend. It was a single lens reflex model, but did not facilitate interchangeable lenses. The lens it possessed produced excellent photographs and, at £30, the offer was too good to refuse. I promptly put the camera to the test with a visit to York, accompanied by Dad. The preserved 'A3' *Flying Scotsman* was the main attraction. It hauled a special from London to York, which I photographed coming off the Doncaster line at Chaloners Whin Junction. Later we saw the engine outside the old York Railway Museum in Queen Street. I also took the opportunity to photograph some of the sights around this famous city. Needless to say, I put the Nikkorex through the rigours at Winwick and Moore. In fact, it was at Norton, a little to the south of Moore, that I saw *Flying Scotsman* again. This time, it was hauling a Gainsborough Model Railway Society special from Lincoln to Chester.

An entertaining, if undesirable, occurrence materialised at Winwick one evening, when Caprotti Standard Class 5 4-6-0 No 73132 stalled on the sharply curved climb following the junction. No amount of effort from the crew could persuade it to restart. During my frequent evening visits to Winwick, there had been a regular light-engine working, normally a Stanier 2-6-0 from Springs Branch returning home. Sure enough, on this occasion, one was following the stalled freight. After liaison with the junction signalman, the 'Mogul', No 42954, buffered up to the rear of the train, and a somewhat comical sequence followed. The 2-6-0's driver decided to push so hard that his steed got left behind as the Standard dug in, momentarily pulling its train clear of the 2-6-0. The 'Mogul' did catch up, however, and probably remained at the rear of the freight as far as Golborne.

An 'A2' 4-6-2, No 60528 *Tudor Minstrel*, traversed the WCML in 1966, hauling a railtour to Edinburgh, and Chris and I took off in the car to Springs Branch, opposite the engine shed, to photograph it. The light was hardly conducive to good photography, but we took our pictures just for the record, something every good camera-owning enthusiast did. A 'V2' 2-6-2 was scheduled to take over at Edinburgh to head the train south to York. So the two of us headed away first to Leeds, and ultimately to York, to see the 'V2' arrive with the special, or so we hoped. At Leeds we bunked Neville Hill shed. Inside was preserved Class 'K4' 2-6-0 *The Great Marquess*, painted apple-green and bearing its LNER number 3442. This loco was one of the earliest BR engines bought in working order for use in private preservation. Keeping it company was another preserved loco, Class 'N7' 0-6-2T No 69621, which I had seen at London's Stratford depot during the South Lancs Club trip recalled earlier.

After taking some photographs in the vicinity, again in gloomy lighting conditions, we popped over to York. We found one of the few surviving 'Jubilee' 4-6-0s, No 45565 *Victoria*, simmering near the engine shed. It was awaiting the arrival of the 'V2' with the railtour from Edinburgh, which it would take forward on the last leg of the tour. We waited for some considerable time, but in vain. Then news filtered through via the bush telegraph that the 'V2' had failed, but just where wasn't clear. Well, not knowing how late the train would be, Chris and I decided to 'call it a day'.

Chris had driven to York before, and knew the route without the aid of a map. In those pre-M62 motorway days, that involved negotiating the one-way systems in Leeds and Halifax and later circumnavigating Manchester. So, getting directions from Chris, I drove the Minx as we set off for home. That was OK until Chris fell asleep. No amount of twisting and turning, braking or bumps in the road would rouse him, so I carried on in the hope that I wouldn't 'come a cropper' in Leeds. As it happened, Leeds was well signposted and there was no problem. I drove on with confidence until we approached Manchester. Incredibly, without any wrong turnings, I eventually found myself back on familiar territory, the A580 East Lancashire Road.

Chris woke up.

'How did you get here?' he enquired. I don't recall what my reply was!

By now I was buying monochrome film in 17-metre bulk lengths, loading it into previously used cassettes with the aid of a photographer's changing bag. This worked out much cheaper than buying ready-loaded films, and I duly took a bunch of loaded cassettes on another run to York. This time the day was bright and sunny, and ideal for railway photography. That is until things became 'unstuck' – in more ways than one. One of my films had become separated from its spool when I tried to rewind it after exposure. Without my changing bag, what could I do but climb into the boot of my car. With the lid closed, I opened my camera and wound the film back into the cassette. I called to Chris to let me out, but he couldn't unlock the boot. The weather was already hot, and I was getting hotter inside that oven of a boot! Eventually, Chris managed to free the lock, don't ask me how, and I emerged looking like the proverbial wet rag. Oh, the pitfalls of running a car! That was something else that had to be put right, but not before it happened again while returning home after a holiday in Plymouth with my parents.

Plymouth? I hardly saw a train while I was down there. I recall walking past Laira diesel depot, but I was not interested. There were other rewards. My parents had never owned a car, and neither had learned to drive. So a car-orientated holiday was a novelty for all of us. We toured many miles around Devon, a whole new scene waiting to be photographed.

But apart from all that, in 1966 football's World Cup was taking place – in England. Our guest house had a TV in the lounge, which filled up at match time as most of the residents followed England's progress. Unfortunately for us, the final took place on the day of our return home. With no car radio and no portable one, we had to rely on listening to those of others each time we stopped for a break. By the time we reached the Midlands and the motorway, we knew that extra time was being played. No more updates then until we reached home. Oh, joy, when we switched on the telly!

So, what else of note had occurred over the previous two years? Perhaps significantly, following a Labour victory at the 1964 General Election, Dr Beeching returned to ICI during June of the following year; the Llangollen-Barmouth line had closed the previous January[34];

---

[34] Services had in fact been suspended in December 1964 following storm flooding, which affected many parts of Wales.

the last two surviving LNWR 'Super D' 0-8-0s, Nos 49361 and 49430, were withdrawn in December 1964; and through electric services commenced between London Euston and Liverpool and Manchester during 1966 itself. That year also saw the severance of through services on the old GCR line into London Marylebone.[35]

Meanwhile, three Class 'A4' 'Pacifics' were simultaneously in Crewe Works. Nos 60010 *Dominion of Canada* and 60007 *Sir Nigel Gresley* were there for restoration. The latter had been purchased from BR by the A4 Locomotive Society Ltd, whilst No 60010 was donated to Canada by the British Railways Board, and has since been on display at the National Railroad Museum, Montreal. The third 'A4' on show, No 60026 *Miles Beevor*, was there to provide a source of spares for No 60007. A visit to Crewe Works during the winter of 1966/67 revealed that *Sir Nigel* had indeed been fitted with the driving wheels from *Miles Beevor*. Crewe Works must have seemed an alien place for these three thoroughbreds from Doncaster, its former rival 'in the east'. Class 9F 2-10-0 No 92220 *Evening Star* was also in the works. It too was being prepared for preservation, just over half a decade following completion as BR's final new steam locomotive.

Musically, Georgie Fame had a hit single with 'Yeh Yeh', the Dave Clark Five were 'Glad All Over', and Sonny and Cher and one Tom Jones emerged on the scene with 'I Got You, Babe' and 'It's Not Unusual' respectively. Meanwhile, established artists like Elvis Presley, the Beatles, and the Rolling Stones continued to flood the music market, each with a quick succession of new releases.

[35] A sad decision – built to continental loading gauge, the line could have had a rosy future as a through route to Europe via the Channel Tunnel.

15
Sounds good to me!

In November 1966 there was a chance to ride behind a Southern 'Pacific', albeit a rebuilt one. No 35026 *Lamport & Holt Line* of the 'Merchant Navy' Class was to haul a Williams Deacon's Bank Club special from Manchester's Piccadilly to Doncaster and York. The route followed the Hope Valley line from Chinley to Sheffield Midland, thence to Doncaster where a stop was made. After running down the ECML to York, return to Manchester took us via Wakefield. It was during this tour that the strains of some sound recordings could be heard, made of the engine from on board the train. It must be said that it wasn't really possible to fully appreciate the sounds, coming as they did from such small equipment in the unfavourable conditions of a noisy train. I remained unimpressed and thought no more about the subject. That is until one evening the following February, when Chris arrived on our doorstep clutching an LP record and a portable tape recorder.

'How about recording some trains from the back?' he asked.

We nipped upstairs, opened the back bedroom window, and waited for a train to pass. The result was quite pleasing – we could tell that it was an 8F 2-8-0.

'You might as well borrow the recorder and tape some more,' Chris suggested, an offer I accepted with some trepidation. But once I'd sampled his LP, my opinions changed. What a superb record! Then on the Argo label, it was a compilation of mono recordings made by Peter Handford, and issued under the stark title of *Shap*. On playing the LP on our radiogram, I couldn't control my enthusiasm. What lovely sounds: the hollow-sounding 'whoof' of an unrebuilt 'Patriot', the staccato beat of a 'Duchess' going all-out at Scout Green, and the intermingling sounds of two engines labouring up the gradient with a freight train, one of them at the rear assisting the train engine. There were other sounds, too: early-morning bird song, bleating sheep and lowing cattle, all helping to set the scene in the mind's eye. I was hooked, and now had to save up and buy myself a portable tape recorder. However, a few months were to elapse before I did so. Right now, though, I was glad to take up Chris's offer to borrow his for a few more 'trial runs' at home.

The weekend of 4/5 March 1967 marked the end of through WR

services between London Paddington and Birkenhead. Although latter years had seen the influx of LMS 'Jubilees' and 'Black 5s' on the Paddington trains between Chester and Shrewsbury, memories of the Great Western presence at Chester in earlier years made the cessation of services over the WR route rather poignant for me.

Preserved 'Castle' 4-6-0 No 7029 *Clun Castle* had already visited Chester on the penultimate weekend with a commemorative special organised by the Locomotive Club of Great Britain. However, both Ian Allan Ltd and the SLS had announced their intentions to mark the event by running special trains on the Saturday and Sunday respectively. Ian Allan advertised its train for the Saturday, utilising preserved 'Castle' 4-6-0 No 4079 *Pendennis Castle*. Such was the demand for seats on this train that *Clun Castle* was roped in to haul a duplicate special. In the event, *Pendennis* ran from Didcot with the 'Birkenhead Flyer', while *Clun* took 'The Zulu' forward from Banbury, both trains initially diesel-hauled from Paddington.

The weather wasn't particularly bright as I found a suitable photographic location, somewhere between Ruabon and Wrexham, at which to capture the two specials on film. From there it was a case of straight to Chester, and to the LMS shed where the two 'Castles' were to be serviced. The sun had broken through by now, but I found it impossible to photograph *Pendennis*; there were so many folk gathered around it, either polishing or just admiring the engine at close quarters. By contrast, *Clun Castle* was almost completely ignored, so it was possible to pick and choose how to photograph it.

The itineraries of the two trains included a run to Birkenhead. However, because of the cramped nature of Woodside station the trains were shortened from 11 to just seven coaches. So, while the two 'Castle' 4-6-0s were being serviced, the tour participants had the option of squeezing into their temporarily shortened trains for the run to Birkenhead. Back at General station, the specials arrived back from Birkenhead behind 'Standard 5' 4-6-0s Nos 73035 and 73038. Then *Pendennis Castle* came steaming through the station to pick up the four remaining coaches prior to backing them onto its train for the return run south. I made up for missing out at the shed, and photographed it with its red mainframe illuminated between the wheels by brilliant sunshine. This shot pleases me no end, as it also includes the substantial LNWR signal gantry, which then graced the western exit from the station. To obtain this shot, I stood with many other onlookers between the tracks, on the boardwalk that protected the signal wires and point rodding. This example of 'open house' attitude became more widespread on BR as time slipped by towards the final days of steam. However, officialdom was always on hand to ensure that enthusiasm did not get out of hand.

Finally, to photograph *Clun Castle* heading the return 'Birkenhead Flyer' (the two engines swapped trains for the return runs), I headed out to the edge of the city, to where the main line cuts through the city walls.

The following day, 5 March, saw the SLS also running two special trains, although on this occasion use was made of 'Black 5' 4-6-0 No 44680 together with *Clun Castle*. These trains ran from Birmingham right through to Birkenhead by using the avoiding lines at Chester. Dad came along with Chris and myself, and we selected the small goods yard close to Bromborough station to witness the passage of *Clun Castle*. I was well pleased with the low-angle shot I took of No 7029. Chris tried tape-recording it, but the result didn't turn out too well. Taking pictures simultaneously made it impossible to monitor the recording level, control of which was manually operated on Chris's machine.

We motored on to an overbridge at Capenhurst for the passage of No 44680. We remained there when the special trains reappeared behind 9F 2-10-0s Nos 92203 and 92234 shuttling the specials to Chester and back, a similar arrangement to the previous day except in reverse, so to speak. In the interim between trains, it was a surprise to see a 2-6-4T hauling two other 9Fs towards Birkenhead, en route to a breaker's yard for scrapping.

The whole day had been blessed with sunshine, which fortunately persisted for our final shots of *Clun Castle*, at a spot on the North Wales main line close to Chester Racecourse. Good fortune prevailed as *Clun* headed appropriately into the evening sun, which reflected brilliantly towards the camera from engine and train.

Also during March 'A4' 'Pacific' *Sir Nigel Gresley* had emerged from Crewe Works after overhaul as a preserved locomotive. At the A4 Locomotive Society's wish, the engine had been outshopped in LNER garter blue livery with dark red wheels, and given its original number of 4498. Unknown to many, including Chris and myself, running-in had taken place at night over a section of the WCML. Having taken an evening parcels train from Crewe to Preston, it returned to Crewe on the 5.35am ex-Preston workers' train. No doubt it created surprise and disbelief among many of the passengers at the sight of an ECML thoroughbred at the head of their train.

The official inaugural run of the 'A4' in preservation was earmarked for 1 April, and Chris and I duly booked seats. The tour's destination was Carlisle via the WCML, with a return to Crewe via the Settle-Carlisle line, Blackburn and Farrington Junction. Chris had become a member of the A4 Locomotive Society and requested seats in one of the end coaches, so that he could tape-record the engine at work. In the event, we found ourselves in the last of 12 coaches going north, which became the first coming back. As circumstances turned out, the arrangement worked quite well. We were able to make use of reasonably good weather to photograph and film from the rear of the train on the northbound leg.

There was plenty of spirited running all the way to Preston. On the four-track stretch out of Crewe, Chris took cine shots from the train, and captured a few steam trains heading south. He then asked me to have a go at filming between Moore and Winwick. We hit 92mph near Moore and hurtled down from Ship Canal bridge into Warrington at 72mph. I could hardly hold the camera still on our descent from the bridge, with the result that Bank Quay station appears to be a little unsteady as we quite literally zoomed towards it! The lightning progress continued as far as Preston, reached 12 minutes before schedule, and the inevitable price was paid with a signal check just after exiting the station. The climb to Shap was topped at 31mph, not bad for an ex-works locomotive with a 450-ton load. Despite further signal checks, Carlisle was reached about 4 minutes early.

At Carlisle our train continued with *Sir Nigel* still at the front to Kingmoor, where it was routed into a loop alongside the engine shed. Having watched the 'A4' being turned and serviced, tour participants had a fine time climbing into the cabs of the many steam locomotives on shed. Whistle-blowing became a temporary pastime; there were the chime whistles of 'Britannia' 4-6-2s, Standard whistles of some 9F 2-10-0s, and of course some hoots from the Stanier 'Black 5s', all calling and answering each other! Chris left his recorder running to capture the atmosphere.

Coming home, Chris tape-recorded *Sir Nigel* from the carriage window. Good progress was made along the Midland line until we were signal-checked at Appleby. From there on the weather turned quite nasty, with snow falling as we ascended towards Ais Gill. Speed dropped to 26mph as the engine repeatedly slipped on the greasy rails. Following a prolonged stop for water at Hellifield, *Sir Nigel* was in trouble again on the climb through Wilpshire on the Blackburn line. On this occasion, speed was down almost to walking pace, but picked up as the 'A4' ran onto drier rails inside Wilpshire Tunnel. Back on the WCML again at Farrington Junction, we continued until stopped at No 7 platform at Wigan, 'round the back' as we called it in our spotting days. This was to let a diesel-hauled express pass us, but why this was necessary I don't know. We were booked to Crewe non-stop, but the operating authorities seemed to think that we wouldn't be able to maintain any daylight between ourselves and the following diesel!

We made it back to Crewe, *Sir Nigel Gresley* having had a trouble-free first outing. There was time for some night-time photography of the engine before we left for the car park. Then, catastrophe! Arriving at the car park, Chris discovered that, having earlier unplugged the microphone on which there was an on/off switch, his tape recorder had started up. Consequently, all the whistle-blowing at Kingmoor shed had been erased from the tape, as had some recordings of the early part of the journey from Carlisle. Thankfully, recordings of the ascent to Ais Gill and the climb through Wilpshire remained intact. A shame really; while not providing particularly interesting listening, the erased sequence would have been a reminder of the crazier things that enthusiasts got up to on their days out!

Later that April the Railway Correspondence & Travel Society ran a special train whose itinerary included some lines around Wrexham. Of particular interest to me was the use of one of the few remaining 2-6-4T engines, together with the fact that the train was to climb the steep branch from Wrexham to Brymbo. With this in mind, I asked Chris if I could borrow his tape recorder, and set off for Wrexham. Arriving first at Croes Newydd East Yard, gravity shunting was in progress in the company of Standard Class 4 2-6-0 No 76037. Not particularly enthralling material for recording, so I moved to the main line, close to South Fork Junction near Croes Newydd shed. LMS Class 4 2-6-0 No 43088 came off the Brymbo branch with a string of wagons, crossed the main line and proceeded to shunt in the up yard. This was more like it; the driver noticed I was recording, and provided some exhibitionism for my benefit. Next, it was time to find a location on the Brymbo branch, as the RCTS special was soon due. Class 8F 2-8-0 No 48697 hammered past me with its train, even blowing off with a surplus of steam. Nothing wrong with the boiler then, even at this late stage in the steam age. Well, I tried to combine photography with tape recording, achieving a reasonable picture, but perhaps inevitably the recording became a little distorted as the train drew close.

Following its return from Brymbo, the 8F headed its train off to Llangollen. I made use of the interlude to venture onto Croes Newydd depot. It had officially closed in March, but most of its locos were still stored outside, cold and forlorn. Among the Standards, which would shortly be dispersed elsewhere, were the shed's 0-6-0PTs, all of them now withdrawn. I just stared at them for a few moments before it dawned on me that, other than preserved examples, no locomotives of GWR origin were now at work on BR. These were possibly the last to do so, albeit it within the LMR since 1963. Just one engine was inside the shed, 0-6-2T No 6697, which was eventually preserved. I mention in passing that Wrexham's Rhosddu shed closed in 1962. Following its transfer from the LMR to the WR in 1958, how ironic that Croes Newydd shed latterly found itself in the LMR!

Back at Wrexham, not one but two 2-6-4T locomotives, Nos 42616 and 42647, relieved No 48697 for the run to the train's next destination, New Brighton (the town situated at the mouth of the River Mersey, not the one near Wrexham!). I took up position by the GCR Wrexham Exchange signal box; situated opposite the GWR's North box, it controlled the connection between the two systems, which the special train was now about to traverse. The train started out from General station, as two signalmen were going about their business close by.

'Have you pulled the starter off, Mervyn?' called one of them.

'Eh?'

'The starter. Have you pulled it off?'

I couldn't hear the reply for the noise of the approaching train. As both tanks powered past, I gather that Mervyn had pulled off the starter. Chris's recorder picked up all this quite well, and this time I was a little more successful at setting the correct recording level and getting a picture into the bargain. Quite happy to have seen the 2-6-4Ts, I didn't bother chasing the train, and returned home instead.

Chris was impressed with my efforts.

'You may as well hang onto the recorder for a while; you'll probably make more use of it than I will,' he remarked.

Chris worked shifts, so we couldn't venture out together as frequently as we'd have liked. It was a very kind gesture, for which I have remained ever grateful, particularly as I actually finished up 'borrowing' his machine until I managed to buy my own the following July!

Well, the next couple of months were spent making recordings mainly in the Warrington area. I soon discovered that Winwick was not one of the better places to record. The proximity of the junction with its associated speed restrictions meant that engines were not working hard enough to provide the desired recording material. Besides, trains coming off the Preston line were usually coasting as they rounded the curve and hit the junction. Acton Grange, near Moore, was more acceptable. Northbound trains off both the Crewe and Chester lines had to work against the gradient up to the Ship Canal bridge, while southbound trains, having negotiated the bridge, were still accelerating as they passed Moore.

On a visit to Moore with Chris, we found the refuge siding provided by the old Birkenhead Railway occupied by a tanker train from Stanlow. And what a 'scoop'! It was double-headed by two 9F 2-10-0s, Nos 92110 and 92020 (the latter an ex-Crosti-boilered conversion). Chris took cine-film while I operated his recorder as, following passage of a DMU, the pair backed out their train before pounding up to the junction at Acton Grange. Once over the canal bridge, the train would leave the WCML again and make the steep descent to Arpley. Visiting later in the year with my own tape recorder, I was pleasantly surprised, if caught out, by the appearance of 'Brit' No 70013 *Oliver Cromwell*[36] heading a Perth-London express. Caught out? Well, unfortunately rain was falling and, having already photographed a few trains, I'd retired to my car to keep dry. So I was quite unprepared for photography when the 'Brit' approached, accelerating down the bank from the canal bridge. I couldn't have wished for anything better than the resultant recording. The engine burst from under the nearby road bridge and the sound of its exhaust echoed back from more bridges as *Oliver Cromwell* continued under acceleration away down the line.

I ventured back to the spot alongside Bank Quay station where, now almost ten years since, I had witnessed with Spike the two 'Southern' diesels swapping a defective baggage car on the 'Royal Scot'. Some reasonable recordings were made here, but I could see steam activity about a mile distant to the south where shunting was apparently in progress, and wondered if I could gain access to the lineside around there. Consultation with a local area map suggested I could. Turning into a cul-de-sac from the Chester road led me to the River Mersey, here merely a tributary as it winds its way from Warrington to become a grander, wider river by the time it reaches Widnes. Here was a location I came to regard as a tape recordist's paradise.

Like the area around Acton Grange on the north bank of the Ship Canal, there is evidence here to interest the railway historian. The place is dominated by a high girder bridge carrying the WCML from Bank Quay across the river, the line climbing at a gradient of 1 in 135 on a sweeping curve up to the Ship Canal bridge. At a much lower level, however, there remains a small portion of the old Grand Junction main line, spanning the Mersey on the original stone bridge of 1837. Often referred to as 'Twelve Arches', the bridge is still in use today carrying loads undreamed of by the early civil engineers who built it, for this little stretch of line now forms part of a link from the WCML down to Arpley, where it joins the line running from Ditton Junction to Stockport. This link descends initially at 1 in 69 from Walton New Junction near the Ship Canal bridge and levels out on the approach to Walton Old Junction just before Twelve Arches. This was where the Birkenhead Railway joined the GJR. Having been superseded by Acton Grange Junction, the stub of the Birkenhead Railway was latterly used to connect with the railway system of the Manchester Ship Canal Company, which ran along the north bank of the canal and passed under the WCML. After crossing the Mersey, the GJR

---

[36] No 70013 was the last BR 'express' engine to receive a major overhaul, being outshopped from Crewe Works during February 1967.

tracks divide; one pair forms a connection with the WCML, the down line burrowing under the latter to join it at Bank Quay station, while the other drops down a further steep incline to Arpley. With its own Low Level station at Bank Quay, the line from Stockport continues westward under the High Level station eventually to connect with the Liverpool-London line at Ditton Junction.[37] In effect, the line formed a second route between Liverpool and Manchester for the LNWR after it swallowed up the St Helens and the Warrington & Stockport companies into its empire. Passenger services on the route ceased in 1962, although the line continues in use for freight traffic. Sidings filled the space between the Bank Quay and the Arpley connection, as did further sidings fanning out from Walton Old Junction, lying in the vee of the two embankments.

So here was scope for a variety of recordings: shunting at both Walton and Arpley sidings, with trains passing on both the WCML and the Arpley connection. Some of the heavier trains took rear-end assistance from Arpley for the climb to the Ship Canal bridge, manna for the recordist with the sounds of two hardworking engines intermingling. Still hanging onto Chris's tape recorder, I made a number of sorties to Walton after work during the summer evenings. Sometimes Dad came along, coming in handy to assist with recording while I took some pictures.

Visits to Walton continued after I purchased my own tape recorder, a Sanyo MR130. Unlike Chris's, it incorporated an automatic volume level control, so not only was I able to take photographs simultaneously, I could also use the recorder at night. One such night turned out to be one to savour for ever, a night on which seemingly nothing could go wrong. Dusk fell on that calm evening towards the end of August when, at around 9.00pm, a sequence of events began to unfold that I still regard as my *piece de resistance*.

An engine was slowly plodding up from Arpley, preparing to take on a bank engine for the climb to the canal bridge, when a Standard Class 5 4-6-0 headed up the WCML with a parcels train bound for Chester. The freight was a little nearer now and, as the banker was now in position at the rear, the pair began to get to grips with tackling the incline, just as an 8F 2-8-0 clanked down the main line towards Warrington. The two engines, both 'Black 5s', of which the banker was No 45055, powered past on their ascent to the Ship Canal bridge. The sounds of the engines continued until they reached the top, providing a lengthy recording of the type I prefer. But this was only a foretaste of what was yet to come. As an interlude a short while later, No 45055

[37] See note [19] on page 95.

returned to Arpley to await its next duty. In fact, I had a stroke of luck before it took up that duty and featured again in my next recording. A young railway employee approached me. (I think he was assisting the driver of diesel shunter No 12032 with the marshalling of some wagons in Walton sidings.) He'd noticed I'd been tape recording, and suggested I should follow him if I wanted a 'variation on a theme' for the next train, which he informed me was due out of Arpley at around 10.00pm. He led me across the tracks by the signal box and away from the illuminated part of the yard. We walked between the lines of goods wagons parked in Walton sidings to a spot just beyond the buffer stops. Here, Walton New Junction, where the two lines converged, was less than half a mile distant, and I was now sandwiched between the two high embankments.

'You'll get some good recordings from here,' the young chap remarked. 'The sound will come all the way up from Arpley tonight. Make your own way back when you've finished. You'll be all right.' I thanked him and off he went.

I stood and waited in this dark eerie place, unable to read my wrist watch to see when 10 o'clock was approaching. I left my tape recorder running to ensure I would miss nothing, also hoping that a train would start out from Bank Quay during my wait. None did; perhaps two or three descended on the main line, but nothing worth keeping on tape. Then the shrill whistle of a Standard came across the still night air from the direction of Arpley. 'I hope this is it,' I thought. Sure enough, the call was answered by the Stanier hooter of No 45055 further down, and the exhaust of the 'Black 5' was heard predominantly at first as the pair set the train in motion. That young railwayman must have known a thing or two, and obviously appreciated the possibilities of tape recording here. As I stood motionless holding the microphone, the sounds of the two engines alternated in prominence, aided no doubt by filtration through the lines of wagons in the sidings; the obvious climax followed as the engines passed above my head. The 9F eased off a little approaching the junction, momentarily slowing the beat of No 45055, still powering away at the back, then quickening before the '5' finally dropped away from the train. Well pleased with the effort, I trudged back between the wagons, glad to get into the dim glimmer of the lights by the junction signal box.

But there was yet further work to be done! An 8F 2-8-0 was standing on the up line by the signal box, its crew discussing matters with the signalman. Acknowledging enquiries from my railwayman friend as to my success, I crossed the tracks to stand close to the GJR bridge to await movement of the 8F. Setting off, it crossed to the down line, no doubt retiring to Dallam shed for the night. Still recording as the engine pattered away into the night, I was startled by the sound of another engine that suddenly exploded into life. My attention being focused on the 8F, I had no idea a train was waiting to proceed up the bank from Arpley. Anyway, after a brief wheel-slip the engine, which turned out to be a double-chimneyed 9F 2-10-0, slowly got its train on the move. I thought, 'I'm going to enjoy this,' and I certainly did. The train consisted of oil tanks bound for Stanlow refinery on the Wirral, and proved quite a load for the unassisted 9F. The engine's exhaust raised echoes as the sounds slammed against the girder bridge supporting the WCML, the engine accelerating on the almost level GJR bridge. As it passed me I could even hear the 'clonk' of the connecting rods. All was brilliantly captured by my tape recorder. As the engine headed away, it appeared to shine in the dim glimmer of the yard lamps, suggesting that it had been 'bulled up'. The 2-10-0 pounded up the 1 in 69 to the Ship Canal bridge, during which diesel shunter No 12032 dragged out a string of wagons from the sidings. My recording concluded with the gentle clicking of wheels over rail joints, the quiet creaking of the wagons, and the clonking of buffers coming together.

What a night! I returned home elated.

In connection with the Chester Arts Festival taking place that July, 'A3' *Flying Scotsman* had been on static display at General station, together with 'A4' *Sir Nigel Gresley*. It was then steamed one Sunday to haul a special train to Blackpool and back. Having seen it leaving the outskirts of Chester on its morning outward run, I elected to go to the top of Frodsham Hill for a bird's-eye view of its return and hopefully get a good recording (this was just prior to my buying my own machine). From here there is a tremendous panorama from Halton (near Runcorn) in the east, out over the plains and mud-flats across the River Mersey to Hale and Speke in south Liverpool, with Helsby and the Wirral to the west. The town of Frodsham is at the foot of the hill and has a railway station, still open today. The A56 main road parallels the railway for much of the way as far as Helsby. On this July day in 1967 it was busy with traffic mainly returning from North Wales at the end of a gloriously fine summer's day. No M56 motorway yet – that was still some time away.

The light was fading when *Flying Scotsman* and its train came into sight, heading down the line from Frodsham Tunnel. It stopped at Frodsham to set down passengers, just as a DMU passed heading towards Warrington. Then the 'A3' set off. Although the line here is on a falling westward gradient of 1 in 240, the driver let rip with full regulator. The engine's exhaust developed into a roaring crescendo, which Chris's tape recorder picked up for some considerable time as the train disappeared into the murk of the evening on its last lap to Chester.

That summer I decided to sample the delights of one of the embryo preserved railways, the Worth Valley line at Haworth in Yorkshire. Following BR's closure of the branch from Keighley to Oxenhope, the Keighley & Worth Valley Preservation Society had been set up in 1962, with the intention of reopening the line. After much hard work, the organisation established its base at Haworth, which was open to the public as a static museum. On selected days an engine and coach ran short trips just beyond the road bridge up to the loop and back. Among the first locomotives preserved at Haworth were Ivatt 2-6-2T No 41241 and 'N2' 0-6-2T No 69523, which I'd seen at Doncaster not so long ago. By now it was owned by the Gresley Society, which had restored it to LNER apple-green livery with the number 4744. No 41241, however, was at the time still in BR lined black, but was later to appear in the KWVR's own red livery. Pleasant times, and interesting to compare with the busy line we can see today.

16
Magnetic Shap, and other points north

The recording of *Flying Scotsman* at Frodsham was the last I made with Chris's recorder, as I shortly purchased my own. I couldn't wait to get to Shap and try my luck at recording engines working hard against the grade. So, following a few satisfactory trial recordings at Acton Grange, I was off for a stay at my aunt and uncle's residence in Dalton, parents in tow, with the idea of visiting Shap foremost in my mind. After threading the beautiful Lune Gorge, the WCML climbs away from Tebay, initially at 1 in 146 for the best part of 2 miles as far as Bridge End, near Greenholme. From there the gradient stiffens to 1 in 75 for the rest of the climb. En route it passes Shap Wells Hotel, before paralleling the A6 road through Shap village beyond the summit. Since the opening of the line, bank engines were provided for the specific task of assisting trains up the steep climb; it was this feature that made the northbound flank of Shap the main attraction for photographers and sound recordists rather than the southbound run from Penrith. At a ruling gradient of 1 in 125, the latter did not warrant dedicated bank engines for up trains. Thus Shap incline became a Mecca for me and like-minded enthusiasts for the remaining months of 1967.

Once or twice I sampled the Settle-Carlisle line, a little over half an hour's drive from Tebay, with its gradients of 1 in 100 on either side of the summit at Ais Gill. But the prospect of the contrasting sounds of two engines struggling against the grade on Shap, coupled with, in many cases, the inclement weather, proved too strong for me to want to spend much time over at Ais Gill. It's a pity really for, as I was later to discover, I could have got some fine recordings on the Settle-Carlisle line. In later years, when I took time to explore it properly, I found the Settle-Carlisle line to be far more photogenic than the route over Shap.

Throughout the line's history, various types of locomotive had been employed on banking duties over Shap. In latter years the task fell to LMS 2-6-4Ts of Fowler and Fairburn patterns. However, from March 1967 Standard Class 4 4-6-0s had taken over the role. (During one visit, I found one of the former, No 42134, still resident inside Tebay shed, although withdrawn from service.) I welcomed the opportunity to record the Standards, at the same time disappointed to have missed out on the 2-6-4Ts.

I took Dad along on my first visit to Shap. After some unremarkable recordings made at Tebay and Greenholme, I got some more impressive results near Scout Green. This signal box is only about 2½ miles by rail from Tebay, but the journey by road is nearer 5. Taking the Appleby road out of Tebay, the route took us through the delightfully sleepy village of Orton, from where the road to Scout Green and Shap diverges to the left. The crossroads beyond Orton, one of which leads to Greenholme, signals the final approach to Scout Green. In those pre-M6 motorway days, the little lane descended diagonally along the fellside towards the railway before passing under the bridge that is still in use today.[38]

I'd heard how bad the weather could be up here, but the day in question was relatively calm with hazy sunshine and a slight north-westerly breeze. Thus I was able to record from the higher ground (now occupied by the M6 motorway) without any interference from wind on the microphone. In such favourable conditions as these, the recorder was able to pick up the sounds from some considerable distance away, both on the approach of the trains and after they had passed. I was aware that I couldn't match Peter Handford's recordings for quality, but at least I achieved similar results with regard to 'content of programme', as they say in other circles. I was very pleased with my first efforts on Shap, which featured 9F No 92227, 'Brit' No 70016 *Ariel* and 8F No 48308, all of which were assisted by No 75024.

While staying at Dalton I had the ambitious idea of visiting the North East. My plan was to photograph and record some of the surviving 'J27' 0-6-0s and 'Q6' 0-8-0s of NER vintage, together with some 'WD' 2-8-0s that were still 'knocking around' up there. (The latter had by now disappeared from the LMR scene.) Still a relative novice at long-distance driving, I grossly underestimated how long it would take to drive to the North East. Maps were not furnished with point-to-point mileages, and fast arterial roads were still rather scarce, especially on the route I'd chosen!

Both Dad and my uncle decided to go with me. As things turned out, I bet they wished they hadn't! I was tired when we had only reached Darlington, and by the time we arrived at West Hartlepool I had developed a bad headache. Mentally exhausted, I trotted around the shed. For the record, just eight engines were there: two 'K1' 2-6-0s, Nos 62026 and 62041, four 'WD' 2-8-0s, Nos 90074, 90309,

---

[38] This road now passes under the M6 motorway virtually at right-angles, before curving right to run parallel with the railway up to the bridge.

90339 and 90695, and two 'Q6' 0-8-0s, Nos 63407 and 63344. No 63344 was in steam, but there was no likelihood of it going anywhere. No 90695 clanked off shed as No 90076 came on, with no exhaust sound to satisfy my recorder. What an anti-climax to my efforts! I tried a location further north, near Sunderland, and succeeded in recording 'J27' 0-6-0 No 65896 restarting a freight after a signal check. I didn't manage to take a photo, though. Although it is not one of my better recordings, I still treasure that of No 65896, as it is the only one I made of a loco from the pre-Grouping era. Well, Disprins not having had much effect on my headache, I decided enough was enough. There was a long journey back to Dalton and, needless to say, it was dark when we got back.

I took things relatively easy the next day. The local village of Pennington lay to the south of Lindal summit on the Furness main line from Carnforth to Barrow. Here, between two reverse curves on the 1 in 95 climb from Ulverston, I achieved a beautiful recording of 'Black 5' No 44825, slogging slowly up with a westbound freight. I liked it so much that I returned the next day. Another 'Black 5', No 45295, attacked the bank rather more briskly, but the recording wasn't up to the previous day's standard. Although it was now afternoon, the day was fine, so I asked if anyone was interested in a run to Shap. Mum and Dad said they'd go, but my aunt decided to stay behind to have a meal ready for us on our return. (Uncle was at work anyway.)

Having cleared Kendal, we followed the A685 Brough road, which passes through Tebay. What a beautiful run it is, with a stunning view of the Howgills just as the road begins to drop into the Lune Gorge. Catching sight of a steam train heading north around the Lambrigg/Grayrigg area, I decided to give chase. Making good progress, we were about to drop down into the Lune Gorge when a British Railways staff bus pulled out ahead from the Sedburgh road, which joins the A685 at this point. I couldn't pass it, and finished up tailing it all the way to Tebay, where it turned into the station yard. The train we'd been chasing was about to restart, having taken on a bank engine. It was actually a passenger train, with a 'Brit' on the front. (The crew couldn't have had much confidence in their steed. Unless the train was abnormally heavy, it was unusual for an engine with the power of a 'Brit' to call on the assistance of a banker.) Well, the extra 2 miles by road to Scout Green took their toll. We arrived just as No 70025 was heading up towards the little signal box – no time for either photo or recording.

I parked as before, high up to the east of the line. The day seemed fated, for rain began to fall just as a parcels train headed up the bank behind 'Black 5' No 45135. The highlight, if one can so call it, as driving rain now smothered the area, came in the form of 'Brit' No 70039 *Sir Christopher Wren*. In common with many engines at this time, it was suffering from poor maintenance, with steam leaking profusely at the front end, shrouding the engine as it forged up the hill. No 75024 was providing able assistance at the rear once again. As the pair passed us a Class 47 diesel rushed down at the head of a Freightliner train.

There was absolutely nothing to do but sit in the car. Mum became frustrated, as she hadn't brought any magazines or a book to read. The only 'literature' we had on board was a Johnson's Road Atlas! So, after yet another parcels train had clambered past (with 'Black 5' No 44911 at the head), we decided to return to our 'digs'. As we passed through Newby Bridge the weather cleared up, and stayed that way all the way back to Dalton.

'Haven't you had a lovely day?' Auntie said.

The Freightliners, or Liner Trains, were one of the fruits born out of Dr Beeching's doctrine. The principle involved the use of box containers placed on long, flat wagons mounted on two four-wheeled bogies. The containers could be transferred between road and rail vehicles, superseding the time-honoured method of wagonload traffic, which it was intended would be phased out. New Freightliner terminals were being built at major centres around the country to accommodate the new trains, replacing hundreds of smaller goods depots. The days were numbered for the pick-up goods trains that plied between various local goods depots. Unwittingly, the liner vehicles caused a little anxiety amongst the population in some parts of the country, Liverpool being no exception. When travelling light without a container, they created a constant whining noise. Some folk telephoned or wrote to the local newspaper, the *Liverpool Echo*, asking what these noises could be. Perhaps something extra-terrestrial? I sat in my bedroom, window open. The sound was so intense that I couldn't decipher what it was or whence it came. All this was because the noise was more intense when heard from a distance, but not so noticeable from close quarters. It's laughable now, but there were a few chills sent down the spine until the mystery of the 'whining' was solved.

The lure of Shap was now becoming irresistible to me. I had by now bought my own copy of Argo's *Shap* LP, and never ceased to admire the recordings at Scout Green of 'Duchess' No 46249 *City of Sheffield* and unrebuilt 'Patriot' No 45519 *Lady Godiva*. Powerful recordings of powerful sounds! I also found fascinating the background sounds of the wildlife, cattle and sheep, which could be heard in relief to the sounds of the trains. It was too late to record the 'Duchesses' by three years now, but the next best thing was to try for a 'Britannia' instead. So, following my Dalton holiday it wasn't long before I returned to Shap with Chris. Once again the weather was clement, even to the point of allowing us some sunshine! At Tebay 'Brit' No 70014 *Iron Duke* took on a bank engine, No 75024 again, the ritual being filmed by Chris and recorded by myself.

Up at Scout Green there was the spectacular performance by 9F 2-10-0 No 92056, which absolutely hammered up single-handed with a freight, following which we saw an unusual working heading north in the form of 'Standard 4' 4-6-0 No 75032 hauling 'dead' Co-Bo diesel No D5714. About this time seven of these Co-Bos were stored at Carlisle's Upperby depot awaiting scrapping, and No D5714 was probably about to join them.

I decided to venture towards the signal box, leaving Chris to his own devices for a while by the little road bridge. The moment I set foot on the terrain below the railway, my feet sank into the waterlogged grass. Being as green as the fells around me, I hadn't realised that, despite the current dry spell, water was still seeping unseen from watersheds on the higher fells. Unbelievable now, but I was wearing casual suede shoes. Suede shoes! Needless to say, they were ruined.

The damage done, I carried on and put up with the discomfort of damp feet! I got my wish. 'Brit' No 70012 *John of Gaunt* powered up the bank with a parcels train, following which 8F 2-8-0 No 48517 provided syncopated sounds with assisting engine No 75024. I had now reached the little signal box. The signalman invited me into the cabin for a chat, and to show me the 'workings'. The box, which was of LNWR origin, was only 12 feet square, and was placed at this location to provide an intermediate signalling section roughly halfway up the bank. The intention was to reduce possible delays to trains ascending Shap by splitting the long section of line between Tebay and Shap Wells. In a while No 75024 returned from assisting No 48517, and I was able to record the bell codes between the signal boxes at Shap Summit, Tebay and this one, together with the pulling of signal levers to let the engine pass.

'What are you doing in there?' came a voice from outside the door as No 75024 clanked away down the hill. For one awful moment, I thought my number was up. But then I just burst out laughing, as did the signalman. The voice belonged to Chris, who was wondering where I was. It's a pity I didn't leave my recorder running to capture the moment for posterity.

There were two more Shap visits interwoven with the night vigils at Warrington, and visits to other locations. Flushed with my success at Warrington, I tried a spot opposite Springs Branch MPD at Wigan, but the results were comparatively mediocre. So, searching for something a little different, I paid a visit to Preston station, and the effort proved quite profitable.

There was still plenty of steam-hauled freight on the WCML

passing by around the west side of the station, and a couple rumbled through on the LYR side. One freight, which was held at signals to the south, started away. I stopped where I happened to be – in the middle of the station, recorder strapped over my shoulder, microphone in hand, and watched the train get under way. Catching sight of me, an elderly gentleman started to walk slowly towards me. Bless him! He wore steel tips on his shoes, and stopped right in front of me.

'And what are you doing?' he enquired.

'Shhhhh!' I whispered quietly, finger over lips and gesturing towards my microphone.

'Ohh!' he whispered just as quietly, and tiptoed away as best he could.

Fortunately, the train was as yet some distance away, so there was no intrusion during the build-up and climax of the recording. The 8F 2-8-0, No 48304, powered by the station and attacked the sharp rise beyond. As a welcome change to all the steam-hauled freights, 'Black 5' No 44872 departed with the Manchester portion of a train from Glasgow, the Liverpool portion continuing its journey with diesel haulage.

Chris heard that some of the surviving 2-6-4Ts were to be found operating between Leeds and Bradford, on the NE Region. So one Friday in August saw us heading for Leeds on a train from Manchester headed by 'Black 5' No 45072. My first attempts at tape-recording from a train were not particularly successful, but I made amends during our trip behind No 42066, one of the 2-6-4Ts. We arrived in Leeds well in time to connect with a London-Bradford train, the rear three coaches of which were taken on to Bradford Exchange by the tank.[39] Out of Leeds there is a continuous climb for 7 miles, the steepest sections being 1 in 50 for just over a mile, then a 3-mile drag at 1 in 100. After Laister Dyke the line drops, mainly at 1 in 50, for the remaining 2 miles into Bradford Exchange.[40] It was a rigorous slog, but the tank made good speed with the three coaches. One stop was made at New Pudsey.

The news columns in the railway journals revealed that Crewe South shed was due to close to steam in November 1967, to be followed by Carlisle Kingmoor at the end of December. The intimation was that a reduction of steam workings on the main line over Shap was imminent. So the pilgrimages to the big incline continued until November when, as events transpired, there was an outbreak of foot and mouth disease among cattle. Travellers were requested to restrict long-distance journeys

[39] Sometimes LNER 'B1' 4-6-0 No 61306 was used, the last survivor of its class. I hadn't managed to record a 'B1', but wasn't going to complain about No 42066.

[40] Since rebuilt as a rail/bus terminal, and renamed Bradford Interchange.

in an effort to minimise the spread of infection, and I chose to honour the wishes of those directly concerned.

On 30 August at 4.00am my alarm clock went off.

'Why was I so determined to go to Shap so early?' I moaned to myself in a daze.

I knew why. My intention was to catch some early-morning birdsong on my recordings, just as Peter Handford had done on his *Shap* LP. So switching to 'autopilot' without giving myself chance to drop off to sleep again, I got ready to leave. Somehow I managed to get out of the house shortly after 4.30am, heading off first to pick up Chris.

On a dry but murky morning just after 5.00am we motored along the East Lancashire Road to gain the M6 northward. Taking with us a portable radio, we listened to songs like 'San Francisco' (Scott McKenzie), 'A Whiter Shade of Pale' (Procol Harum) and 'All You Need Is Love' (the Beatles). The year 1967 saw the Beatles making their last public performance as a band before splitting up. Pop music was emerging from the raucous era of the mid-'60s into the more sedate 'pretty' style symbolised by the Scott McKenzie song above[41], the Woodstock Festival, Hippies, and Flower Power.

As we approached the end of the M6 as was, we looked over towards Carnforth. There was some smoke. It wasn't coming from the MPD either, but from an engine working hard, heading a train northward. I drove to one of the lay-bys on the A6 from which there was a good view of the WCML. There was hardly any road traffic around, so we were struck with disbelief when, with my tape recorder switched on, a van promptly pulled up behind us.

Imagine our thoughts at that moment. Fortunately, the van driver switched off his engine. Apparently there was some concern about one of the tyres. While the driver was checking around, I got a decent recording of 'Black 5' No 45212 hauling the lengthy freight. As the sound of the train faded away towards Burton and Holme, believe it or not the van started up again and left. Good timing indeed!

We continued north ourselves, arriving at Tebay just after 7.00am, well before No 45212. We took up position north of the station, close to the cutting through Loups Fell. Around 7.30am No 45212 arrived and called for a bank engine. What happened next was almost a carbon copy of a Peter Handford recording from the *Shap* LP. As No 45212 approached, a 'Britannia' 'Pacific' dashed southward with a freight, sounding its chime whistle on approaching the station. (On the LP a 'Black 5' is heard speeding southward, as another slows to take on a banker for the big climb.) Having seen off train and banker, which

[41] The exception being the Rolling Stones, who just carried on...

turned out to be No 75037, we retired to the station.

Tebay was once a junction for the NER line from Darlington. Originally opened in 1861 by the South Durham & Lancashire Union Railway, the line's raison d'être was for the transportation of coking coals from the North East to the ironworks at Lindal and Barrow-in-Furness. Iron formed a balancing traffic in the reverse direction. But there was also a passenger service, hence three platform faces at Tebay, the eastern face of the island platform serving the NER trains. Although passenger services between here and Kirkby Stephen ceased in 1952, the station remained open for WCML services until July 1968. We found the station buildings still intact, but now being used for storage purposes and closed to the public. Both platforms once possessed canopies, but these had been removed in the mid-1960s, leaving scant protection from the elements for intending passengers (and for ourselves, as we were to discover very shortly). Within the station buildings on the down platform was a stairwell connected to a footbridge spanning the tracks, by which access to the station was gained from the station yard. Tebay's engine shed was situated behind a high wall that extended beyond the buildings at the southern end of the down platform; the wall provided limited protection for passengers from the smoke that would otherwise smother the platforms due to the prevailing winds.

Although NER engines worked through to the Furness area initially, in later years they were exchanged at Tebay, whose shed provided locomotives to relieve the incomers. Freight continued over the NER line at a dwindling rate up to 1962, when it was closed completely between Tebay and Kirkby Stephen. Passenger excursion traffic between the North East and Blackpool, Morecambe and Southport also continued up to this date. The appearance of NER engines continued until they were mostly supplanted in the 1950s by Standard and LMS 'Moguls'. Larger engines were precluded from the route, owing to weight restrictions over the slender lattice girder bridges at Belah and Deepdale. As a consequence the heavier trains were double-headed. 'If only we'd been born five years earlier!'

Before long, the wind freshened up from the south and it began to rain. The wind roared up through the confines of the Lune Gorge and through the station with constant force, carrying with it the 'horizontal rain' renowned in this area. For a time we had to take shelter on the leeward side of the station buildings, or in the stairwell on the down platform. Despite the rain it was possible to take some photos of 'Standard 4' 4-6-0 No 75026 pottering about with a breakdown crane in what remained of the old NER goods yard. Some trains passed on the main line, mostly southbound, but it was useless trying to record the one down freight that turned up. It was headed by a 'Brit', which pulled up for a bank engine. Except for No 75032 leaving the shed, and the exchange of whistles between it and the 'Brit', the wind didn't allow any sound to reach the microphone as the pair set off from Loups Fell. Meantime, No 75026, which incidentally was one of a few 'Standard 4s' to receive a double chimney, trundled through the station with the breakdown crane to gain entry to the depot yard. Notwithstanding one or two 'hiccups', there then started one of those sequences that constitutes the tape-recordist's dream.

Having descended from Shap, 'Black 5' No 44878 halted its partially fitted and lengthy freight in the station to take water. (Good judgement here by the driver, as he stopped his train with the tender filler opposite the water crane.) Its tender replenished, the engine then eased its train on the move, and we thought that was that. At this point I needed a change of film, but for some reason I'd left all my fresh films in the car. Leaving Chris on the down platform, I made for the footbridge. On reaching the top of the stairs I noticed that No 44878 had stopped its train clear of the station.

'Stay where you are,' I thought to myself. 'She's going to reverse into the yard.' And I switched on my recorder. Just then Chris came thudding up the stone steps in his wellies, the stairwell acting like a huge echo chamber so that each 'thud' went booming into my microphone!

'Shhhhhh!'

'Oh, sorry!' he whispered, and quietly made his way to the island platform. What resulted was a super recording of the 'Black 5', the southerly wind enhancing the sound waves, to the background of the rumbling and clanking of goods wagons as they entered the old NER yard on the far side of the station. I had now run out of tape as well as film. Back at the car I'd just loaded a new tape when came the shrill sound of a 'Brit' chime whistle. It belonged to none other than No 70013 *Oliver Cromwell*, hurtling around the curve from Loups Fell. So, with recorder switched on, I ran hell for leather to the footbridge, but managed only a third-rate recording, despite capturing 'Black 5' No 45279 powering a parcels train northward into the bargain. Thankfully, Chris managed to snap 'Olly Crom' from the down platform. So much for the 'hiccups'. There was better yet to come.

More horizontal rain started to blow up from the south, so we both ventured back onto the down platform, sticking as close as possible to the wall at the south end. 'Brit' No 70024 *Vulcan* and 9F 2-10-0 No 92004 both rushed through with up freights before No 44878 was signalled away. As it eased its train out onto the main line, a Brush Type 4 (class 47) diesel hurtled northward through the station with a down express. The 'Black 5' was then really opened up. Once again the wind played its part, bringing back the sound of the engine for some considerable time, during which the starter signal clattered 'on' and a railwayman remarked (politely) about the weather as he passed. Background sounds to all this were provided from the engine shed behind the wall. Superb stuff!

Next, after capturing an 8F 2-8-0 'taking off' from Loups Fell – and almost leaving the bank engine standing ! – Chris expressed a desire to visit the Settle-Carlisle line over at Ais Gill. So we set off along the old A685 towards Kirkby Stephen.[42] The visit was not at all profitable, with only a 'Black 5' materialising, heading up to a rain-sodden summit with a solitary open wagon and a brake-van.

Back on the WCML, another drama was about to unfold. Chris and I arrived back at Tebay just in time to see 'Brit' No 70035 *Rudyard Kipling* leading a freight out of the down loop to the south. This was a case for an 'about turn', and we were soon haring along the Orton road, destination Scout Green. I parked close to the little signal box just as the 'Pacific' emerged from the road bridge near Greenholme. As well as providing an intermediate block post for trains on the bank, this tiny box controlled a level crossing[43] for the narrow lane where I was parked. This lane led back up the fellside to the direct road from Orton to Shap. Although the rain had by now ceased, the wind was gusting quite strongly at times. With no time to test for interference from the wind, I quickly secured the microphone to one of the windscreen wipers and, hoping for the best, nipped up onto the trackside with Chris to join a few other lineside observers.

The 'Brit' seemed to be limping, with clouds of steam emitting from its front end. To our surprise, and no doubt to the consternation of the driver, the Scout Green signalman kept his signal at 'danger'. The driver hung on the whistle a few times, but to no avail; the signalman had to deliver a written message to him. I guess there was a feeling of apprehension all round as to how this ailing 'Brit' would restart its train, notwithstanding the bank engine at the rear. There wasn't a problem, although great clouds of steam appeared. But without a trace of a slip, *Rudyard Kipling* got steadily on the move again, ably assisted by No 75037. The total duration of this recording is just under 10 minutes.

Next came a no-nonsense ascent by 'Black 5' No 44834 with No 75037 again assisting at the rear. But then came another little drama. Another train was on the tail of the 'Black 5', but it didn't seem to have a banker. Dead right! Class 9F 2-10-0 No 92208 was tackling the bank solo with a fairly long freight. It began to slow down noticeably on the long left-hand bend between Greenholme and Scout Green, and was

---

[42] The 'new' A685 utilises the trackbed of the old NER line for most of the way.

[43] The crossing was closed following electrification of the WCML.

almost down to walking pace when No 75037 dashed past it, returning to Tebay after assisting No 44834. Coming off the bend, No 92208 amazingly accelerated its train and really hammered past the recorder. The shallow cutting by the signal box and the few trees that graced the lineside just here all enhanced the sound of the exhaust to varying degrees, as the engine forged onward towards Shap Wells. It treated with contempt an unsecured brake handle on one of the wagons, which wasn't exactly helping matters by bouncing up and down, as if attempting to retard the train's progress.

No 92208 was heard for some time after passing Scout Green. It would have been passing Shap Wells when another train came bounding round the curve from Greenholme. This turned out to be another parcels train, headed by 'Brit' No 70022 *Tornado* galloping up single-handed. Once again the driver hung onto the whistle, but the Scout Green signal wasn't 'pulled off' until the train came off the curve, and No 70022 then powered past. There was repeated whistling again, this time for the Shap Wells signal. Alas, the 'Britannia' shut off steam, so No 92208 was obviously having a struggle on the final stages of the climb. After a lull, 9F 2-10-0 No 92017 headed a lengthy mineral train, banked once more by No 75037. I recorded this one from close to the trackside, and as a result it is not one of my favourite recordings. Positioning the recorder at least 50 yards from the track gave better results, since there was not such a severe change in volume as experienced when recording from close to the trackside. We then concluded our day with 'Black 5' No 45135 storming the bank with yet another parcels train, rain beginning to fall again during its passage.

Chris and I had been in the area for about 10 hours, and didn't we know it? Nevertheless, we returned home well contented with our efforts for the day. But what about the early morning birdsong I'd hoped to record? We were not early enough. I did manage to include a few bellows from cattle when recording No 45212, together with a herdsman and his collie, out to round them up. A few sheep starred as 'extras' on some recordings made later in the day at Scout Green.

I returned to Shap myself the following weekend, but by way of Ais Gill. In conversation during our visit to Leeds, Chris and I learned that during the summer 'Jubilee' 4-6-0s had been seen hauling a passenger train over the Settle-Carlisle route. This was the Saturdays-only 10.17am Leeds-Glasgow service, which the 'Jubilee' hauled as far as Carlisle. By now there were just two of these locos surviving, Nos 45562 *Alberta* and 45593 *Kolhapur*. The first weekend in September, the final weekend before the cessation of the summer timetable, was possibly my last chance to record one of these three-cylindered LMS 4-6-0s before they were withdrawn.

On that wild, blustery Saturday, I got to Selside in good time to see the train, but when it came what should be heading it? Not a 'Jubilee', but a 'Peak' diesel, either a Class 45 or 46. 'You can't win 'em all.' But drat it! I determined that I hadn't come all this way for nothing, so headed up to Ais Gill in the hope of recording one of the Lazonby (Long Meg)–Widnes anhydrite trains. Not as much freight ran at weekends in those days, but on the way north I caught sight of 9F 2-10-0 No 92017 heading south near Ribblehead with a freight – not one of the anhydrite trains though.

At Ais Gill I chose to record just beyond the summit, at the now hallowed location where the Kirkby Stephen road crosses the line, and waited. Looking to the north, the line sweeps round to the right, then is carried on a ledge along the slopes of Mallerstang Common below Wild Boar Fell. At Ais Gill the wind on this day seemed to swirl around unpredictably, and during the long period of waiting I became a little apprehensive as to what sort of recording would materialise. I needn't have worried. Hitting on the idea of placing the microphone in my camera bag brought terrific results. The long-expected freight eventually appeared from round Wild Boar Fell. To a background of the wind rustling the long grasses surrounding the microphone, the exhaust of the locomotive, 9F 2-10-0 No 92077, was carried in alternating waves of sound across the landscape from Mallerstang. Distances are deceiving in the vastness of mountainous country such as this, and a full 4 minutes passed as the big 9F slogged up the 1 in 100 towards me and emerged from under the road bridge. With the summit now only half a mile away, the engine accelerated a little before the regulator was eased for the run down through Shotlock Hill and Moorcock tunnels. After these the train would swing to the right across Dandry Mire Viaduct to pass through Garsdale station and on towards Blea Moor Tunnel and Ribblehead.

On that same day another piece of history was about to be made on the WCML, with the passing of the last express passenger train rostered for steam haulage over Shap. So, flushed with my success at Ais Gill, I headed off westward along the A685, finishing up at Scout Green – where else? The wind was still pretty fresh, but it had broken up the clouds to give plenty of sunshine with some fluffy white clouds specially for photographers; and the tape recordist could pick up the sound of telegraph wires humming in the strong wind, close to the bridge spanning the little lane from Orton. Such was the setting for 'Brit' No 70025 *Western Star* as it came, right on cue, roaring up the bank with its six-coach train.

Not a great deal was achieved that day, but to revamp a certain catchphrase, 'Never mind the quantity, feel the quality'. I returned home contented with the results attained. Despite the very limited variety of locomotive types now surviving, I had thoroughly enjoyed my tape-recording exploits. At home I could connect my tape recorder to the speaker in our radiogram, and drive my parents to despair with 'Sounds of Shap', etc. Dad didn't mind up to a point, as he was interested himself, but it goes without saying that I had to limit my listening to when it was convenient. The sleeve notes that accompanied the Argo records stirred the imagination as to the setting for each recording. Listening to my own recordings took me back to the time and place I made them. Shutting my eyes, I was virtually there, waiting for all the background sounds that helped to set the scene in my mind's eye.

Following its busy involvement with the Paddington-Birkenhead specials in March, preserved *Clun Castle* was in demand for more special workings during September. In the wake of its run up the ECML between King's Cross and Gateshead[44] earlier in the month, the 'Castle' was in use again on the 17th hauling an Ian Allan special from King's Cross to Leeds. Chris and I nipped over to Holbeck shed to see it being serviced, and later, at Beeston on the outskirts of the city, saw it heading its train over GNR metals back to London. An overcast day, the light by now was inadequate for photography but, needless to say, a good recording resulted, my first of a 'Castle' 4-6-0.

For the weekend at the turn of the month, the business continued for *Clun Castle*. The A4 Locomotive Society Ltd ran two trains between Peterborough and Carlisle, via Leeds and the Settle-Carlisle line. That meant Ais Gill was in the offing, with the prospect of seeing both *Sir Nigel Gresley* and *Clun Castle* in one day. But which day, Saturday or Sunday? Chris, who was now a member of the A4 Society, was determined to be 'in' on this particular weekend, but could only make it on the Sunday. For me, the temptation to go north on the Saturday as well was too great. I could nip over to the Settle-Carlisle by way of Shap.

I was at Scout Green by about 9.00am. The weather was atrocious – over the whole weekend as it happened. Conditions were indeed similar to those I'd experienced with Chris in August, so I knew that some pretty dramatic recordings could result in adverse weather. Awaiting the first train, I sat in the car and watched the 'horizontal rain' sweeping across the landscape from the south-west. I tried to imagine the scene when the railway was being constructed. These were the same hills the railway builders had to negotiate, and my heart went to those hardy individuals who would have been bombarded by the same sort of weather (and worse) from which I was thankfully sheltering in my car. Not surprisingly, I was

[44] *Clun Castle* was barred from entering Newcastle Central, having failed clearance tests in August. A 'K1' 2-6-0 relieved the 4-6-0 at Gateshead to take the train on to its destination.

the only soul around, save for the Scout Green signalman. Even the sheep had vanished, no doubt to seek what shelter they could find on the lee side of some wall or other. If you wanted solitude, this was a good place to be right now.

Wedging my microphone in one of the windows, I positioned the car appropriately to minimise interference from wind and rain. The first recording was a gem: a double-chimneyed 9F 2-10-0 (whose number was unreadable) heading a train comprising 44 mineral wagons and a brake-van, and banked by the double-chimneyed Class 4, No 75026. I couldn't have asked for better. Despite the bad light and the sweeping rain, I did get a photo of the whole ensemble from the car. After that, I ventured up to the signal box, but the person on duty showed no leaning towards hospitality. No chance of a chat by a coal fire today, so I hurried back to my car, bemoaning the fact that I'd received a soaking for my trouble! The rain abated later on, and 'Black 5' No 44775 hammered up with another freight. (Goodness knows why the driver had summoned the assistance of a banker. No 75032 was cruising, just about keeping pace with the brake-van!)

The rain had started again when I got to Tebay station. What were the recording prospects on this day? I was in luck. No 92128, one of the 9F 2-10-0s fitted with a single chimney, restarted its freight train from the loop south of the station. Whistling up for a banker, it pulled through the wet and windswept station. No 75026 answered the call. Once again I was thwarted as I tried to record the two engines getting the train on the move, the wind playing its part adversely.

Now it was time to head for the Settle-Carlisle line to see the first of the specials from Peterborough, which would be headed by *Clun Castle*. Although the new road is much faster, it was quite a pleasant drive along the old A685 through Kelleth and Wath to Ravenstonedale. The railway trackbed was still intact at this time and, together with the River Lune, it paralleled the road almost as far as Ravenstonedale. From here the road, since modernised, still climbs over Ash Fell before dropping down to Kirkby Stephen, passing under the Midland line from Settle about 1½ miles west of the town. En route the rain continued relentlessly. Just before entering the town a road to the right signposted 'Nateby' leads to Ais Gill. I didn't stop here today, though, as my destination was Dent station. I continued to Garsdale station, from where the 'coal road' climbs steeply along Widdale Fell before dropping down even more steeply to join the Ribblehead-Dent road. About halfway down is Dent station.

There was plenty of room to park in the station yard. Although there were a number of folk around to watch the special, it didn't compare with the crowds that were to frequent such vantage points in the years from

1978, the year steam returned to the Settle-Carlisle in the preservation era. Miraculously, the rain stopped briefly as two freights to passed, 'Black 5' No 45145 heading south and 8F 2-8-0 No 48077 passing northbound. Then, guess what? More rain, and with a vengeance. I took shelter under one of the three arches of the bridge carrying the 'coal road' across the line, finding myself completely out of the wind at the same time. So far so good, for tape-recording at least, but the light deteriorated unbelievably, making photography rather difficult. I decided to pan the train and snap it at 1/125th second as it tore towards me through the station, the lens set wide open at f2.8. The result is unusual, but very pleasing.

Up at Ais Gill it was time for a butty break before *Sir Nigel Gresley* appeared with the return leg to Peterborough. The rain stopped. Better pick my spot like everyone else. However, many of us were caught completely by surprise as, oh so quietly, 'Jubilee' 4-6-0 No 45562 *Alberta* suddenly emerged from the shallow cutting at the summit. There was no time to grab my camera for a photo, so I just switched on my recorder, microphone in hand, as *Alberta* clinked away down the hill with its freight.

Sigh! Pity I hadn't 'stayed for tea' at Dent station.

A good many more spectators were now gathering, taking up positions for their photographs and recordings. Then the heavens opened once again, sending us all scurrying back to our cars. Time progressed, and the rain stayed away as *Sir Nigel* rounded the bend from Birkett. Unfortunately I didn't get such a good photo, but the tape recording is superb. The engine surprised many with its deep-toned chime whistle, the sound of which came loud and clear across the valley in contrast to the loco's exhaust chattering away with comparative softness. The whistle had obviously been fitted since I rode behind *Sir Nigel* with Chris in April. Regretfully (from a personal view) this whistle was later removed in favour of one giving the standard 'A4' chime.

A glutton for punishment, I was back on the S&C with Chris for the Sunday trains, and the weather was just as foul. We decided to head for Kingmoor shed, hoping to photograph *Clun Castle* in preparation, but found our way barred at the end of the access track from Etterby Road. British Transport Police were patrolling the site. In the distance we could see No 7029 standing outside the shed, but it hadn't yet been turned to face south. So it was back to Ais Gill for the pair of us after this fruitless episode. Who would spend hours on a wet Sunday waiting for just two trains? Thousands would. Little did we know that, when steam returned to the S&C in 1978, the tradition would continue, even beyond the Millennium. The wait in driving rain for *Sir Nigel Gresley* at Shotlock Hill Tunnel soaked us to the extent of the proverbial drowned rats, all the worse as the train was half an hour late. All too quickly, it came and was gone. Pictures and recordings were 'in the cans'.

One down, one to go. It was waiting time again. But the light was fading fast, aided and abetted by the inclement weather, not really good enough for photography. Another hefty downpour sent everyone scurrying back to their cars, and there we stayed, rather fed up. My tape recording had better be good! It was. The wait was worth the trouble. At around 5.30pm *Clun Castle* came forging up the hill with the final leg of the two-day specials. It whistled triumphantly as it passed us and strode on towards the summit. Photographically, all we had were some rather underexposed broadside pictures.

Madness prevailed! I couldn't resist sampling what Shap had to offer following the closure of Crewe South depot in early November. I waited opposite Loups Fell, and waited a long time. The line seemed absolutely dead – nothing was coming north nor going south. There was no activity around the engine shed either, until at long last one of the 'Standard 4' 4-6-0s dragged out a train of hoppers from the sidings and headed away up towards Shap.

Enquiries at Tebay station revealed that a derailment had occurred near Shap Summit early in the day, and the 'Standard 4' was taking up ballast to pack the realigned trackwork. Undaunted, I went up to Scout Green. Apart from Class 47-hauled passenger trains, two diesel-hauled freights appeared with steam bankers. One was headed by a Class 40, the other by a 25. The magic had gone. I went home.

Postscript: on reflection

There wasn't anywhere near the variety of motive power that existed in Peter Handford's tape-recording days. In the North West, with the preserved examples excepted, I had been able to record just six different types of steam engine: 'Britannia' 4-6-2s, LMS Class 5 4-6-0s and 8F 2-8-0s, Standard Class 9F 2-10-0s, and Standard 4-6-0s of Classes 4 and 5. My one big regret was that I wasn't able to record any Southern steam. Steam had come to an end on the Southern Region during July, thus scotching any ideas I might have had about heading down south to tape-record a few examples, and now there would be no more forays north by Bulleid 'Pacifics' hauling enthusiasts' trains. As related above, I got some 2-6-4Ts on tape, but if I'd been a little more enterprising I could have obtained sounds of the last of the LNER 'B1' and LMS 'Jubilee' 4-6-0s that were operating out of Leeds. It was too late for the 'B1s', but an opportunity arose in October to record both of the surviving 'Jubilees' on the same day.

During 1967 there was an increase in the number of steam-hauled railtours run for enthusiasts. At this 11th hour were born a number of locomotive preservation societies, with the intention of saving this engine or that. They placed advertisements in the railway journals, begging readers to join. Some of the railtours were promoted for the benefit of raising funds for the various projects. One such was the Jubilee Railway Society, whose aim was to preserve either *Alberta* or *Kolhapur*. This society had already run a railtour special over Shap with *Alberta* in February 1967, and was now advertising in the railway press a repeat run for September, using the same engine. I rather fancied that, and booked for the trip. In the event, a train guards' strike led to postponement of the train until 7 October. As I had already booked onto two tours for the following weekend, I would now have to endure, if that is the right word, three railtours in nine days.

The Jubilee Railway Society's train originated at Bradford Exchange, and would pick me up at Manchester after traversing the Pennines over LYR metals through Halifax and Rochdale. Meanwhile, Chris had booked onto another railtour that was to run on the same day. His train started from Stockport Edgeley, so I volunteered to drop him off there before heading off into Manchester for my train. I watched his train depart behind No 70013 *Oliver Cromwell*, then sought a multi-storey car park in the big city. A day's parking cost 10 shillings, I recall.

My train rolled into Manchester Victoria with No 45562 *Alberta* at the head as anticipated. At the time the engine seemed to be everybody's favourite of the two surviving 'Jubilees'. The train was made up of six coaches, one of those at the centre being reserved for passengers boarding at Manchester. However, I wanted to tape-record, so headed off through the corridors to the first coach to record at a drop-down window.

The train followed the LYR route via Bolton and Chorley, and at Euxton Junction we joined the WCML. The 'Jubilee' made a spirited run with its six coaches, making good speed on the easy stretches of the route. However, with such a light load there hadn't been much for my tape recorder to hear from the soft three-cylinder exhaust. The northern fells would change all that.

But first there was a stop at Carnforth to enjoy. Permission had been obtained for us to roam around Carnforth shed, where we were greeted by the presence of *Oliver Cromwell*. The 'Brit' had been relieved here by a 'Black 5' 4-6-0, which then took Chris's train around the Cumbrian Coast to Ravenglass (where its passengers were to enjoy a ride to Dalegarth on the narrow-gauge Ravenglass & Eskdale Railway). Otherwise the shed was host to some Standard Class 4 4-6-0s, together with the inevitable 'Black 5' 4-6-0s, 8F 2-8-0s and 9F 2-10-0s. Depressingly, the 'back road' contained some withdrawn engines, more of the same.

The shed 'done', some of us reboarded our train, which was parked at the still open main-line platform. While awaiting departure, steam proved to be very much in evidence on the main line. 'Black 5' No 44902 drew up on the up line and stopped in the station; on leaving, we passed another Class 5 recovering from a signal check and, further on at Milnthorpe, a 9F 2-10-0 passed heading another up freight – good tape-recording material.

Following the assault of Grayrigg bank, we descended at speed into the Lune Gorge to pick up water from the famous troughs on the level stretch at Dillicar. Our fireman was a little late in raising the water scoop under the tender, so as the tender tank became full to overflowing I was drenched as the water cascaded in through the open window! I had had no option but to curtail my recording for a little while and shut the window. *Alberta* then made a full-blooded assault on Shap, but it soon became evident that the engine was mechanically run down, as speed had fallen away considerably by the time the summit was reached. Thoughts were evoked of stories from bygone years, when 'Jubilee' 4-6-0s took nine- and ten-coach trains up Shap unaided. But given the circumstances, this was a game performance by *Alberta*.

At Carlisle time was allowed to visit Kingmoor shed. A sunny autumn day resulted in some pleasing photographs taken on shed, particularly of our engine awaiting its turn in the queue for servicing. Ahead of it was 'Brit' No 70012 *John of Gaunt*. Time to return to Citadel station came all too soon, but there was the assault of the climb to Ais Gill to look forward to.

Having passed Appleby, *Alberta* was going 'great guns' when suddenly her driver eased up on the regulator. Rumours began circulating. Was there trouble with the injectors? Or maybe the engine was becoming winded on the big climb. We crawled up to Kirkby Stephen station, where the opportunity was taken to make an unscheduled stop to take on water. So perhaps *Alberta* had used more water than was anticipated. Anyway, after about 20 minutes we set off and our 'Jubilee' breasted Ais Gill Summit in good style.

Somewhere between Skipton and Leeds news spread through the train that *Kolhapur* was to take us on the final leg from Leeds to Bradford. This surprised a good many of us, myself included, for I was prepared to catch a service train directly from Leeds back to Manchester. But I couldn't forsake a run behind the other remaining 'Jubilee'. What a bonus!

Darkness had fallen by the time we reached Leeds. Sure enough, there was No 45593 *Kolhapur* waiting to back onto the rear of our train. The train almost emptied at Leeds, as some unfortunate individuals had long-distance connections to make; thus I had the luxury of a choice of seats from which to tape-record. The route to Bradford was the same as that taken by No 42066 in August, except that this time there was no stop at New Pudsey. Once clear of the maze of pointwork out of Leeds, *Kolhapur* was opened up. We then heard that beautiful six-beat rhythm of an LMS three-cylinder engine in synchronisation with the clonk-clonk of its connecting rods. When steam was shut off for the descent into Bradford, other sounds were allowed to take over – the 'rat-tat-tat tat-tat' as the tender wheels and front coach bogie clattered over the rail joints. Sophisticated syncopation!

At Bradford it was difficult to let go once again, and I recorded *Kolhapur* backing out the empty stock, its exhaust reverberating around the cavernous interior of the station. I'd had a marvellous day but, being rather shattered, was glad to find a convenient DMU that would take me back to Manchester. The raison d'être was now over and done with. In pitch darkness, save for the occasional lights from habitation and road lamps, the journey seemed to take an interminable time. My thoughts turned to wondering how Chris had fared on his railtour; would I have to wait, and for how long, before we were reunited? I needn't have worried. Having alighted from the DMU, the shrill chime of *Oliver Cromwell's* whistle greeted my ears. Having set down passengers at Exchange station, the 'Pacific' appeared, marching its train along the centre road through Victoria en route to Stockport.

Chris had had a reasonable day, and achieved some nice cine-film footage on the Ravenglass & Eskdale Railway. *Oliver Cromwell's* performance, though, hadn't been up to expectation, until a change of crew at Preston produced some fireworks on the final leg back to Manchester.

So the end of another era had come and gone, for both *Alberta* and *Kolhapur* were officially withdrawn on that night. *Alberta*, however, was used to steam-heat the stock of the Royal Train later in October, during stabling near Harrogate. The Jubilee Railway Society eventually secured *Kolhapur* for preservation, and in 1968 the society became associated with 7029 Clun Castle Ltd, custodians of the engine I was to ride behind the following weekend.

The North West branch of the Locomotive Club of Great Britain promoted the railtour. Although the train commenced from Liverpool, we had to wait until we got to Preston before enjoying the privilege of having *Clun Castle* on the front. Initially we were to sample the horsepower of 9F 2-10-0 No 92091. The itinerary was just as varied. Departing from Liverpool's Exchange station on a gloomy, windy morning, the 9F took us along the electrified line to Southport. There the avoiding line was used and we proceeded through Wigan Wallgate, Black Rod and Chorley to join the WCML at Euxton Junction.

Clun Castle was waiting at Preston, but before we departed, catastrophe! My recordings of No 92091 were intermittent, sometimes crackly, indicating that there was a break in the microphone lead. Fortunately Chris was also recording, so all was not lost. Or was it? As it unfolded, the run seemed to develop into an anticlimax. We had looked forward to this trip behind No 7029, the first time a 'Castle' had run up the WCML since the LMS trials of 1926.[45] The LCGB had hoped that bookings would have filled ten coaches, but in the event only seven proved necessary. As with my run behind *Alberta*, with such a light load for a Class 7P locomotive there was not much voice from *Clun Castle* until we got into the hills. Even then the 'Castle' just seemed to 'walk' over them. Then, with the eagerly awaited climb to Shap looming, insult was added to injury. As the train cleared Loups Fell and swung right towards Greenholme, a gale-force wind blew across from the west. It hit the train broadside, forcing rain through the open window to which Chris's microphone was secured. With the window now practically shut, only minimal sound from the engine could be picked up by his tape recorder. Not funny at the time, but the rain crackling on the microphone is now recalled with some amusement.

At Carlisle the sun had broken through the clouds and shone for the rest of the afternoon. Avoiding the station, our train took the goods lines, from where Ivatt 'Mogul' No 43121 took over for a tour over local lines as far as Longtown and Riddings Junction near the Scottish border. Returning to Carlisle via the goods lines again, we proceeded onto the Newcastle lines and Petteril Bridge, where No 43121 ran round the train before dragging us back into Citadel station. *Clun Castle*, having been serviced at Kingmoor MPD (and how some of us wished we could have been there), we set off in glorious sunshine

---

[45] The LMS borrowed the GWR's No 5000 *Launceston Castle* in an effort to determine a suitable 4-6-0 design for its principal expresses. The end result was the 'Royal Scot' Class 4-6-0s of completely contrasting design.

along the Settle-Carlisle line. The late-afternoon sun enabled Chris to obtain some fine cine shots of our engine from the rear of the train, as we followed the River Eden towards Appleby. At Appleby there was a stop for photographs and for *Clun* to take on water for a non-stop run to Hellifield. Up front, the coaches were rather crowded with tape-recordists. Our seats were now at the rear of the train, and it was 'every man for himself' to get a decent position for recording. Once again, the 'Castle' was not particularly extended, so we decided that recording was now more trouble than it was worth, and retired to the back coach.

At Hellifield *Clun Castle* was relieved by yet another 9F 2-10-0 for the run to Liverpool. There was a little matter of dragging brakes on the train at Blackburn; other than that, the run to Liverpool, via Wigan Wallgate and the direct line through Kirkby, was incident-free.

The last of my trio of railtours was an SLS affair. Much to my shame, it was now six years since my one and only tour with this honourable organisation. There was no Chris this time as I headed for Crewe to join the train. This was my first ride behind *Oliver Cromwell*, which provided the motive power for the ten coaches. At least a reasonable load, I thought. Our destination was Carlisle, out and back via the S&C line. The run was also my first over the line in the northbound direction, albeit from the rear coach. Thus, for me, the run was about as inspiring as the weather, which, like the previous day, had started on the dull side. The only incident of note was a stop near Selside for the driver to check the engine's big ends, following suspicion that one of them was running hot. All was well, though, and the 'Brit' restarted its train without any fuss.

As with our run behind *Sir Nigel Gresley* in April, the train ran directly to Kingmoor shed. I don't know what Carlisle's secret was, but the sun shone once again as the shed became swamped with photographers. My tape recorder was back in action with a new jack plug on the microphone lead. Sitting in the first coach on the return run, there was a distinct fore-and-aft sensation from the engine, a result of being driven very hard with the reverser wound back to give a short steam cut-off in the cylinders. I wasn't disappointed with the sounds! A water stop at Hellifield took an interminable time, and this was followed by a frustrating run all the way down to Wigan, where we were held at signals. However, our spirits were uplifted when there came a climax to the whole run: 84mph beyond Weaver Junction, as our driver informed us on arrival at Crewe. Busy weekend, wasn't it?

18
Countdown

While the Southern Region and North Eastern Region sheds had closed their doors to steam during 1967, the New Year dawned with the closure of the sheds at Carlisle Kingmoor, Tebay and Workington on the LMR. What was left was a pocket of 13 working steam sheds in the North West bounded within the triangle formed by Carnforth, Liverpool and Stockport/Manchester. The remaining steam locomotives were generally not well cared for. 'Unkempt' would be a mild description of the appearance of most of them. Work-stained, and with their paintwork now more of a shade of grey than black, those that were left soldiered on until each was finally withdrawn. However, there was an anonymous band of enthusiasts who became known as the Midnight Neverers Association. Members of this dedicated bunch stole themselves onto selected steam sheds at the dead of night, specifically to clean up certain locomotives they knew would be out on the main lines hauling trains. The two 'Jubilee' 4-6-0s were just two cases in point, but the band's work also showed up on 'Black 5s' and 8F 2-8-0s. I'm sure I speak for many photographers in wishing to thank them for their efforts in providing a few clean engines to photograph.

One locomotive that didn't need MNA attention was 'Britannia' 'Pacific' No 70013 *Oliver Cromwell*. The rest of its class having been withdrawn from Kingmoor at the turn of the year, this engine was transferred to Carnforth, whose staff maintained it in a reasonable condition for use on special trains. Indeed, I don't believe it was used in general traffic at all during 1968.

Workington shed may have closed, but steam was still rostered along the Furness coast of Morecambe Bay as far as Barrow, where the now closed shed was still in use as a stabling point for steam locomotives. Notably, the 8.15am Barrow-Euston continued with steam haulage for some time into 1968. During March I made a point of travelling on this train, and duly booked my lodgings with my aunt and uncle in Dalton for the occasion. I was on the platform at Barrow in good time on a very foggy and damp morning. 8.15 came and went, and a station announcement informed a fairly large contingent of passengers that there had been an engine failure, and that it was anticipated that the train would depart about 20 minutes late.

'That's it,' I thought. 'Diesel haulage!'

But no. What eventually loomed out of the fog was another 'Black 5', No 45342. I was elated and bagged the front seating bay in the first coach. The best recordings produced on this run followed the start from Dalton station and the climb to Lindal summit. The train stopped at all stations to Carnforth, following which there was a spirited run to Lancaster, where I alighted. Despite the conditions, No 45342 lost no more time on the run. At Lancaster the 'Black 5' was removed, and its train was combined with another from Carlisle and taken forward to London by a Class 47 diesel. I decided to stay on at Lancaster, as the fog began to clear. But apart from watching another 'Black 5', No 45001, shunting in the yard opposite, there was nothing worth recording or photographing, so I returned straight to Dalton. Decisions, decisions! How I rue my decision not to stop off at Carnforth on the way.

Back in January Chris and I had made it our business to go and see the 8.15am ex-Barrow from the lineside. Thus early on a dull and cold morning we set off for Grange-over-Sands. The train appeared right on cue, headed by 'Black 5' No 45287, and we duly photographed it from the footbridge east of the station.

Having got the main attraction over and done with, we meandered off to Carnforth. Tebay's 'Standard 4' 4-6-0s had migrated here to join others of their class, and we hoped to see one or two of them in action. No such luck. Anything that moved was either a 'Black 5' or a 9F 2-10-0. Disappointingly, there was nothing to provide good material for photography or tape-recording, so off we sped down the M6 to Lostock Hall MPD. Approaching the shed, we caught sight of a 9F 2-10-0 heading a freight onto the Blackburn line.

'Turn round! Turn round!' Chris urged. 'We can get that further up.'

We retraced our steps, and crossed the motorway junction whence we had come. With Chris directing me from a Bartholomew's half-inch map, we motored along various lanes, eventually stumbling upon a level crossing about 1¼ miles from Hoghton summit, well ahead of the train. A number of cars were already parked in the narrow lane on either side of the crossing, their occupants by now dotted about the embankments awaiting passage of the 9F. The engine, which was devoid of a front number plate, was leaking steam profusely at the front end, a common malady from which many engines were now suffering through lack of maintenance. It clambered past up the 1 in 99/101 with its load, shrouded along its offside by the escaping steam.

At this time a cluster of trees occupied an area on the south side of the line close to the crossing, and these produced a marvellous baffling effect on the sound of the 9F's exhaust, as the engine approached from

Bamber Bridge. A crossing-keeper resided in the cottage just across the road, and he manually operated the gates whenever a train was due. At night, however, the gates were generally closed to road traffic. Today the trees have gone, leaving a green field, and the crossing now has lifting barriers. They are normally closed to road traffic, which is pretty infrequent (except when steam railtours are run up the line!), and a phone call to the signalman at Bamber Bridge is required before vehicles can cross the line.

I was impressed with my tape recording, and decided to return and explore this line further for alternative photographic and recording locations. February brought a fair quantity of snow, something that comes when you least want it, and rarely at a convenient time when you could make good use of it for some creative photography. Fortunately, after a midweek fall, the weather settled to give a fine, clear weekend, and the temperature dropped to maintain a good covering of snow over the countryside. I went back to the Blackburn line, but the day was to prove disastrous as far as tape-recording was concerned.

Another lane branches off eastward from close to the level crossing, and runs more or less parallel with the railway for about a mile. Roughly halfway along I set up the recorder in the car for a train that was on its way up from Bamber Bridge. I got a reasonable photo of the engine, another anonymous 9F 2-10-0, but when I returned to the car – oh, woe was I! Somehow I must have caught the microphone lead on closing the car door, for I found it unplugged from the recorder. Never mind. Onward to Hoghton summit.

Close to Hoghton Towers[46] a cul-de-sac crosses the railway just below the actual summit. From the bridge there was an excellent view of the line curving away to the west, under a farm access bridge and away down towards Bamber Bridge. (Today the view is severely restricted by 30 years' growth of trees on the railway embankment.) The sun continued to shine as another train plodded up the hill, and at nearby Hoghton church bell-ringing practice was in progress, a nice little background sound to accompany the train. This time the engine was 8F 2-8-0 No 48258, and my photos, both colour and monochrome, turned out excellently. But as for the tape recording – I guess the recorder's motor must have been suffering from frostbite! The intense cold had caused it to run erratically during the recording so that, upon playback, bouts of wheelslip seemed to emanate from the 8F, while the background bell ringing, as reproduced, would have turned the stomach of any campanologist!

My photograph of this train led to a new friendship, but there is a

[46] Here, at a banquet in 1617, King James I knighted a portion of steak, which gave us the name 'sirloin'.

strange twist to the tale. I entered a few photographs, including the one of No 48258, for a competition sponsored by the Ian Allan journal *Railway World*. While I didn't win, the effort sparked off a friendship that lasts to this day. Alan was one of the sorters engaged by the organisers. He liked my photo of the 8F at Hoghton, and requested a print for himself. A correspondence commenced, and discussions turned to tape-recording. After swapping lists of our best recordings, we each dubbed selected recordings onto fresh tapes and duly exchanged them. Judging from the engine numbers on Alan's lists, I realised that he was 'on Shap' during that same wild day at the end of August as Chris and myself! And it just so happened that Alan briefly visited Scout Green when we were hurtling back and forth on our unprofitable visit to Ais Gill![47]

One night in March I'd gone to the Blackburn line after work with Chris, when once again I was scared out of my wits when tape-recording. First, we attempted some night photography at Lostock Hall shed, following which we tape-recorded one of the surviving steam-worked passenger trains, the 17.25 Glasgow-Liverpool. This left Preston at 21.25, and we taped it traversing the chord connecting the WCML with the LYR line from Preston to Liverpool. As at Warrington in 1967, the night was starry but without a moon to light our way. Up at the little level crossing on the climb to Hoghton there was only the faint glimmer from a window of the crossing-keeper's cottage in the otherwise pitch darkness. Chris and I separated as we heard a train start down in the Farrington/Lostock Hall area. By torchlight I made my way onto the trackside close to the crossing. Shortly afterwards there was a 'swishing' noise, which seemed to come from all around me. I momentarily froze. Anyway, the 8F clambered past with its lengthy train, after which a Preston-bound DMU came hurtling down the hill. Ah! Another of those little strokes of luck that enhances many a recording. But what had caused that 'swishing' noise? It was a signal wire pulling 'off' the nearby Distant signal for the DMU. I'd missed it earlier, because the wire was covered with ballast, applied periodically over the years during track maintenance. The sound of the wire sliding among the stones was quite 'stereophonic'!

Meantime, BR had relaxed its embargo on steam-hauled railtours, imposed in November 1967, although with one exception the ban continued on the use of preserved main-line locomotives on the network. That exception was 'A3' 'Pacific' *Flying Scotsman*, whose owner, Alan Pegler, had earlier signed a contract with BR allowing the use of his engine on BR's lines until 1973. Williams Deacon's Bank Club, whose

[47] I eventually met up with Alan in 1969, at an open day at the old Tyseley MPD (latterly known as the Birmingham Railway Museum).

railtour we had enjoyed with *Lamport & Holt Line* in November 1966, was first off the mark with another tour lined up for 17 March. A rather intricate itinerary was devised, and there were two trains involving six locomotives! Dad accompanied me for this one, but Chris decided he would catch a glimpse of us from the trackside somewhere en route.

On board train No 1, we enjoyed the voice of the 'A3' as far as Bolton, where 'Black 5' No 45290 was inserted behind it. The pair trundled, for that is the appropriate word, through Entwistle to Blackburn, and onward to Accrington. The spectacle of an 'A3' piloting a 'Black 5' may have proved interesting to lineside photographers – indeed, Chris snapped us near Entwistle – but there wasn't much material for those of us on board with a leaning for tape-recording; the load of ten coaches was insufficient to tax the motive power up front, despite some adverse gradients. From Accrington *Scotsman* was swapped for another 'Black 5', No 44899. This was an ex-Kingmoor engine, still clinging onto its bufferbeam snowplough[48], and it 'helped' No 45290 get us to Skipton over the now severed route via Colne. *Scotsman*, having turned meanwhile on the Accrington triangle, followed us to Skipton tender-first before hauling us single-handed once again to Carnforth. Departing from Skipton, we passed the second train waiting on the Colne line with two more 'Black 5s'. The inevitable *Oliver Cromwell* was the sixth engine involved in the day's activities.

At Carnforth everyone sampled the delights of watching the servicing of two 'Pacifics'. More depressing, however, was the awesome sight once again of more Standard 2-10-0s, 'Black 5s' and 8Fs lined up for scrap. For the return journey motive power was swapped between the two trains, so that we had No 70013 departing from Carnforth. For me this proved to be the highlight of the day, as the 'Brit' dragged our train around the sharply curved gradient out of the station and onto the old Furness & Midland Joint line, heading for Settle Junction and Skipton.

On 4 May 1968 steam activity was due to come to an end in Liverpool in respect of the sheds at Speke Junction and Edge Hill. Apart from a handful of recordings made at home, I hadn't really bothered with what was 'on my own doorstep'. Chris heard that Pighue Lane was worth a visit, so maybe here was a chance to redress the balance somewhat.

This road (need I add that it is known locally as 'Piggy Lane'?) was situated on the opposite side of the 'gridiron' embankment I first saw from the trains I used to ride between Broad Green and Lime Street. (Close by is Binns Road, where Hornby model trains were made at the works of Meccano Ltd.) There was scope at Pighue Lane for some excellent

---

[48] Probably a relic from its winter forages into Scotland, very likely to clear snow from the Waverley Route to Edinburgh.

tape-recording: the departure of main-line trains, arrivals climbing what we christened 'the hump' to the upper reception sidings at Olive Mount, and the shunting movements of wagons as they trundled under gravity down into the sorting sidings, clanging into other wagons already there. Within earshot of all this activity, streets of terraced housing abounded around the perimeter of the complex of lines, sidings and engine sheds. How could anyone sleep at night with the sporadic clatter of wagons and train movements going on? Speaking with folk from earlier generations reveals that they considered the railway's presence gave a sense of security. An air of satisfaction ('If we could hear the trains moving, the world was OK') would seem to have prevailed. I have to agree up to a point, having lived in a house backing onto a railway line.

To gain access from the south to the Edge Hill/Olive Mount complex, freight trains used a double track that diverged at Wavertree from the Crewe-Lime Street line. In the shape of a huge question mark, this line twisted around Edge Hill engine shed, then across the L&M tracks, emerging at mid-level from the hump opposite our Pighue Lane viewpoint. It then continued down-grade to the lower reception sidings at Edge Hill. From there, arrivals were either pushed or pulled up to the upper reception sidings at Olive Mount, from where wagons were uncoupled as required and allowed to roll down into the gridiron sidings.

After sorting at the gridiron, wagons were taken to local depots such as Spekeland Road (via the aforementioned circuitous route through the hump), Edge Hill Goods, or the Fruit & Vegetable Depot. Those destined for the docks were then marshalled into new trains for 'trip' working along the Bootle branch (see below). The procedure was reversed when wagonloads of imports were brought to Edge Hill for resorting into trains for destinations elsewhere. In bygone years, when some local stations still possessed a goods yard, wagons were despatched and empty wagons picked up and brought to the hump for resorting. By 1968 the pick-up goods trains had almost disappeared, and much of the docks traffic had fallen away, mainly in favour of road transport. Alexandra Dock had closed in January of the previous year.[49]

Pighue Lane spanned two lines that formed a giant triangle with the Liverpool & Manchester main line. One emerged from Olive Mount Tunnel underneath the upper reception sidings; the other connected with the L&M at the west-facing Bootle Branch Junction opposite the MPD and, after passing under both hump and Pighue Lane, joined the

[49] Canada Dock closed in 1982, but the survival of the Bootle branch was ensured by the opening of the Seaforth Container Depot, from where containers are moved to the Freightliner terminal at Garston.

Olive Mount connection at Edge Lane Junction. Known as the Bootle branch, this line continued northward through Bootle itself to serve the LNWR's Canada and Alexandra Docks, and also connected with the former LYR system of lines.

A further pair of tracks connected the Olive Mount line at Pighue Lane Junction to the reception/departure sidings at Edge Hill away to the west. Most of the trains that we saw, however, were to or from the Crewe line. Engines were invariably in good voice for the tape recorder as they climbed up from Edge Hill and swung away into the tunnel through the hump towards Wavertree.

The Bootle branch was also used by the 'through coaches' service to London Euston, mainly worked by Stanier Class 3 2-6-2Ts, which worked them to and from Lime Street. With the advent of electrification in 1960, the through coaches ceased, and Southport passengers were obliged to use a DMU service over the same route, changing at Lime Street for the London service.[50]

So what of my activities at Pighue Lane? The inevitable dark night figured once again, this time in March – cool, starlit, and with a gentle breeze coming up from the direction of Edge Hill. The stage was set for a dramatic recording of a 'Black 5' 4-6-0 setting out from the departure sidings with a southbound freight. The engine slipped on starting, but was soon into its stride, pounding up towards me. As the train approached wagons were heard thudding into each other in the sorting sidings, after rolling down gradients of 1 in 60/74, and a 350hp diesel shunter (Class 08) emerged from under the hump with a few vans, passing the 'Black 5' lower down. Finally, the '5' itself dived under the hump, providing a fitting climax to the recording.

By now I'd got every kind of background sound I could have wished for on my recordings. Road vehicles (inevitably), aeroplanes, people, dogs barking, a saw mill (on the Blackburn line), and church bells (well, almost) had all found their way onto my tapes; I'd even captured some early-morning birdsong on a couple of recordings made from my bedroom window prior to leaving for work. But there was one sound that I had not yet managed to record – thunder. We were experiencing quite a storm in Liverpool one evening at the end of April. It happened to be the final week for Liverpool steam, so I asked Dad if he fancied a run up to Pighue Lane.

'What! In this?' he queried.

I explained all, and off we went, arriving in about 10 minutes. The

---

[50] This arrangement ended in October 1977 when the underground electrics began serving Lime Street. Since then Southport passengers have had to change trains twice, using the Wirral Line services to connect with Lime Street.

rain was still falling 'like stair-rods', but – the thunder had moved on!

'Oh, well. Better tape than never!' I thought.

Dad hadn't been before, and I was certain he would be impressed with a sample of the action from Pighue Lane. Scope for photography was very limited here anyway, so I was quite content to just sit in the car and keep dry while recording.

Two freights in succession were pushed up the hump by 8F 2-8-0s Nos 48722 and 48715 respectively. Space in the reception sidings at the top seemed to be at a premium just now, as both trains were stopped on the incline, the 8Fs level with my recorder. In such wet conditions I expected some wheel-slipping when they restarted, but was disappointed as both made perfectly clean starts – all due respect to the drivers for their skills in getting their run-down steeds on the move so successfully. The various factory and warehouse buildings dotted around the place served to effect some remarkable echoes of the hardworking engines climbing to Olive Mount. The added ingredient of the teeming rain plopping around the microphone served to create some very 'atmospheric' recordings. Having deposited their trains at the top, the 8Fs trundled all the way down the hump to gain access to the 'question mark', which would take them to Engine Shed Junction[51] at Wavertree. Before we headed back home, 'Black 5' No 45284 departed with a freight for the Crewe line.

Edge Hill and Speke sheds were to close to steam on Sunday 5 May. I therefore returned with Chris on Friday the 3rd for the last rites, as did a fairly large contingent of other mourners. 8F 2-8-0 No 48056 opened our account that evening by climbing from Pighue Lane Junction with a brake-van and heading in the Edge Hill direction. 'Black 5' No 45231 arrived from Wavertree with a freight, which it eventually pushed up to the Olive Mount reception sidings. Sister loco No 45284 did likewise and later headed off to the shed. Other steam engines in evidence on that final night were 'Black 5' 4-6-0s No 44877, which headed a freight out towards Wavertree, and No 45055 (previously encountered on banking duty at Warrington); 8F 2-8-0s Nos 48096, 48168, 48169 and 48529; and, with Class 08 diesel shunter No D4155 pulling, No 48715, banking its heavy freight up to Olive Mount. As the last few hours of steam ebbed away in Liverpool, diesels were more in evidence than on previous visits to Pighue Lane, probably because most of the steam engines were required to remain at the shed at the end of the night. In evidence were Class 25s Nos D7509 and D5155 and Class 40s Nos D210, D267, D343 and D370. And finally, as No 48056, the engine we saw at the start of our evening, disappeared through the hole in the hump, spectators

---

[51] Also known as Lodging House Junction.

began to disperse, realising that there wasn't much point in staying on. Another stage of the countdown was complete.

I returned the following day – a curious decision, perhaps. That bright and sunny Saturday was officially the last day for Liverpool steam and I didn't really expect to see anything. But I found difficulty in letting go of something I'd been so used to, and just wanted to stare at the lines around me, trying to imagine a scene from earlier years when I thought steam was a permanent feature of our railway – the 'Super D' 0-8-0s, for example, barking up to Olive Mount. 'If only I'd been…' Nothing was moving on the hump; there seldom was at weekends. There was some banging and hammering going on and a few lorries came and went, as industrial life continued as before. Then all this was interrupted by the sound of a train approaching on the Bootle branch. A pair of 8F 2-8-0s (the leading one was No 48467) emerged from under Edge Lane bridge, double-heading a long train of bogie wagons loaded with fabricated lengths of track. They took the Olive Mount line and dragged their train through the hump to head east along the L&M main line. I sighed and went home.

Talk about the 'highs and lows' of life! Shortly after the 'big exodus' at Pighue Lane came a double disaster. For a start, the motor in my tape recorder finally expired. Catastrophe! I'd planned to stay with my relations at Dalton again early in May to record on the Furness line and around Carnforth. Some Standard Class 4 4-6-0s were still active, and I wanted some sounds of these on duties other than those I'd recorded on Shap. Chris came to the aid of the party yet again, and off I went with his recorder.

Next day, having just set out for Barrow, my car ground to an inglorious halt with a rather ominous grating sound. A good-natured guy at a nearby garage offered to take it in and see what could be done. The news wasn't good. Somehow, the drive to the distributor had shattered, damaging the distributor itself and the oil pump in the process. As things turned out, the premises were really only a used car showroom, and didn't carry out mechanical repair work on a general basis. No one could guarantee when the work would be done, but I didn't fancy stumping up towing fees to another garage and left the car there in optimistic innocence. This episode really knocked the enthusiasm out of me. Motivation had disappeared and I returned home after just a couple of nights in Dalton. The saga of the immobile Minx lasted six weeks, by which time I had bought the parts necessary to get the car on the road and posted them up to Dalton. A few days later I collected my car.

In the meantime my tape recorder had also been repaired, but it packed in again on 20 April while Chris and I were chasing a railtour in his Vauxhall 101. Sitting in the back of the car, I managed to coax the recorder back to life, using pieces of string and a little jiggery-pokery with some electrical connections inside. It seemed to work all right. The tape was transported at more or less the correct speed, as long as power was provided by a mixture of new and spent batteries! Reluctant at this late hour to leave my recorder for further repair, I put up with this arrangement through to the final curtain in August. It proved a little expensive on batteries, but it was worth it!

The railtour in question was 'The Lancastrian', promoted by the RCTS, which commenced at Liverpool Lime Street behind 'Black 5' No 45156 *Ayrshire Yeomanry*. We saw it at Garswood, between St Helens and Wigan. *Oliver Cromwell* took over at Fleetwood, and in very windy conditions we saw the 'Brit' storming through Staveley on the Windermere branch. To finish off our exertions for the day, we waited at Oxenholme for the 'Pacific' to return. Little did we know at the time that 'Black 5' No 44874 was at Windermere acting as station pilot. Apparently it shunted the empty stock while No 70013 was turned ready for the return run.

Another railtour was run on the same day, which included Liverpool in its itinerary. Locomotives involved with this one were 'Standard 5s' Nos 73069 and 73134 double-heading (the latter with Caprotti gear), 'Black 5s' Nos 44949 and 45110, also double-heading, and 8F 2-8-0 No 48773. But you can't be in two places at once.

Having become mobile once again, I was able to see the Warwickshire Railway Society's North Western Tour on 18 May. This train was double-headed by two 4-6-0s, 'Black 5' No 44949 and 'Standard 5' No 73069. The latter also figured in the LCGB 'Two Cities' railtour, which made two round trips between Liverpool and Manchester on 23 June. Three routes were used – CLC, L&M and LYR. A good recording and photograph resulted from the 'Standard 5' powering through Kirkby on the LYR line. The other engine involved was 8F 2-8-0 No 48033, which I saw arriving at Lime Street on the final leg (which was by way of Stockport, Northwich and Runcorn). The empty stock was hauled clear by an electric loco, and in a feat of exhibitionism the 8F roared away light-engine into the tunnels, probably heading for Newton Heath, then the nearest steam shed to Liverpool.

Time was getting short. Following closure of the sheds at Edge Hill and Speke, Bolton and the Manchester sheds of Patricroft and Newton Heath closed at the end of June. Just Carnforth, Lostock Hall and Rose Grove remained to see out steam to the end. There was time for one more visit to Hoghton with Chris. At about 9.30pm on the evening of Wednesday 17 July, Chris and I waited at the summit. The dusk gathered as we heard the faint strains of a steam train beginning the climb from Bamber Bridge. The available light was unacceptable for photography, but the calm, still evening made the prospects excellent for a first-class recording. At an early stage in the recording, a Colne-Preston parcels train headed by 'Black 5' No 45388 approached from the Blackburn direction. Emerging from under the road bridge, the train clattered away into the distance, its fading sound merging with that of the hard-working engine climbing in the opposite direction. That engine was 8F 2-8-0 No 48775, one of the three taken into BR stock in 1957. It slogged steadily past, its big ends clanging noisily, then the noise was cut off abruptly as the engine dived under the road bridge. Now muffled, the exhaust was briefly heard again before steam was shut off, the train accelerating beyond the summit. This was an experience to savour for the rest of my life. Never again would I be able to make a recording such as this, with a lengthy build-up to a dramatic climax. I have always preferred listening to long recordings, like those made on Shap or at Warrington, to those where a train is speeding by and the enjoyment is quickly over. This final effort at Hoghton perhaps compensated a little for my misfortune in February when my recorder became rather tipsy!

Railtours with steam haulage were by now thick on the ground, but it was impossible to see them all. Still a member of the SLS, I had already booked places for Chris, his brother Ian and myself on the society's 'Farewell to Steam' tour of 4 August. But another railtour attracted our attention. This one was advertised by the Roch Valley Railway Society for Sunday 21 July, with just a fortnight to go before 'D-Day'.

The Roch Valley tour turned out to be a real bonanza. Commencing from Manchester's Victoria station, we set out ordinarily enough along the L&M line to Liverpool. With nine coaches trailing, immaculately turned-out 'Black 5' No 44888 hammered its way up the 1 in 90 from St Helens Junction to Rainhill. At Olive Mount Junction we swung off the L&M and dived under the gridiron hump to gain the Bootle branch. Exiting the tunnels at Bootle, we were held at signals at the junction with the electrified LYR line to Southport. No 44888 made a clean start on this difficult exit from the branch and, after a brief compulsory pause at the station, we proceeded uneventfully to Southport. Instead of entering Chapel Street station, our train pulled up on the chord connecting the Liverpool and Wigan lines. No 70013 *Oliver Cromwell* was waiting to relieve our 'Black 5'. That done, and once clear of the speed restrictions around the horseshoe-shaped route through Meols Cop, the 'Brit' treated everyone to an exhilarating run to Wigan. The line is pretty well straight as far as Parbold, and 'Olly Crom' accelerated along the level stretch to Bescar Lane, where speed must have been nudging 70mph. Speed was more or less maintained, despite the line rising slightly to Burscough Bridge, where it dives under the Liverpool-Preston line. Our driver then opened up his charge still further, and it responded with a roaring exhaust accompanied by a spitting cylinder drain cock, as speed increased towards the 80mph mark along the level section to Parbold. Thankfully, my recorder picked up all these sounds beautifully. Non-stop through Wigan Wallgate, we were next treated to a foretaste of the hard work to come later, as our engine slogged up through Hindley on gradients ranging between 1 in 98 and 1 in 130.

With the engine refreshed after a water stop at Manchester, our train swung left onto the LYR line leading to Newton Heath. But *Oliver Cromwell* then got into difficulties, continually slipping on the brief 1 in 59 gradient until we could make no more forward progress. It so happened that just outside Victoria station was Class 25 diesel No D5153. This came in handy, for it was called upon to provide rear-end assistance up to Newton Heath. We then sailed up the hill past the recently closed engine sheds.

Our route then took us climbing past Rochdale and through Summit Tunnel, then dropping down through Todmorden to the junction of that name. From there the main line continues to Wakefield, while we turned left through Stansfield Hall on the line to Rose Grove near Burnley. What happened next was to be the climax of the whole tour, the climb on gradients of 1 in 65 and 1 in 68 to Copy Pit summit. With the corridor of our coach now crammed with tape-recordists, *Oliver Cromwell* didn't let us down. But in response to being opened up, it slipped violently upon entering Lydgate Tunnel, where the climb starts in earnest.

'Here we go again,' we thought, recalling our exit from Manchester. Not so. The 'Brit' settled down and fearsomely attacked the climb, shouting at the sky as we passed by Portsmouth and Holme Chapel. Hundreds of onlookers littered the surrounding countryside, photographing and recording us as we progressed towards Copy Pit. Undoubtedly this was the climax of the tour. Our engine then took things relatively easily down through Burnley. We then joined the line from Skipton and Colne at Gannow Junction and proceeded on to Rose Grove, where a stop was made for watering the engine and for the 'tourists' to visit the engine shed.

The shed was functioning just as a steam shed always did, as though there was no impending doom. Admittedly, most of the engines appeared woebegone, with the exception of 8F No 48773, which was spotlessly spruced up, maybe as a result of the efforts of members of the MNA. With a sense of irony, someone had painted a diagonal yellow stripe across its cabsides, supposedly barring the locomotive's use south of Crewe, a restriction from which the 8Fs were in fact exempt. Then, after a few shots of *Oliver Cromwell* in brilliant sunshine, we were off back to Lostock Hall for our last water stop before returning to Southport.

I would have been happy if the Lostock Hall stop had been omitted, for I was now eagerly anticipating the final leg of the tour, which was to take me down the CLC branch past my home. The obligatory photographs were taken of *Oliver Cromwell* resting at the buffer stops in Chapel Street station, before all reboarded for the run to Manchester Central. 'Black 5' No 45110 was on the front. Little did any of us know at the time the fame destined for this locomotive, nor its eventual destiny in preservation.

Having used the north chord at Burscough to access Southport, we now used the south chord to get to Aintree, where our train diverged from the LYR Liverpool line onto CLC metals. We trundled through the desolate abandoned platforms of Aintree Central, then passed into the deep cutting and through the tunnel under the line that used to serve Racecourse station (with its memories of times spent there on past Grand National days). No 45110 took a leisurely pace through the northern suburbs of Liverpool, with me at a window on the right-hand side awaiting my chance to photograph our back garden and home. We passed through West Derby where Dad used to live, then came the bridge carrying the L&M tracks across our path at Broad Green. After the two farm access bridges came the anticipated view of home. It was not exactly as I had imagined, actually – the house seemed much further away, yet the trains as viewed from the window seemed to be so close. Mum and Dad were in the garden waving, and I snapped them, a poignant photograph to keep for posterity. Very shortly we crossed the main road to town climbing steeply over the ridge from Woolton (recalled earlier in this story). A little further down I photographed the platform at Gateacre station on which I had waited with my parents all those years ago for the 4F-hauled train to Southport. I felt as though I had come full circle, and was now on my way home.

Joining the main CLC route at Halewood East Junction, we continued to Manchester. There the cafeteria was soon filled, as most of us had run out of drinks and scoff by now on this hot July day. In the middle of all this came the sound of the exhaust of our 'Black 5' erupting into the station. The performance was repeated – what was going on? We all rushed out onto the station concourse. No 45110 couldn't get the empty stock on the move out of the station. There was no station pilot as in times past, and the engine had stopped too close to the buffers to inch up and try again from a different position. There were more bouts of slipping and the engine began to prime, engulfing us in sooty water, before it eventually got the empty train on the move. What a way to say 'Farewell', we thought.

19
Valete!

With just one week of steam left, I couldn't resist joining the flock chasing yet another special on Sunday the 28th. *Oliver Cromwell*, together with a couple of 'Black 5s' and two 'Standard 4' 4-6-0s, Nos 75019 and 75027, were used on various sections of route between Carnforth and Skipton.

Into the final week of steam, Chris and I took ourselves to Rose Grove, inspired by the stop made during the Roch Valley tour. Before visiting the shed we took up position well to the west to photograph and record trains on the main line. A good many like-minded folk gathered, and engine crews responded by coaxing some vigorous performances from their charges. Venturing onto the shed, we discovered that the Letters of the Law had been relaxed. An open-house policy prevailed as the general public were allowed to roam responsibly around the site. The Police were on hand to oversee matters, however, as the shed still had to function as it had always done.

I joined a small band of other recordists, standing on hillocks of coal dust and oil, compacted between tracks over a period of time. From this vantage point we captured two 'Black 5s', Nos 45073 and 45156 *Ayrshire Yeomanry* (devoid of its nameplates) being prepared for stopping over at the shed. They had been coaled and watered, and were now standing over the ash pits having their fires dropped.[52] Sounds of fire-raking and the general clatter of irons continued for some time; simultaneously, another 'Black 5' could be heard shunting wagons in the goods yard close to the station, and an acetylene torch was crackling as a shed fitter cut through the securing bolts to remove the front number plate from 8F 2-8-0 No 48340.

Having completed their task of fire-dropping, the crew from No 45073 went off duty, leaving the crew of *Ayrshire Yeomanry* to shunt its sister to the neck of the shed yard before dragging it down into the shed. The young fireman from No 45156 coupled the two engines together and climbed back into the cab.

'Are ye tapin'?' he called to his audience.

---

[52] There was no disposal staff as in years gone by. The engine crews now had to do this dirty work themselves.

On receipt of acknowledgement, he told his driver 'Right away', but there was no movement from the engines. The fireman then deftly ran to the cab of No 45073 to release the handbrake. A blast on the whistle followed, and *Ayrshire Yeomanry* strode vigorously up to the top of the yard.

'Tea time' was approaching and word got around that a train would soon be due off the Padiham branch. So before leaving the MPD, Chris and I soaked up more of the atmosphere as engines were coming on shed for the night; very few of them would be venturing out again today, as there were now no servicing facilities for them outside the triangle of the three surviving steam sheds.

The Padiham branch joined the main line just west of the shed. It once formed an alternative through route west, which continued beyond Great Harwood to connect with the Accrington-Blackburn line at Daisyfield East Junction. At this time the truncated branch served the power station at Padiham, whence came the train of empties we were about to see. We positioned ourselves on a bridge that crossed the branch close to the Leeds-Liverpool Canal. The train duly appeared, with 8F 2-8-0 No 48493 running tender-first and with full regulator, hammering away as far as the junction with the main line. What a fitting finish to the day!

We vowed to return to Rose Grove on the Friday, two days before general steam activity was officially to cease. However, there was the small matter of the transfer of preserved 'A4' *Sir Nigel Gresley* to its new home in the North East. Following the loco's last charter, which had taken place the previous October, it had been housed in the old steam sheds at Crewe South, together with the now preserved 9F 2-10-0 No 92220 *Evening Star*. Agreement had been reached with the then National Coal Board that accommodation would be leased to the A4 Society to accommodate *Sir Nigel* at the NCB's Philadelphia Works for the foreseeable future. On Wednesday 31 July the 'A4' was scheduled to leave Crewe at 8.00am to travel north under its own steam. I thought I would nip across to Moore to photograph it, and arrived there at 8.20 only to be told that it had passed about 5 minutes earlier! I couldn't believe it, but I should have known it could fly, as it did the previous year during its inaugural trip in preservation!

I knew the 'A4' was to call at Carnforth for water, but decided to give up the chase and called in at Lostock Hall shed instead. I was glad I did, despite my mixed feelings. The as yet insignificant 'Black 5' No 45110 was on shed, and in a good position for a photograph among the other occupants of the yard. Sister loco No 45305 was also present, looking very spruced up inside the shed. Compared to the hive of activity at Rose Grove the previous day, it seemed like a Sunday morning at Lostock Hall. I was surprised, however, to find in steam Ivatt Class 4 2-6-0 No

43106. Shed staff informed me that it had been bought for preservation, and was being prepared to run under its own steam to Stourbridge the next day. The day after, Friday the 2nd, it would move to the embryo Severn Valley Railway, which would reopen under preservation in the summer of 1970[53], the third standard-gauge railway to do so. The only object that moved during my visit to Lostock Hall was an anonymous and extremely work-stained 8F 2-8-0. The engine groaned woefully as I recorded it reversing its train into the goods yard beyond the road bridge. To my regret I didn't photograph it.

Before going to Rose Grove on the Friday, Chris and I decided to visit the Grassington branch to try and catch one of Carnforth's 'Standard 4' 4-6-0s working the morning stone train to Skipton from the works near Threshfield. We sourced some timings, from where I cannot recall, but saw no movement on the branch. Another one that got away!

As we headed over to Rose Grove, the sun appeared, and was with us for the rest of the day. This time we selected a perch on the embankment opposite the engine shed. After contentedly taking pictures and making a few recordings, a Stanier hooter was heard – continuously. We thought one of the whistles was stuck, but it was soon apparent that an engine had derailed in the shed yard, and the driver of the recalcitrant had wedged open its whistle to warn of the obstruction. From our position we couldn't identify which engine it was, nor the 2-8-0 that coupled up to try and drag it back onto the rails. It didn't succeed, and more time elapsed before No 48773, easily identifiable by its yellow cabside stripe, was attached ahead of both 8Fs. Together, with a little wheel-slipping, they succeeded in their task. Chris and I succeeded in getting to the shed in time to see the culprit, No 48666, thudding over the turntable and into a siding, there to die. It appeared that authority had decided to withdraw the engine there and then. This was a shame, for it was obvious that No 48666 had been well and truly cleaned up. Maybe the intention had been to use it on 4 August as one of the pool of locos rostered to haul the 'farewell' specials.

As on the previous Tuesday, the same family atmosphere was prevalent at the shed. We bought a copy of the local newspaper, which was full of railway-related reports of the week. It also contained brief histories of and interviews with local railwaymen; some were sorry, others glad, to see the steam engines go.

Soon it was time to go ourselves, and it was difficult once again to accept that never again would we be able to make any more spontaneous shed visits. At least we were contented to have been there practically to the last. We would briefly call at Rose Grove again in two days' time, courtesy of an SLS 'Farewell to Steam' railtour, but that was another

---

[53] With passenger services between Bridgnorth and Hampton Loade.

matter.

But there is always another side to every coin. Regrettably, neither of us saw either of the two passenger turns that remained steam-hauled right up to the end. These were the 8.50pm from Preston to Blackpool and the 9.25pm Preston to Liverpool Exchange (ex-Glasgow). On Saturday 3 August, their final night of steam operation, these trains were hauled by 'Black 5' 4-6-0s Nos 45212 and 45318 respectively. We decided against going to Exchange station to witness the 'last rites', as there was a long Sunday ahead of us. We needed to be on the road to Birmingham by 5.00am to catch our SLS special.

Sunday 4 August arrived at last. Officially labelled as the final day for general steam operation on British Railways, in fact the only trains rostered for steam haulage on the day were six 'farewell' specials. They were to tour around various routes in Lancashire and across the border into Yorkshire. The SLS found it necessary to run two trains, such was the demand for seats; three were sponsored by the RCTS, the LCGB and the Stockport Bahamas Locomotive Society/GC Enterprises group; while the remaining special was organised by BR itself, and ran from Manchester to Southport and back.

I was away to pick up Chris and Ian at goodness knows what time of the morning. Chris told me what he had heard a few hours earlier – a light engine had headed east along the LYR Manchester line close to his home. If this was No 45318, where was it going? To get to Lostock Hall, or even Rose Grove, the obvious route should have been straight back up the Preston line to Farrington Junction.

By now, thankfully, the M6 motorway came within reasonable distance of the centre of Birmingham, but we still had to find a suitable car park in an unfamiliar city. We arrived at New Street station with half an hour to spare, but became a little concerned at being allocated seats in the last coach. All was well, however, as we learned that ours would now be the leading vehicle out of Manchester. This came as a bit of a surprise, because steam was originally advertised to take over at Stockport, from where the intended route would have been via Reddish and Dukinfield to gain the Manchester-Huddersfield line at Stalybridge. In the event BR insisted that all of the special trains running via Stockport should be diesel-hauled from there to Manchester Victoria.

At Stockport diesel No D7588 was attached for the run to Manchester Victoria. Photographers lined the route as far as Denton Junction, expecting to see steam on the front. One poor guy had set up a substantial wooden tripod with a plate camera perched on top. Double thumbs-down was his reaction as we swept past. From Denton Junction we ran via Droylsden and Miles Platting before dropping down the steep descent into Victoria station. Our motive power, 'Black 5' 4-6-0s Nos 44871 and 44894, was waiting just outside the station, standing on the

Cheetham Hill tracks. Having pulled up in the station roughly half an hour late, passengers were warned not to detrain, as we would soon be on the move again. This was a pity in some respects, for also in the station were two more 'Black 5s', Nos 44874 and 45017, awaiting the arrival of the second SLS special. Anyone attempting to photograph these risked being left behind!

The situation was one of wishing you could be at the lineside as well as on board one of the trains. Remaining at Manchester Victoria station for the day would have guaranteed sightings of all six trains. To those who did, it must have seemed like a summer Saturday from a previous age, when holiday specials passed through heading to and from the coasts of Lancashire and North Wales. Light-engine movements at the station added to the spectacle.

Our exit from Victoria was spectacular to say the least, with an initial climb at 1 in 59, followed by about a third of a mile at 1 in 47. The gradient then eased to 1 in 118 up to Miles Platting, after which the '5s' settled down to negotiate the various gradients up through Diggle to Standedge Tunnel. Beyond Huddersfield we continued to Bradley Junction, swinging left to gain the LYR route from Normanton and Mirfield back towards Todmorden. We wouldn't be long in reaching what many would regard as the climax of the whole tour – the climb to Copy Pit (as on the Roch Valley tour of a fortnight ago). By now I had used a considerable amount of tape from my 5-inch reel, and decided to load a new one before getting to Stansfield Hall and the line over Copy Pit. That done, I settled back in my seat to enjoy the sounds of the two 'Black 5s' charging the bank. Once again, the corridor in our coach was crammed with recordists, and we let one or two into our compartment to record from 'our' window. Managing a glance or two from the window, we could see that the countryside was blanketed with people, intent on enjoying the spectacle of this, the first special of the day to assault the bank. The train rolled towards Rose Grove, where there was the obligatory stop for water. Entering the station, no one took much notice of Class 8F 2-8-0 No 48519, in steam and seemingly standing at the head of a freight train in the goods yard alongside. It was reported later that the last steam-hauled freight had left Heysham for Carnforth the previous day. So what was the significance of the presence of No 48519? No one has yet come up with an explanation.

During the break at Rose Grove, Chris and Ian went off snapping their cameras around the shed while I took the opportunity to try my recording. Consternation! In my eagerness I had twisted the recording tape during reloading just as the train passed through a short tunnel before reaching Stansfield Hall, and thus paid the penalty for not waiting until I was in daylight. A very muffled recording of the ascent resulted, made through the non-magnetic side of the tape. By the time I sorted myself out, there wasn't much time to view the proceedings outside, but I do remember seeing 8F No 48773 depart from the shed, heading for Blackburn. There it would relieve *Oliver Cromwell* from piloting 'Black 5' No 44781 on the LCGB train. The 'Brit' was then to head light-engine to Lostock Hall to take over haulage of the RCTS train.

On the move again, we headed through Accrington and down the line to Bolton. No 48773 would have a long wait at Blackburn, for we sighted the LCGB special standing in the centre of Trinity Street station at Bolton as our train passed by on the avoiding line to the north. Sure enough, *Oliver Cromwell* was the leading engine. Excepting the BR special, this was the only sighting we had of any of the other special trains run on that Sunday.

Pausing at Wigan Wallgate, our crews photographed each other in their respective cabs, no doubt intending their pictures for the family albums. Continuing along the Liverpool line, we next took the docks branch, which diverged at Fazakerley. This time we passed close by Aintree shed, getting a good look at the building that was to remain standing, empty and unused, for more than two decades. After dropping down at Bootle onto the electric line from Southport, our train then retraced the path taken by the Roch Valley tour by diverging onto the branch from Edge Hill. Burrowing under part of Bootle, this line also passed under the LYR direct line from Wigan to Liverpool and the CLC branch from Halewood to Huskisson Dock. The latter two were themselves at different levels, indicating the deep level at which this part of the line was constructed.

Our drivers encountered a slight snag on arrival at Edge Lane Junction. The colour-light signal was showing red and the signal box was empty. A few minutes elapsed, but there was still no sign of the signalman. A call to control from the trackside phone revealed that he had 'gone home'! After about a 20-minute delay, our drivers received dispensation to proceed with caution past the red light. Fortunately, the junction points were set to path us under Pighue Lane and through the Olive Mount Tunnel to gain the L&M line to Manchester.

We were now about 40 minutes late and, after crossing over at Huyton from the Wigan to the Manchester tracks, our drivers opened up their steeds. We hurtled up the 1 in 90 to Rainhill as though it didn't exist. Then the brakes were applied hard as we approached the station. Coming to a halt some way beyond, our two drivers were in conversation. A photo-stop at Rainhill had been scheduled, but the second driver called 'Go on!', probably in view of our imposed lateness, and off we set again. There was nothing spectacular now, though, as engineering work beyond Newton-le-Willows enforced some 'wrong line' working, putting us further behind time.

Crossing over onto LYR tracks beyond Salford, our train eventually entered Manchester Victoria, our crews exchanging whistles under the train shed as we trundled along the curved platform. We halted alongside another train of maroon coaches. The very moment we stopped, an unfamiliar whistle sounded, and the train alongside moved off, accompanied by the exhaust of another steam engine. This turned out to be 'Black 5' No 45305 taking out the empty stock of BR's Southport special to the carriage sidings at Newton Heath. Good timing! I just left my tape recorder running. A photograph would have been the icing on the cake, but in the circumstances this wasn't possible.

A 10-minute stop ensued before the final steam leg to Stockport. Out on the crowded, cramped platform, I managed a photograph of our two 'Black 5s' raising steam for their final assault on Miles Platting. The whistles blew, and it was 'all aboard' for that final fling. And what a fling it was! Setting off under the wide bridge carrying Miller Street across the broad expanse of trackwork, there was much exhibitionist wheel-slipping and whistle-blowing, the engines playing to the crowd of onlookers, many of whom had spilled onto the trackside beyond the end of the long through platform. On the steep rise to Miles Platting, our 'Black 5s' raised tremendous echoes, shouting at the sky as they passed between the various buildings and underbridges, thus giving the illusion that there were more than just two engines at work! After Miles Platting, the show was virtually all over. There were no more fireworks from the front now as we cruised along to Stockport Edgeley. The time was around 6.00pm when we rolled to a stop. The 'Black 5s' were unceremoniously uncoupled, then everyone watched them pass light-engine along the opposite side of the station, heading back to Lostock Hall shed. All excited enthusiasm and anticipation was now finished.

The three of us were exhausted. My car was in Birmingham! How we wished it was in Stockport, or even Manchester. Reluctantly, we reboarded our train, with the memories of that final exit from Manchester still reverberating in our heads. Although the electric 'governor' whisked us along, it seemed an age before our arrival back in Britain's second city. On the M6 Chris and Ian fell asleep, and slept most of the way home, while I had to call in at every motorway service station to freshen up. Thankfully, I had booked the following week off work, so I could enjoy a sleep-in on the Monday.

I had become used to the absence of steam locomotives at home since May. However, after all the activity of travelling to and fro during the preceding months, there was now an indescribable feeling that something was missing. True, there was BR's own final farewell act to look forward to, the renowned 'Fifteen Guinea Special', on the following Sunday. During the intervening 'steam-dry' week, the local press had a 'field day' relating snippets of history, and informed readers of the historical event that would take place come the weekend.

20
The Glorious Eleventh

Sunday 11 August 1968 dawned rather dull and overcast; maybe it was going to be a gloomy day all round. Chris was going to make his own arrangements for seeing the 'Fifteen Guinea Special', so I headed down to Lime Street station with just my parents. They were pleased to be invited, particularly Dad, who himself had had a lifelong fascination for trains. Dad and I left Mum in the car, which I parked in Skelhorne Street by the side of the station, and made for the top of Platform 7. It soon became quite crowded with onlookers, as did No 6. 'Black 5' No 45110 was standing at Platform 5 with its train, whose reporting number, 1T57, was affixed to the smokebox door. There was no headboard to proclaim the significance of the train. The 9.00am to Newcastle left Platform 8 behind a 'Peak' diesel; then the stage was set for the departure of the 1T57, the 'last' steam-hauled special. As the engine started in motion, I couldn't help wondering why No 45110 had been chosen. It seemed to be leaking steam from every conceivable place, but nevertheless, with a few bouts of wheel-slip, it succeeded in crawling into the tunnels and thereafter managed some acceleration – a good example of driving indeed. I obtained a good recording by stuffing the microphone in my jacket pocket, and managed to take some reasonable photographs as the ten-coach train exited the station.

Stops were scheduled at Rainhill or Parkside, but I decided to head straight for Ribblehead and Blea Moor. Were my eyes deceiving me? As we surmounted the final crest on the B6255 from Ingleton, I was sure there were wisps of smoke hanging in the air. As is well documented, two 'Black 5s', Nos 44871 and 44781, were allocated the task of hauling the special back to Manchester. We had just missed them heading light to Carlisle for the purpose.

During our journey north the grey skies had given way to broken cloud and there was now plenty of sunshine. A gentle breeze wafted around, but not too much to cause any anxiety when tape-recording. The public descended on the place in droves, with cars lining the cart track leading under the famous viaduct from the Ingleton road. There was a general buzz of conversation as people gathered on the hillsides on both sides of the line north of the viaduct, very likely discussing the prospects of what they were shortly to witness. Incredibly, apart from passing on my way to Ais Gill, this was my first visit to Blea Moor. What a vista! What had I missed by concentrating my attentions on Shap?

All conversation was hushed as soon as the exhaust from *Oliver Cromwell* was sighted down beyond Ribblehead. The sound of the engine, quiet at first coming across the westerly breeze, climaxed as the train crossed the viaduct and the 'Brit' strode purposefully past with the coaches clattering behind. Then quietness resumed, as the breeze once again played its part, cutting off the sound as the train curved away to the north. The buzz of conversation resumed as a mass exodus began from the whole area. Some people calmly made their way back to their transport; others hurried back as though their lives depended on getting to their next planned location before anyone else.[54]

Seemingly, everybody decided to head for Ais Gill, where 1T57 was scheduled to stop for a photo call. There are two ways of getting to Garsdale Head, from where the B6259 Kirkby Stephen road leads off to Ais Gill. One is via Hawes, the other via Dent Head, the two routes running on either side of Widdale Fell. Regrettably, I followed the convoy turning left off the Hawes road and dropped down into Dentdale. Progress is always slow along this road at the best of times. After it descends under the railway, the road follows the River Dee along the valley bottom. The railway is by now high on a ledge skirting first Wold Fell and then, after crossing Artengill Viaduct, Dent Fell. A mile or so further, the road to Dent village veers west towards Cowgill, and the 'coal road' to Garsdale station branches off to the right. The procession of cars duly turned into the 'coal road', which zigzags initially between 1 in 5 and 1 in 7 to gain some height. It then straightens out a little, crossing the railway by Dent station. Just before the bridge, traffic came to a standstill. Someone's car had become stuck in the gulley at the roadside, and a group of willing helpers were trying to heave it out onto the tarmac. They succeeded eventually, and the tailback that had formed got on the move once more. By this time, of course, we couldn't expect to get to Ais Gill in time to see 1T57 but, on reflection, it was perhaps a little naive to believe it would have been possible anyway because of the sheer volume of traffic.

The convoy turned left by the Moorcock Inn at Garsdale Head. Beyond Shotlock Hill, we were greeted by lines of cars parked on both sides of the road as far as the eye could see. Nearing the summit, I suggested to my parents that it would be best to park in the first available space, which I did. Loaded with camera and tape recorder, I started walking between the lines of cars as far as the now familiar bridge where the road crosses the railway. From there, I climbed to a spot high up on the slopes of Wild Boar Fell. Viewed from here, the track appeared so small, like

---

[54] Nothing changes!

a model, but I wanted to be fairly isolated for my tape recording, away from the hubbub of conversation and traffic noise. In fact, the murmur of conversation developed again, just as at Blea Moor, as more and more spectators gathered on the slopes. We waited. We waited a long time, then 1T57 was sighted 'coming round the mountain'. A 'spooky' gasp filled the air, as though everyone to a person exclaimed, 'There it is!' The expected hush followed, leaving Nos 44871 and 44781 to do the talking. They certainly did that, storming around the final bend, and over the viaduct that crosses Ais Gill itself. They duetted on their whistles before the road bridge, and again on approaching the summit. Once again, the coaches clattered past, then the sound faded. 1T57 disappeared into the cutting and subsequently past the spot where my parents were waiting with the car.

I thought, 'That's it! So ends a fine innings by steam.'

I felt privileged to have been around at the right time. The crowds were present at the end, just as they had been at the dawn of railways when the Stockton & Darlington and Liverpool & Manchester Railways opened. 'Those Were The Days' sang Mary Hopkin, who was shortly to top the pop charts with that number. The Beach Boys called 'Do It Again'. But we couldn't. An era had ended – a way of life for those in the job, as well as others looking on from the outside. The 'cheese butties' had lasted well, but the feet were a little tired as the 'grandstand' facilitated by Wild Boar Fell emptied of people. I made my way back to the car. Slowly, I think.

'What's going on?' a local farmer had asked Dad during the wait. He'd seen the occasional enthusiast over the years, but had taken no notice of the trains they photographed. He took notice of this one, as Dad enlightened him of its significance. Dad had heard that *Oliver Cromwell* was to return light-engine over Ais Gill, making its way to East Anglia for preservation at the Bressingham Museum near Diss. But we'd had enough; we were ready for a good meal. Besides, I wanted to remember the 'Fifteen Guinea Special' as my last view of a BR steam train, rather than a light-engine movement. With that, we headed for Kirkby Stephen and a restaurant. Retracing our steps over Ais Gill en route home, there were still many onlookers gazing over the tracks. Had No 70013 gone past? Or was it that they found difficulty in letting go? I don't know; we didn't stop to find out.[55]

Arriving home, we found Chris and his brother Ian waiting in their car. But there wasn't time for much conversation initially, as a special programme was about to be shown on television. It told the story of *Flying Scotsman*'s commemorative non-stop run between London and Edinburgh, which had taken place on 1 May. A fitting end to a momentous day. Needless to say, much discussion and storytelling followed the programme.

21
Aftermath

'4472 *Flying Scotsman* Climbs Shap, Ais Gill, and Standedge' – so read an advertisement headline in the October 1968 issue of *The Railway Magazine*. The advertisement referred to a tour, organised by the RCTS, to be run on 26 October between Liverpool and Carlisle. The 'A3' was still permitted to run over the network, thanks to owner Alan Pegler's contract with BR. Despite the fact that his contract was valid until 1971, Mr Pegler had decided to send his engine for a tour of the USA in 1969. Thus the advertisement in *The Railway Magazine* had also noted: 'This WILL be 4472's last tour on BR before leaving on a nine-month visit to America'. In fact, this statement turned out to be premature. The engine's departure for the States was postponed from the following spring until September, allowing for a few more appearances on railtours over here in the interim. The October tour was given the title 'The Moorlands'; it would run northward to Carlisle over the WCML, returning to Liverpool via the Settle-Carlisle line, Leeds and Manchester. I couldn't miss this, could I?

My ticket cost £6 10s 0d, received together with a very comprehensive itinerary. In addition to the usual pick-up and set-down timings and seating allocations, information was given as to where to find representatives from the four railway preservation societies participating in the tour, and the names of no fewer than 11 eating places in Carlisle were listed for those wishing to take meals 'on terra firma'. An interesting sentence relating to photographers urged them 'to consider others who may wish to take photographs from a similar vantage point, and not to monopolise positions in such circumstances.'

As usual, I'd requested a seat near the front of the train for tape-recording purposes, and was a little dismayed to learn that I was allocated a seat in the second coach. Being the length of two tenders[56]

[55] Of the four locomotives involved with the 'Fifteen Guinea Special', only No 44781 didn't survive into preservation. It was used in a crash scene during shooting of the film *The Virgin Soldiers*, and was cut up on the spot after sustaining some damage.

[56] *Flying Scotsman* had been running for some time with two tenders. As watering places were now few and far between, Alan Pegler acquired the second one and had it converted as a water carrier of about 10,000 gallons capacity.

and one coach away from the engine, I was concerned about the ability of the recorder to pick up the sounds above the clatter of the coaches. I needn't have worried. The 'A3' came through 'loud and clear'. The load was ten coaches, the second tender adding the equivalent of two more.

The tape recorder was borrowed from Beaver Radio in Liverpool. I'd submitted my MR120 for repair again, now that BR steam had ended, but it was not ready when the trip with No 4472 came along. After a little forceful persuasion, Beaver Radio was good enough to lend me an MR 130 model. Reluctantly, I had to return it after my trip. It was superior to my own!

I have taken the liberty of quoting, with slight modifications, from an account of the trip I sent to my friend Alan to describe the run:

'We departed from Liverpool at 7.53, and there were more spectators than I expected along the route at this early hour. As we stormed through Edge Hill station, a driver stopped his DMU on the approaching line, obviously showing consideration for the photographers. The train passed through Broad Green, about half a mile from my home (more people, as on just about every station – not all enthusiasts either…).

After joining the Crewe-Carlisle line at Golborne, Wigan was our first pick-up point. Leaving Wigan (which looked like the "Spion Kop"[57]), the engine had to tackle the 1 in 104 gradient to Coppull. Fantastic sounds from 4472!

"Wow!" I thought. "If this is only Wigan, what's Shap going to be like?"

Once over the hill, speed rose to around 70. It seemed as though everything had to stop for *Flying Scotsman*, as people were hanging out of bedroom windows, in gardens, not to mention the embankments littered with spectators. Someone held up a giant notice 'PLEASE WHISTLE', and 4472 obliged! It was amusing to pass the Leyland Motor factory … employees were in the works yard to see us pass…

If Wigan was like the "Spion Kop", Preston station was like Wembley! On leaving Preston I left the tape recorder on until we were level with the M6, where speed could not have been far short of 80 (the maximum allowed for 4472). It must have looked a stirring sight for anyone travelling north on the motorway.

We were signal-checked just outside Oxenholme and the climb to Grayrigg. This threw my timing right out and I had to change tapes before we got to the summit! (I had wanted to do this between there and Low Gill, in time for Shap.)

[57] A reference to the crowded 'Kop' end of Liverpool FC's Anfield stadium, before the enforcement of seated accommodation.

How disheartened I was to see the Lune Valley cut up in preparation for the M6 extension. For some reason our driver let speed drop considerably before Tebay … our ascent [of Shap] was spectacular all the way…

From Shap onwards it was fast running all the way to Carlisle (with hardly a soul in sight at the lineside!).'

The train arrived at Carlisle about 8 minutes late, having made up 2 minutes from a 10-minute late start at Preston. Passengers had nearly 2½ hours to sample the delights of Carlisle. I took photographs of our engine after it returned from servicing, but otherwise my recollections of what I did during that time are blank.

For the run back home via Leeds, my coach had of course become the last but one. So, armed with recorder, I positioned myself in good time at a drop-down window in the front coach. Alan had mentioned that he may travel north to see the train, but in the event couldn't manage it. Thus my letter continued:

'Did you go to Birkett Tunnel? If you did, you will have seen us moving at little more than walking pace. Someone had put three detonators on the line further down. An inspector on our train thought it was the work of a practical joker, as it had happened before to other specials at the same spot. After the tunnel, 4472 was opened up and made great acceleration to breast the summit at about 50.

After Ais Gill, I left the "sardine can" at the front of the train and returned to my seat in the next to last coach… At Leeds I returned to record the journey up to Standedge (more crowds of people all the way up, and it was quite dark by now). At Manchester the front coach practically emptied, so I had a seat from there to Liverpool, arrived 1 minute late. Even on this last lap, speed must have been in the 70s at times, and still the platforms were thronged at every station.

So that was it, for me a thrill-a-minute trip!'

My letter omitted mention of the climb from Lime Street station to Edge Hill. The sound of an 'A3' exhaust would have been alien to the tunnels as it reverberated through them. Nevertheless, I was pleased to be able to make a recording of any engine climbing through the tunnels, be it of LNER origin or otherwise. Regarding the slowing near Birkett Tunnel, the placement of detonators was more likely made by someone waiting at the south end of the tunnel, expecting to see the engine opened up as it emerged. As it was, that someone may well have been disappointed, for our driver kept just enough steam on to continue crawling for some distance beyond the tunnel before letting rip. *Flying*

Scotsman was blowing off furiously, the fireman having maintained the fire in anticipation of an uninterrupted climb.

It's just as well I was blessed with some excellent results from the tape recorder, as carelessness prevented me from realising any fruits from my photographic efforts. At home, my film emerged from the developing tank completely imageless following a 45-minute processing procedure. Why? Only because I'd tried to develop it in washing solution instead of developer! All I was left with was a colour transparency taken during a photo-stop at Blea Moor.

And so we passed into January 1969, and Chris I paid a visit to the Keighley & Worth Valley Railway, which had reopened under the banner of preservation the previous June. The day was atrocious, rain teeming down for most of the time. No 31 *Hamburg*, an 0-6-0T bought from the Manchester Ship Canal Co, was operating a two-coach train service over the whole line. Thinking back to those early days, everything seemed so basic. The general public could wander at will around the site at Haworth, where the locomotive stock was restored, maintained, or just 'kept', mostly out in the open air. Little did we realise that this was only the start of something very big. No one in their wildest dreams, not even the most ambitious of preservationists, could have foreseen how their little pastime would develop into the massive tourist industry we see today (accompanied of course by strict rules and regulations tied to Health and Safety). Gratitude and high praise will be due indefinitely to the dedicated generations of hard-working enthusiasts who have made it all possible.

With the knowledge of *Flying Scotsman*'s impending departure to the United States, I set about making the most of seeing what I could of the engine's remaining railtours on this side of the big pond. Following visits to Blea Moor, Kiverton Park (Sheffield) and Shap, a glorious day on 29 June heralded another 'A3'-hauled railtour sponsored by the North Eastern Locomotive Preservation Group, a body that became inextricably associated with the North Yorkshire Moors Railway.[58] Originating in the North East, the tour was circular, taking in Leeds, Manchester, the WCML and Carlisle. A pause was made at Keighley, junction with the KWVR, where a train was laid on to connect with the special, giving passengers the option to ride up the line. The KWVR train was double-headed by two ex-BR locomotives, 0-6-0Ts Nos 69023 *Joem* and 72, which I photographed approaching Oakworth.

On leaving Keighley, *Flying Scotsman* headed for the WCML and Shap. I drove over to Greenholme, as a change from Scout Green where

---

[58] This was another infant preserved line, which was to commence public operations in 1973, initially between Grosmont and Goathland.

I'd photographed No 4472 on 1 June. The sun brilliantly illuminated engine and train as they rounded the bend from Loups Fell at a fair lick. *Scotsman* whistled as it roared past me and under the road bridge, the coaches whining on the welded rails. The whining faded and the train was gone. A fitting curtain call, I thought, for all my visits to Shap. This particular train proved to be the last to be steam-hauled over Shap until steam was allowed back over the line in the 1990s.

For its final tour before leaving for America, *Flying Scotsman* hauled its own farewell special over the ECML on 31 August, between King's Cross and Newcastle, stopping off at York en route. By now an American-style whistle and bell had been fitted to the right-hand side of the smokebox. A little bit of disfigurement, perhaps, but it allowed the chance to take what would become rare photographs.

I saw the train first north of Selby on its northbound run, then watched the engine being serviced at York MPD before going to Thirsk to see it returning. Unfortunately, the train was running late on its return run. During the wait I managed to obtain yet another variation on the theme of background sounds for my tape-recording – turkeys – which started gobbling from a nearby farm. While waiting I recorded my first (and last) 'Deltic'-hauled train. It absolutely flew past me. As always, the distinctive 'Deltic' hum sounded very impressive, but there is no conception of speed on my recording until the locomotive actually passes the microphone. Doubtless it would have sounded better in stereo. Darkness had fallen when *Scotsman* appeared, taking things rather leisurely on the slow line. Paradoxically, if only for myself, this was something of an anticlimax to what was supposed to be the climax of main-line steam.

For that was the end of main-line steam in the UK. Or so everyone thought. 1970 was a dry year, following *Flying Scotsman*'s departure from Liverpool aboard the *Saxonia* during September. However, BR had second thoughts over its ban on main-line steam, resulting in its pioneering return the following year in the form of GWR 'King' 4-6-0 No 6000 *King George V*. Like the events of 1968, this momentous event is already a well-related story, and will no doubt be retold many times more for as long as there are railway enthusiasts.

During this period there was time to reflect on what I had achieved, and what I could have achieved. Regarding missed opportunities, there are more to add to the references I made towards the end of Chapter 13. Regretfully, I did not return to Birkenhead to where many 9F 2-10-0s had migrated by the late 1960s; nor did I venture to record the iron-ore trains associated with the John Summers steelworks, which those 9Fs worked; I didn't visit the Peak District where 8F 2-8-0s worked trains of limestone; and of course I made a hash of visiting the North East as recollected in Chapter 16. Thus the 'five-year syndrome' raises its head for the last time. More shutter-clicking and less number-spotting? Perhaps. On the plus side, it was a fun life. In fact, I did manage to accumulate hundreds of photographs over the years, including a fair number taken during the recording era.

Following all that, I married in 1973 and moved out of Liverpool to St Helens, while my parents remained at Childwall for the foreseeable future. A decade later I was fortunate to have some of my tape recordings published on vinyl. My first visit to Shap was featured, as were the recordings made on that starry night near Warrington, and steam's final hours at Rose Grove. Meanwhile, the 'winds of change' continued to blow across our railway system. Some familiar landmarks disappeared completely, like the 'hump' at Olive Mount, and Liverpool's Central and Exchange stations. Most significantly, the CLC branch through Childwall, singled in 1971, finally succumbed to closure in 1978. In time, the route right through from Halewood to Aintree was converted into a linear park. There *was* a railway at the bottom of our garden, and I can still hear those 'O4' 2-8-0s clanging up and down.

Appendix
Glossary and abbreviations

In the decade preceding the Millennium, our national railway system experienced a revolution in the form of privatisation, just 70 years or so since the first revolution, when a host of small independent railways had been 'grouped' in 1923 to form the 'Big Four', and some 50 years since the next revolution in 1948, when the 'Big Four' had been nationalised to become British Railways (which was renamed British Rail in the 1960s).

The principal constituent companies of the 1923 'Big Four' were as follows:

GWR – Great Western Railway

LMS – London Midland & Scottish (Railway)
    CR –Caledonian Railway
    FR – Furness Railway
    GSWR – Glasgow & South Western Railway
    HR – Highland Railway
    LNWR – London & North Western Railway
    GJR – Grand Junction Railway
    L&M – Liverpool & Manchester Railway
    LYR – Lancashire & Yorkshire Railway
    MR – Midland Railway

LNER – London & North Eastern Railway
    GNR – Great Northern Railway
    GCR – Great Central Railway
        (formerly MSLR – Manchester Sheffield &
        Lincolnshire Railway)
    NBR – North British Railway
    NER – North Eastern Railway

SR – Southern Railway
    LBSCR – London, Brighton & South Coast Railway
    LCDR – London, Chatham & Dover Railway
    LSWR – London & South Western Railway
    SECR – South Eastern & Chatham Railway

CLC – Cheshire Lines Committee (GNR/GCR/MR, later LNER/LMS) – remained independent until nationalisation

In 1948 these groups were nationalised to become

BR – British Railways (later British Rail)
    ER – Eastern Region
    LMR – London Midland Region
    NE Region – North Eastern Region (later combined with ER)
    S Region – Southern Region
    ScR – Scottish Region
    WR – Western Region

The five English Regions of the former Big Four companies fell naturally into the London Midland, Eastern and North Eastern, Western, and Southern Regions. North of the Border, however, the LMS and LNER routes were so interwoven that a single Scottish Region was formed to embrace the lines of both. In England, the newly formed Regions of 1948 overlapped in certain areas. For example, at Leeds the LMS had rubbed shoulders with the LNER, while between Birmingham and Bristol the LMS and GWR possessed separate routes. In time the LMR administrations at these places were transferred to the North Eastern and Western Regions respectively, and there were similar 'adjustments' in other areas during the course of time.

Other abbreviations used

BTC   British Transport Commission

CME Chief Mechanical Engineer. This position was held by whoever was selected by the company management board to take charge of design policies for locomotives and rolling stock. Living in an area principally served by the former LMS, I and my friends greatly admired the locomotives attributed to William Stanier. Sir William, as he later became, was CME of the LMS between 1932 and 1941 and, although no design is the result of one man's sole efforts, he has gone down in history as being responsible for creating a stud of locomotives in the medium to high power bracket to plug a chronic shortage of suitable motive power for the LMS. Stanier's counterpart on the LNER was Nigel Gresley, who was also later knighted. Some of his engines, too, made early impressions on me, as they passed my home in Liverpool.

D(E)MU Diesel (Electric) Multiple Unit. As an alternative to locomotive-hauled trains, production of diesel or electric multiple units, consisting of powered cars and trailers, was commenced in the 1950s. However, EMUs were nothing new, London Transport 'tube trains' and the Mersey Railway 'underground' system being early examples. More EMUs were produced as lines became electrified. The diesel sets were intended mainly for short-haul and suburban services, although some Cross-Country and Inter-City units were built for selected routes of medium distance.

E(W)CML East (West) Coast Main Line. Both terms are comparatively modern parlance for two of the three principal trunk routes from London to Scotland. The LMS route from Euston became the WCML, passing through Rugby, Crewe, Preston, Carlisle and over Beattock to Glasgow Central; the ECML was the LNER's route from King's Cross to Edinburgh Waverley via Grantham, Doncaster, York and Newcastle. Neither route is truly coastal, although the latter does actually skirt the North Sea for some considerable distance between Newcastle and Edinburgh. On the opposite side, however, for only a few miles around Bolton-le-Sands and Hest Bank does the WCML view the Irish Sea. The third route to Scotland was former MR main line from London St Pancras via Leeds and the famous Settle-Carlisle line. Through trains from this route continued north of Carlisle, either to Glasgow St Enoch via the old GSWR line, or to Edinburgh via the former NBR Waverley Route.

EEEnglish Electric Company, builder of the prototype 'Deltic' diesel locomotive and a supplier of many diesel types for BR's Modernisation Plan

KWVR
Keighley & Worth Valley Railway

LCGB
Locomotive Club of Great Britain
MoS   Ministry of Supply, the Government department that, among other matters, ordered the supply of locomotives for the war effort, which saw service at home and overseas. Many of those that returned to the UK after the war found service with the 'Big Four', and were subsequently taken into British Railways stock.

MPD Motive Power Depot

RCTS Railway Correspondence & Travel Society

S&DJR
Somerset & Dorset Joint Railway

SLS   Stephenson Locomotive Society

WCML See ECML

Classification of locomotives

Each of the old railway companies applied its own classification system for locomotives. After the 'grouping' of 1923, the LMS developed a system the basis of which was eventually adopted by British Railways following nationalisation. This system comprised a power figure, from zero for the smallest engines to 8 or 9 for the most powerful passenger or freight engines respectively. A suffix, P or F, designated passenger or freight. However, a figure without a suffix designated a locomotive's suitability for both passenger and freight work, and at first these carried the suffix MT (for 'mixed traffic'). An example of the latter is the ex-LMS Class 5 4-6-0, commonly known to enginemen and enthusiasts alike as the 'Black 5'. However, the original 5MT classification of these engines probably gave rise to the spotters' nickname of 'Mickey'.

Although BR applied these power classifications to all the steam locomotives inherited from the Big Four companies, engines of the former LNER, GWR and SR still retained their former company classifications, probably for ease of identification.

Bibliography

Adley, Robert *In Search of Steam 1962-68*
    (Blandford Press (BCA), 1981)
Anderson, Paul *An Illustrated History of Liverpool's Railways*
    (Irwell Press, 1996)
Aughton, Peter *Liverpool: A People's History* (Carnegie Press, 1990)
Awdry, Christopher *Encyclopaedia of British Railway Companies*
    (PSL, 1990)
Barker, Eddie *In and Around Broad Green, Liverpool*
    (Edward Barker, 1991)
Baughan, Peter E. *A Regional History of the Railways of Great Britain
    Vol 11: North & Mid Wales* (David St John Thomas, 1991)

Beck, Keith M. *The Great Western North of Wolverhampton*
(Ian Allan, 1986)

Biddle, Gordon *Scenes from the Past: The Railways Around Preston*
(Foxline Publishing, 1989)

Bonavia, Michael R. *British Rail: The First 25 Years*
(David & Charles, 1981)

Boocock, Colin *BR Steam in Colour 1948-1968* (Ian Allan, 1986)
British Railways in Colour 1948-1968 (Ian Allan, 1988)
BR Main Line Gradient Profiles (Ian Allan, 1997 (1966))

Christiansen, Rex *A Regional History of the Railways of Great Britain
Vol 7: The West Midlands* (David St John Thomas, 1991)
Forgotten Railways: North and Mid Wales (David & Charles, 1976)
Regional Rail Centres: North West (Ian Allan, 1995)

Clarke and Patmore *Railway History in Pictures: North West England*
(David & Charles, 1968)

Corkhill, John and Hanson, Peter *Classic Steam*
(Silver Link Publishing, 1995)

Cox, E. S. *British Railways Standard Steam Locomotives*
(Ian Allan, 1966)
Locomotive Panorama (Ian Allan, 1965)

Davies, R. and Grant, M. D. *London and Its Railways*
(David & Charles (BCA), 1983)

Dyckoff, Nigel *The Cheshire Lines Committee* (Ian Allan, 1984)

Edwards, D. and Pigram, R. *The Final Link (The GWR & GCR Joint
line)* (Midas Books, 1982)

Ferneyhough, Frank *Liverpool & Manchester Railway 1830-1980*
(Robert Hale Ltd, 1980)

Fields, Gilbert and Knight *Liverpool to Manchester into the second
century* (Manchester Transport Museum Soc, 1980)

Gahan, John W. *Rails to Port and Starboard* (Countyvise Ltd, 1992)
The Line Beneath the Liners
(Countyvise Ltd & Avon AngliA, 1983)

Glover, John *British Rail in Colour 1968-1980*
(Ian Allan, 1988)

Griffiths, R. P. *The Cheshire Lines Railway*
(The Oakwood Press, 1978)

Hardy, R. H. N. *Beeching: Champion of the Railways?*
(Ian Allan, 1989)

Hawkins, Hooper and Reeve *BR Engine Sheds: London Midland
Matters* (Irwell Press, 1989)

Holt, Geoffrey O. *A Regional History of the Railways of Great Britain
Vol 10: The North West* (David St John Thomas, 1986)

Hoole, K. *A Regional History of the Railways of Great Britain
    Vol 4: The North East* (David & Charles, 1978)

Johnson, E. M. *Scenes from the Past 8: Manchester Suburbs*
    (Foxline Publishing, 1989)

Jowett, Alan *Jowett's Railway Atlas* (PSL, 1989)

Joy, David *Cumbrian Coast Railways* (Dalesman, 1968)
    Main Line Over Shap (Dalesman, 1967)
    Railways in the North (Dalesman, 1970)

King, Peter *71000 Duke of Gloucester: The Impossible Dream*
    (Ian Allan, 1987)

Larkin, Edgar *An Illustrated History of British Railways Workshops*
    (Oxford Publishing Co)

Marshall, John *Forgotten Railways: North West England*
    (David & Charles, 1981)

Nock, O. S. *The Royal Scots and Patriots of the LMS* (David & Charles)

Pearce, Kenn *Shed Side On Merseyside* (Sutton Publishing)

Pixton, Bob *Warrington Railways* (The Chalford Publishing Co, 1996)
    Widnes and St Helens Railways
    (The Chalford Publishing Co, 1996)

Preston Hendry, R. and Powell Hendry, R. *Paddington to the Mersey*
    (Oxford Publishing Co)

Rear, W. G. *Scenes from the Past: The Conwy Valley Line*
    (Foxline Publishing, 1991)

Rear and Jones *Scenes from the Past: The Llangollen Line*
    (Foxline Publishing, 1990)

Reed, Brian *Crewe to Carlisle* (Ian Allan, 1969)

Rowledge, J. W. P. and Reed, Brian *The Stanier 4-6-0s of the LMS*
    (David & Charles, 1981)

Simmons, Jack and Biddle, Gordon *The Oxford Companion to
    British Railway History* (Oxford University Press, 1997)

Singleton, David *Liverpool & Manchester Railway* (Dalesman, 1975)

Smith, Steve (ed) *British Hit Singles* (Guinness Superlatives, 1985)

Timetables, London Midland Region 1958 and 1963
    (British Railways)

Tolson, J. M. *The St Helens Railway* (The Oakwood Press, 1983)

Various, *Wrexham Railways Vol 2* (Bridge Books, 1993)

Index

Roman numerals refer to the pages of illustrations

Further reading from Silver Link...

Horton's Guide to Britain's Railways in Feature Films
Updated 2nd edition
Glyn Horton

The first movie guide for the British railway enthusiast!

Railways and the cinema have a long association, from early silent films to Harry Potter. This enlarged second edition lists almost 1,000 feature films that have British railway content, and gives details of where the sequences were filmed, whether on the contemporary railway or more recently using the facilities of today's preserved lines.

The first film to use a railway as part of the storyline was the saucy A Kiss in the Tunnel in 1900. Since then hundreds of feature films have used railways as a backdrop or as an important plot ingredient, including Train of Events, The Titfield Thunderbolt, The Ladykillers, Oh Mr Porter, The Railway Children and, more recently, several of the 'James Bond' and 'Harry Potter' films, as well as many where the railway – steam, diesel or electric – makes a brief and tantalising appearance, unwittingly providing a living archive of railway footage.

- Enlarged and updated second edition
- The railway element of almost 1,000 films described, from 1900 to the present day
- Steam, diesel and electric – contemporary scenes and preserved railways
- Includes trams, the London Underground and Irish railway scenes
- Filming locations identified
- Howlers, continuity errors and fascinating trivia

Glyn Horton is a lifelong railway enthusiast with a degree in Film Studies. He contributes to film websites, and lives and works in South Wales. His book is the result of 10 years' research.

234 x 153mm   208 pages   40 b&w illustrations 24 pages plates
978 1 85794 334 4   Paperback   £17.99